A DELICIOUS WAY TO EARN A LIVING

A collection of his best and tastiest food writing

Michael Bateman

Grub Street · London

For Alex, Georgia, Dan, Paul, Simon, Sarah, and Fay

Published in 2008 by
Grub Street
4 Rainham Close
London
SW11 6SS
Email: food@grubstreet.co.uk food@grubstreet.co.uk
Web: www.grubstreet.co.uk

Keying by Richard Davie
Formatting and layout by Sarah Driver

A CIP record of this book is available from the British Library

ISBN 978-1-904943-92-1

Printed and bound by MPG, Bodmin, Cornwall

This book is printed on FSC (Forest Stewardship Council) paper

Contents

Acknowledgements

Thanks to family and friends for their encouragement; to my mother and to my sister Ruth for her patience and great listening skills; to Angela Wrapson, Hilary Adamson, Sue Malden, Ellen Nall and Ingrid Selberg for invaluable help at critical moments; and to publisher Anne Dolamore for her enthusiasm, commitment and hard work in creating this delicious and fitting memorial to Michael.

Editorial Note
Michael was a prolific writer, producing a weekly column for most of his career, as well as articles for magazines, and over a dozen books. This collection ends shortly after he began working at the *Independent on Sunday,* but we intend that another volume will follow containing his weekly pieces from his 14 years there.
Illustrations
Michael was also a talented artist, though not many people knew about this. He always took a sketch pad with him on holidays and press trips; his notebooks were covered with drawings; and his dinner menu planners –often in the form of cookstrips – were decorated with pictures of the food, seating arrangements and even the guests. His sketches embrace his wit, humour and great sense of fun, and we have included some of them here.

Heather Bateman

Publisher's Note
The articles collected here have been transcribed directly from their original publications.

Foreword

Michael Bateman wrote about food, becoming one of the most eminent and admired of present-day food writers. But it was a strange thing to want to do, back in the 1950s, when he started out. Britain was still suffering from post-war austerity. A meal out meant roast beef and cabbage cooked to death, with none of that funny stuff foreigners ate, such as garlic - ugh, horrible. He wanted to write about food as a subject, not in the sense of recipes, but food, the eating of, the contents of, the use of, the history of – a subject worthy of serious space.

It was during his National Service in Hong Kong, as a second lieutenant, where he first became interested in cooking and after that he saw food as a serious subject. I first met him in 1958, when he was a young journalist on the *Durham Advertiser*, and I was a student at Durham, editing *Palatinate*, the university newspaper. He invited me for a meal in his hovel on Claypath. He made a curry, something I'd never had before, presuming it was merely a funny foreign powder, not a dish, and insisted on telling me its history, where he had got each ingredient, how he had cooked it. Later, at a lunch for several people, he made a paella, which again was new to me. It seemed to take him for ever, but he kept everyone amused with stories and drinks and bits, though, after three hours' waiting, I went out secretly for a meat pie, then returned for the paella.

Potty, I thought. Real men, in 1958, were not interested in food, either cooking it or talking about it. And, as for real journalists, I couldn't see how anyone would ever survive as a hack by writing about such a pansy, piddling subject.

In Durham, he was a familiar sight around Palace Green, walking about with his flaxen hair and his scruffy, second-hand overcoat which seemed to make his shoulders about six feet wide. We organised skiffle parties together. I passed on student stories for his newspaper and he told me, to my amazement, that there were two national graduate training schemes for would-be journalists, neither of which I had known about, one run by Kemsley Newspapers (later Thomson Newspapers), the other run by Westminster Press –

the one he had joined.

From the local paper in Durham, he eventually moved to Fleet Street and then *The Sunday Times,* where we met up again as colleagues. He started writing about food on the features pages, where I was in charge at one time of his articles. He would produce long pieces on saffron, a new substance to most people, but made it totally riveting. He was the first journalist I was aware of to write detailed exposés of food additives.

He clearly loved researching his food articles, disappearing for days if not weeks, covering every possible angle, talking to every expert. In those days on *The Sunday Times,* you were allowed to take forever, if it sounded a reasonable story. But, to many other journalists, Bateman's obsessions were pretty daft, if not weird. Then slowly they began to realise that he had become an expert in, perhaps even the creator of, a new branch of journalism - food journalism. It was a subject national newspapers had scarcely bothered with before.

Later, while still on *The Sunday Times,* where he became editor of Lifespan on the magazine, he launched a national campaign for Real Bread, which later, in 1982, turned into a book, *The Sunday Times Book of Real Bread.*

His first cooking book appeared in 1966, *Cooking People,* which was an ingenious idea, combining biographical interviews with the main cookery writers of the day, such as Elizabeth David, Robert Carrier and André Simon, plus some of their recipes. Getting a proper interview with Elizabeth David was a coup in itself.

It wasn't his first book. Michael Bateman's other, if minor, passion was cartooning and he had already produced a book about leading cartoonists called *Funny Way to Earn a Living* (1966). In all, he published around a dozen books on cooking. His last book, *The World of Spice,* was published in September 2003. 'Best thing I've done,' he told me. 'I loved every word.'

Michael Bateman was the food writer of *The Independent on Sunday* from its creation in 1989 and during that time won many awards and commendations, notably the Glenfiddich Food Writer of the Year in 2000. He was a great traveller, determined, if he was writing about coffee, for example, to get to Brazil and see the stuff growing. He would even pay his own way, if he couldn't wangle it otherwise. Now that's something journalists rarely do.

His personal life was at one time very complicated, not to say shambolic. When his first marriage disintegrated, he was alone for some time, in some chaos, living a fairly wild life. On his travels, which included Latin America, he started a collection of plastic bags, trying to get one each from some of the world's major shops, mainly in the food line. A unique collection, which no one else had thought of. They were all thrown out one day by his cleaner, who thought she was doing him a favour, trying to reduce the squalor in his flat.

For 25 years, he had been a model of healthy living, sensible drinking and eating, with lots of exercise. When I last had lunch with him, he looked as fit and vibrant as when I had first met him in his twenties, his face no more crinkly, still liable to be convulsed with laughter at the slightest excuse, still as enthusiastic as ever, without an ounce of cynicism. When I was ill once, with jaundice, he arrived at my sick bed, where I was surrounded by flowers, holding an enormous cabbage. It sat at the end of my bed for three weeks.

The accident which led to his death was sudden, banal and appalling. In September 2003, he was walking across a quiet rural road outside his country home in Norfolk, having said goodbye to some friends, watched from the house by his wife Heather, when he was hit by a motor car. He never recovered.

This collection of articles follows the development of Michael's career spanning over thirty years from the 1960s, when he began a syndicated cookery strip, to the early nineties, when he became Food Editor of *The Independent on Sunday*. It also includes his award-winning article on Rio is Cooking (Glenfiddich Food Writer of the Year 2000) and the introduction to the last book he wrote, *The World of Spice*. It can be seen as a telling record of the first years of food journalism in the UK.

Hunter Davies

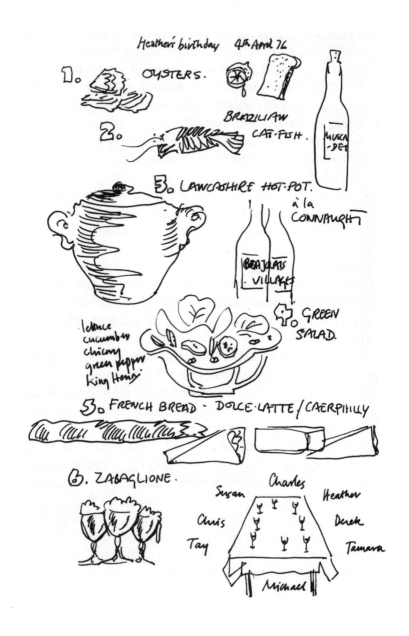

Heather's birthday   4th April 76

1. OYSTERS.

2. BRAZILIAN CAT·FISH.

MUSCA-DET

3. LANCASHIRE HOT·POT.
à la CONNAUGHT

BEAJOLAIS VILLAGE

4. GREEN SALAD.

lettuce
cucumber
chicory
green pepper
King Henry

5. FRENCH BREAD · DOLCE·LATTE / CAERPHILLY

6. ZABAGLIONE.

Susan   Charles   Heather

Chris   Derek

Tay   Tamara

Michael

A Hack's Lament

They come into my office, bronzed and sleek: the fashion correspondent from Barbados, the motoring man who has been testing a
Ferrari in North Africa, the travel writer who has been comparing
sunbathing facilities in Ipanema and Copacabana beaches. 'Where
have you been?' you ask. 'Oh,' they reply, 'the South of France – working.' Or occasionally, 'Oh Bali – working.'

Then there are the wine correspondents, who not only visit the
world's vineyards, but many of the local wine bars. They sway in,
wreathed in bucolic smiles. 'Huh, where have you been?' 'Ah – working, old boy.'

My turn came recently. Would I join a party visiting the
Armagnac area in Southern France? Why not. 'Is it a working party?'
I asked.

We were five at Heathrow. We all had such responsible jobs, editing this and that, doubling as motoring correspondent and diary
editor, writing reviews and administrating, it was surprising any of
us could find time for this three day trip. But find it we did.

Our plane was so late to leave London that when we got on
board, Margaret, from Food and Wine from France, counselled us to
eat from the plastic trays which had been filled by the Trust House
Forte staff. Tucked in our seats like babies in high chairs, we ate
every scrap, even those of us who had not long finished breakfast.

In France our host was M Ledun, an archetypal Frenchman
whose ample frame testified to the goodness of the French way of
life. 'Now we will have a little light lunch,' he said, as we came off the
tarmac. We explained that we had just eaten. 'Psssh,' he said. 'We will
have just a *little* lunch.'

This is the part of France where they produce fine *foie gras*, by
giving geese more to eat than they actually want. He sat us down
and fed us, and a few hours later fed us again. And each day, again
and again and again, with all the fine delicacies that Gascony has to
offer, *ragouts* of pigeon, and salads of *foie gras*, and croustade
Gasconne (a rich apple tart with puff pastry); *civet de lièvre* and
boeuf en daube and *gâteau gersois*.   In between meals we were
shipped from one distillery to another, tasting the light, aromatic

eau-de-vie, which for me is more delicate and flavoursome than its cousin cognac. Kindly distillers thrust bottles into our hands and wished us good drinking.

On the last night M Ledun took us to a fine two-star restaurant in a converted mediaeval chapel in Condom, and treated us to *nouvelle cuisine.* A sea-food soup under a pastry hat; a gamey mousse of hare in pastry; a plate of grilled thrushes...this was too much for the senior wine writer, a lady of seventy. 'How can you do this to your little songbirds', she implored, and aside to me, hissing: 'The French, if it moves they will eat it.' I'd already eaten mine.

On the last day M Ledun took us round the local stores to buy garlic, shallots, wine, sausages and pâtés, and sent us off with a farewell lunch at Toulouse Airport (he recommended the rich and heavy cassoulet); then he waved us into the sky, where immediately French air hostesses tucked us into place and slid a tray of food in front of us.

At Heathrow I declared my three bottles of Armagnac and paid the excess. The excess round my middle took some weeks to disperse.

No sympathy at the office, of course. 'France – I bet you had some wonderful meals.' 'Yes,' I said, 'but I was *working.*'

Poor Old Potato!

Which of the following are the most fattening? Cheddar cheese, lamb chop, fried onions, bread, grilled steak, mashed potatoes, cream crackers, baked potatoes, new potatoes, chips?

It's a fair bet you've placed the three kinds of potatoes high among the fatteners. But you're wrong: the chips, the boiled potatoes and the jacket potatoes all contain less calories than the other foods named.

Getting down to detail, let's take the average sized portion (3 ½ oz) of each. Chips are high enough, true, at 230 calories, but still not as high as bread with 243. Cream crackers are 557. Cheese is 425. Fried onions 355. Grilled steak 304. The fried chop is 629 calories – but the mashed potatoes are only 120, the baked potatoes 104 and the new potatoes 75.

And how many times have you heard friends say they are cutting out potatoes in order to slim? Yet they still go on consuming chocolate, Coke, biscuits, cake and booze – all with high calorie counts.

Poor old potato! Perhaps – but things *are* changing.

If you had to choose between sugar and potatoes in a diet, you'd be mad to drop the potato. Sugar provides energy, but is otherwise useless. The potato provides carbohydrate and more. It provides Vitamin C, some of the Vitamin B group, iron, and there's even some protein – four per cent of your daily needs.

Scientists still disagree over the exact value of Vitamin C, but they don't disagree that the lack of it leads to scurvy, which rots the gums and afflicted sailors as late as the 17th century. Vitamin C certainly keeps the gums, muscles, skin and bones healthy.

Dr Linus Pauling, the Nobel Prize-winner, goes even further. He takes massive doses himself in the belief that it keeps the common cold at bay.

This is by no means proved in clinical tests. But, on the basis of Pauling's recommendations, chemists do a roaring trade in Vitamin C powder and tablets. If you want to follow his advice, though, you can save more than a few pence by shopping for Vitamin C at the greengrocer, not the chemist. The potato alone will give you one third of your daily Vitamin C needs.

What else? Well, there's iron, nearly 10 per cent of your daily needs; that's what you require to keep your blood corpuscles tingling. There's thiamine, which keys up your appetite and digestion; potatoes give you 12 per cent of your daily needs. And there's niacin (sometimes called nicotinic acid but nothing much to do with the stuff in cigarettes) which is especially valuable to growing children. (If your child's tongue were to become red and sore, it would mean he wasn't getting enough niacin. Lack of niacin is also responsible for diarrhoea.)

But these are scarcely the most exciting reasons for eating potatoes. The fact is they are really *marvellous* to eat. If you were to become an expert in cooking potatoes, and only potatoes, you could delight your family continuously. But because potatoes are so common in Britain (and Britain is the only country in the world where potato consumption is going up), we have never greatly prized it in the kitchen. The French, though, with their superior culinary standards, rate it very highly, and have hundreds of sophisticated potato recipes. We just boil and mash them, or we make them into chips – and that's about it. A terrible waste.

Marcel Boulestin, a Frenchman who came to England and opened restaurants in our parents' and grandparents' day, wrote a book about potatoes, and gave a hundred charming recipes. The Potato Marketing Board (50, Hans Crescent, London SW1), naturally, puts out potato recipe books. The prettiest – unfortunately nearly out of print – is *The Midweek Cookbook* by Elizabeth Gundrey, the fierce champion of consumer rights and the driving force behind *Which?*. This book (for 50p and 10p postage) gives 200 recipes. The Board's new book is *Spuds Galore* by the eminently sensible Zena Skinner, giving 84 recipes for 20p (and 5p postage).

Four centuries ago, in Tudor times, the British had rather more respect for the potato, but those were exciting days and the potato was a romantic, exciting object from distant climes. In the absence of pot, they had the potato to turn them on. Falstaff is wishing sexual satisfaction on his friends when he cries: 'Let the sky rain potatoes.' And there is also rude and ready reference to potato fingers – neither potatoes nor fingers in this context.

Sir Walter Raleigh may have introduced the potato into Britain from Virginia in the Americas, but the vegetable is generally believed to have come from Peru. In fact, I once drove through the village famed as the birthplace; it lies between two mountain passes high in the Andes. The potatoes there were tiny compared with the monsters we know, and were light, dry and wrinkled like brown puffballs. These were dried potatoes. Seems they invented the concept of freeze-drying a few thousand years before we did; in this case, because of a natural combination of effects – freezing cold nights and blisteringly hot days.

The English were extremely slow to take to the potato. These white tubers with peculiar growths resembled the pale skins caused by leprosy, a disease feared with good reason in Tudor times.

In a sense, their fear of the potato itself was not unreasonable.

One story has it that, when the Royal cooks at Ham first picked their potato crop, they cut the green stems and leaves, cooked these and ignored the rest. People were very ill – not at all surprising, since the leaves contain a poison called solanine.

In the potato, also, there are about 90 parts of solanine per million, but this is a level with which we easily cope. But potatoes left in the sun turn green and build up this toxic matter. In a greenish potato, the solanine content can increase to 400 parts per million.

Dr Magnus Pyke, the distinguished food scientist and writer, is fond of pointing out that if Raleigh brought potatoes over today, the food and drugs authorities and the Food Standards and Labelling Committee would require him to spend about £50,000 or more on testing for toxic acceptance. And then the potato would not pass our laws. But, as he points out, the extreme rarity of illness from eating potatoes shows there's little real toxic danger. Common sense prevails.

It's a mark of the desperation and poverty of Ireland that this is where the potato first became established in the British Isles. Irish dependence on it was so great that, when the crop failed due to potato blight throughout Europe in 1845, the effect was disastrous. It wasn't just a question of going without potatoes; there was nothing to fatten the cattle, and without cattle nothing to pay the rent, and no rent meant evictions.

While Vitamin C deficiency led to scurvy, many who didn't die were forced to leave their homes and thus Ireland began the first of many mass emigrations which have produced a larger Irish population abroad than on native soil.

That's what the potato did to Ireland. Obviously the potato can have no very lofty place in Irish cuisine.

The potato was introduced with far more determination in France by the man who gives his name to several potato dishes, Auguste Parmentier. He even persuaded Louis XVI to wear the yellow-and-white potato flower in his buttonhole to help popularise it.

But it wasn't actually a cake-walk, even for Parmentier. He believed potato flour could replace wheat in bread – reckoning without people's simple, natural prejudices – and he had little success with this in his own day. He grew the tubers along the Seine under armed guard – not, as some historians have recorded, because people would steal the precious potato, but because he feared the sabotage of bakers and millers who were intent on destroying the crops.

Parmentier's enthusiasm did eventually catch the French imagination, however, though it wasn't until a century later that the greatest chefs of the day – the greatest era of French cooking – blessed potatoes with their genius, and found ways of serving them as specialities... *Pommes Duchesse, Pommes Anna, Pommes Dauphinoise, soufflé* potatoes and so on.

And it was the French who evolved the chipped potato. While Londoners were still buying baked jacket potatoes from street vendors, *pommes frites* established a beach-head in the North of England in the 1780s – and they've never looked back. Now there isn't a café in the land that doesn't offer chips.

Unhappily, though, we haven't taken to many of the other ingenious inventions of the French chef, and there may be a reason for this. Potatoes are basically of two kinds – floury and waxy. Our cookery writers are often very careless when they transcribe recipes from other countries (or perhaps they know the housewife hasn't much hope of getting what she asks for at the greengrocer), so they don't often specify exactly what potato is required.

Even the Potato Marketing Board is blameworthy here. I asked them for a *soufflé* potato recipe, a delightful, original way of cooking them. The PMB gave me a recipe all right – and I followed it to the letter, my wife at my side, watching out for innocent blunders. We carried out each step exactly, from the immersion of the sliced chips in iced water, to the exact temperature for the fat (measured with a cooking thermometer). But only one of the fifty slices ballooned up into the *soufflé* shape. Only one.

Well, we amateur cooks do experience failure and presume it reflects our lack of expertise. But, having eaten *soufflé* potatoes in a restaurant, I knew what they should be, so I searched for some other recipes.

I found the answer in Marcel Boulestin immediately. The Potato Marketing Board hadn't specified the kind of potato you must use. Boulestin says it's very important to use a waxy potato, a potato he

calls the 'yellow, soapy kind'. Now, we can't even buy these (two varieties are Record and Bintje) in Britain, but a new potato is the next
best thing, and the PMB should have specified this.

All right, but *why* can't we buy the waxy potatoes? Ask a greengrocer and he'll tell you there's no demand – and that's because the
housewife doesn't know what she can do with them. And she does-
n't know what she can do with them because she's never had them.
It's a vicious circle, within the circumference of which British culinary interest has gone to sleep, if not died.

So, which potatoes can we buy in Britain?

Well, it's the old story. The most available potato is the one that
gives farmers the biggest yield and the biggest profit. Number one
on the farmer's hit-parade, then, is the big, bland Pentland Crown, a
pale, creamy, thinnish skinned variety. It is far from being the tastiest, far from having the best texture – and far, even, from being ver-
satile. It's also a pale ghost of the number two variety, the King
Edward, a floury potato which we do use well, especially in mashed
and jacket form.

Third is Maris Piper – not quite so mealy; number four is
Pentland Dell – rather like number one, a good cropper, but lacking
character; number five is the pretty, blush-pink Desiree – also
floury, but not as sound as the King Edward.

The Scots have different tastes; they're more likely to be eating
Golden Wonder, the variety which gave its name to the crisp compa-
ny (although crisps are actually made with Record potato) and
Kerr's Pink, and Redskin – all rather floury.

All of this may be good news for those who use their potatoes for
soups, baking and purées. But no good for those who'd like to
explore the delights of potato salads, *soufflé* potatoes, many *sauté*
dishes, and many of the other French specialities mentioned
already.

One thing no-one can complain about is the price of potatoes.
We do get good value, and there's little saving in growing your own,
especially since you can use the ground for other more profitable
vegetables – courgettes, for example.

Potatoes keep well (except in extremes of heat or cold), just as
long as they're kept well out of the light. Otherwise, they'll start to

go green. If you eat as much as 7lb a week you should think about buying in bulk, 56lb at a time.

British farmers grow 6 million tons a year, a trade which is worth £140 million to them. But the percentage of this crop that goes to the shops costs us about £240 million. The moral is clear: cut out the middlemen and the processors and you'll make a good saving. Happily, a large number of Britons do just that; nearly half a million tons are bought over the farm-gate, direct from the farmer.

Most potatoes go to the wholesale trade, which also supplies the caterers and fish-and-chippers; but over half a million tons go for processing into crisps and frozen chips and powders which are quite the most expensive ways to eat a potato today.

There's nothing wrong with the modern instant potato if it's handled right; nothing except the price. There's certainly nothing wrong with a modern crisp, a miracle of technology which keeps crunchy in its film bag for up to ten weeks; nothing except the price – nearly a shilling for less than an ounce of potato. (And you're not giving your children Vitamin C in a bag of crisps, by the way; that vanishes in the processing. In fact, what you're paying for is the oil – a crisp contains 40 per cent oil.)

Actually in Britain, we don't make the most of our potatoes in any way. The Danish and, likewise, the Polish and Russians, treasure potato water, which is both starchy and full of nutrients; they keep it for making soups and boiling other vegetables. They also use potato starch in their cooking; we do sometimes, but not that many people know it. (Potato flour is the main ingredient of Bisto, the gravy mix some people religiously pour over their potatoes.)

The Russians even drink potatoes! They make some of their famous vodkas from them. And, just for fun, Merrydown (the Sussex cider firm) is making a potato wine this year and it will go on display at exhibitions. Some home-wine makers make potato and raisin wine. The only drawback to potato wine, which packs a good alcoholic punch, is that it tastes absolutely filthy. Poteen the illegal Irish whiskey, is based on a kind of potato wine.

Pan's People

They are to television what *Penthouse* and *Playboy* are to magazine publishing. They've even been described in a book as the 'pornography of television'.

Ruth Pearson, one of the five girls, says they get frequent letters from a Mrs Savage, who's convinced they are five whores. 'She says we're obscene. And the way we dance is responsible for the spread of teenage motherhood.' All because Mrs Savage's teenage daughters copy the girls' routines from Top of the Pops, when they pick up pop song themes to illustrate. 'Once we did a dance in Spanish costumes, throwing the skirts above our heads,' says Ruth. 'Mrs Savage said her daughters immediately went out into the streets and threw their skirts over their heads in front of the boys.'

The girls may only be on the air for two and a half minutes, but they put in the same amount of work in rehearsal, perhaps more, than the 'legit' dancers of Sadlers Wells, who do the two and a half hour bit, for Swan Lake.

They rehearse three or four days a week in a boys' rugby club, in a deserted street not far from Shepherds Bush TV studios, under their American choreographer, Flick Colby, one of the original Pan's People. There's a day of rehearsal under the lights at the studio, then the performance itself. Some nights they dance in cabaret. They train as hard as most footballers, perhaps harder.

You can't do that on a Mars Bar. So we wondered, what powered their exciting little frames? Would they be slimming conscious? Would they need special foods to sustain them for long hours of athleticism? Or would they, being the sexy girls they are, be tuned into all the aphrodisiac foods? All three, in fact.

Penthouse, in a spirit of inquiry, invited the five to dinner at the Penthouse Club to sample the new menu provided by Ben Puricelli, who comes to the club with rather a special reputation. He helped cook the famous banquet for 600 when the Shah of Persia held his 2,500 year celebrations in Persepolis a year or two ago.

Penthouse editorial director Steve Ashworth came along too. He was already waiting in the dark of one of the candlelit bars when I arrived. The girls, seen without the usual flickering 625 lines running across their faces, looked stunning. They also appeared taller than the tiny figures on your screen, but not much. Pan's People are not very tall. The amount they consumed was therefore impressive.

Dee Dee Wilde is the spokesgirl for the group. She's the one who marches forward on the screen, leading with her bosom, like the figurehead on an 18th century sailing ship. She's already decided what she wants to say: 'I love all food. It's the next best thing to being with your man.' Dee Dee is 29, and Libra.

Provocative stuff. Babs Lord is the blonde one, who swings her hips in a slow thoughtful way, implanting suggestions more interesting than those in the music she interprets. 'It's not what you eat,' she says, 'but how you eat it and where you eat it.' Babs is 29, and Sagittarius.

Ruth Pearson, the smallest and darkest of the group, is the one whose eyes invite you to some wild, insane orgy. 'If a man I met didn't like food I'd be put off. I'd immediately presume he wouldn't be very imaginative about sex.' Ruth is 29, and Cancer.

Sue Menhenick is the athlete of the group; on the screen she's the one who'll drop to your feet in a submissive slave-girl posture, and hurl her body back in an acrobatic arch. She doesn't think too much about the sexual role of food. For her, food's a power pack. Sue is 20, and Virgo.

Cherry Gillespie is the one who closes up on the camera to mouth a kiss which would melt a choc-ice. She's the only one of the group who's married, and food's been important in her marriage. 'I'm turned on by food. My husband David and I recently zoomed off to France and just ate for three days.' She goes along with Dee Dee, too. Food can be a substitute for sex. Cherry is 20, and Aquarius.

Now they ask Steve Ashworth his views on food. Steve gives a sample menu designed to turn him on.

His favourite meal is half a melon, scooped out to make a pool into which he pours his favourite liqueur, Kummel. You drink the Kummel, leave the melon. Followed by a good rare steak with Brandy sauce. You drink the sauce, leave the steak. Finishing with pancakes stuffed with fruit, served with a sauce of Brandy and Grand Marnier. Drink the Brandy and Grand Marnier, leave the pancakes.

The girls observe that you can tell a lot about a person by his tastes in food. They have come to certain conclusions about Steve already.

Frankly, say the girls, eating is their life, next to working. Ruth: 'When we're travelling we always take our Egon Ronay guide. It's very important to have a good meal. We really spoil ourselves. It doesn't really matter about the atmosphere of a restaurant, the food itself is the important thing.'

By now we're sitting at the table and demolishing chef Puricelli's finest offerings. First there's pâté and Parma ham and a plate of garlic buttered snails. Ruth's verdict: 'The snails aren't garlicky enough. Garlic is an aphrodisiac. You can't have too much of it.'

The thin slices of buttered bread which accompany it, cause merriment. As they pick them up, they droop. A slice of bread should be firm and stiff, they agree. These must be made from Mother's Pride. (Voice from the back: Mother's Shame.)

For the main course, some have duck with orange, some have chicken in sauce, the rest have huge chunks of châteaubriand steak, brown on the outside, bursting with red juice inside. Dee Dee says the most important thing for her is Béarnaise sauce: 'I like food which is gooey and juicy and *bunjery*.' Cherry: 'I like something I can lick and suck and roll around in my mouth. And I go for the smell.'

For the pudding most of them go for the cheesecake. Dee Dee was most critical, since she'd expected most. Licking her lips after the last crumb had gone, she sighed: 'Not very successful. I love a good cheesecake. Or chocolate cake. I'll die eating chocolate cake. Ah. I love all the things which make me fat.'

Cherry says: 'The cheesecake's too chewy.' And Babs: 'Not a hit the cheesecake, but a miss'. All this time, other guests have been noticing the celebrated five and are sending over bottles of champagne. These are hurriedly and appreciatively despatched, not without help from Steve, who's enjoying the liquid side of the meal. He's already introduced Cherry to a Harvey Wallbanger, which tastes very much like it sounds, and now he's got her on to Kummel on the Rocks; double Kummel on the Rocks. The evening is passing into a kind of euphoria.

The girls' verdict on the meal: good. But it didn't have their group favourite, which is Peking Duck. Nor did it have their group hate which is potted shrimps, thank goodness.

What was it about dancing which gave them such hearty appetites? Basically, the demands of their rehearsal. They probably have a light breakfast, then rehearse all morning, and all afternoon too. Dee Dee: 'We have soup for lunch in the winter, salad in the summer. You couldn't dance after a heavy meal. And salad is so sexless.'

It's late. I'm searching for some way to mark this unique occasion, Babs agrees to dance with me. As we go out on to the small floor I feel like an L-driver taking out a Formula One car for a spin round Brand's Hatch. Or trotting out with the England side at Wembley. And there's no-one to comment on my shortcomings, only a man gripped in the deadening power of a Harvey Wallbanger; and the girls, who've seen it all before.

Babs is Ginger Rogers dancing a Fred Astaire number. I'm Fred. A table and a chair by the dance floor serve as studio props and I tap dance elegantly to the top. Then crash. Fancy lights spin in front of my eyes. I have danced into the strobe lighting. Babs returns me to the girls: 'He's a proper Fred.'

Steve rings to say the next day that the £6 for the strobe lighting can come off the fee for the interview. And look, would I interview the chef about the girls' opinions of his cooking?

I ring up and arrange the interview, but when I get to the Penthouse Club kitchens, he isn't there. 'I have come about the interview,' I explain to his assistant chef. 'I will interview you,' he says graciously, 'What experience do you have washing dishes?'

Ben, when I do find him, turns out to be younger than most of the girls. He accepts their comments with good humour. 'I cook to the specifications of the club. Ninety per cent of the customers don't want to smell of garlic, so I don't put too much garlic in the snails.' Mother's Pride with snails? He didn't comment.

Ben then produced one of the great menus of the century, the one he'd helped cook for the Shah of Persia. It reads: Caviar served in halves of hard-boiled quails' eggs. Mousse of crayfish, with

Nantua sauce. (That's made from the shells pounded with butter, cooked with cream and brandy.) Saddle of lamb stuffed with mushrooms. Then a sorbet, spiked with a 1911 vintage champagne from Moet. Then Peacock Imperial, a baby peacock to each guest, served with choice blue and green tail feathers from a large male peacock. Then an Alexandre Dumas salad, lettuce hearts, sprinkled with sieved hardboiled yolks of eggs to look like mimosa blossoms. Finally, a turban of figs, piled high, and served with fresh raspberries.

Ben had eaten some of it, and it was pretty good. As for the guests, he didn't really notice them. And in any case he's been on culinary terms with the very famous for many years, since he used to be a chef at one of the world's most expensive hotels, the St. Moritz in Switzerland. He's cooked for most of Europe's royalty, and President Ford and Italy's Fiat Boss, Umberto Agnelli, and Sophia Loren. Even Ringo Starr.

He said he was very honoured to have cooked for Pan's People. 'Could you just say who they are again?' he asked.

What Kind of Eater Are You?

How much do you reveal about yourself by the kind of food you eat? Are you a Moody Eater or an Eager Eater? Are you a Fussy Eater, or a Showy Eater? Or even an Alarmed Eater? Try this quiz to test your own rating, then see how your tastes compare with those of six celebrities.

The psychologists who helped me compile the quiz did so in light-hearted vein, but in some parts of the world the new science of foodology is taken very seriously by sociologists and psychiatrists.

In America, for example, the Pentagon has been using foodology to select the best recruits for the Army. They gave a grant to two psychologists, Dr Howard Schulz and Dr J Kamentsky, at the National Institute of Health, for the investigation of food preferences of officer candidates.

The men most likely to make war, not love, the men discovered, were those with a preference for rare steaks. Fish-eaters had less drive than meat-eaters. Those who liked starchy foods lacked the character to make decisions. Those who drank a lot of milk, the psychologists concluded, shouldn't be considered as officer material at all. They disliked complicated situations and sought the comfort and security of childhood.

In another military experiment Dr Richard Wallen investigated the food tastes of two groups of American Marines. Half were normal, the other half were due to be discharged from the service on psychiatric grounds. Dr Wallen tried out 150 different foods on them. Normal Marines accepted most of them, but declined some twenty percent of the more peculiar dishes. The disturbed Marines couldn't stomach even half the food they were given. They rejected over sixty percent. It seems that they, too, yearned for a simpler life.

Japan was one of the first countries to exploit the potential of foodology. Dr Kiichi Kuriyama, head of the Food Research Institute, Tokyo, created a delightful sensation a few years ago when he said he could tell people's sex characteristics by their food choices. People who eat steak (American Marine officers, for example) are selfish in bed, and think only of their own satisfaction. Spinach eaters are quite good lovers, peanut-eaters are indiscriminate. Cottage-cheese eaters are moody in bed, and turnip-eaters are dull and unimaginative in bed. (He seems not to have put baked-bean eaters to the test.)

It's not only the Americans and the Japanese who have investigated foodology. One of the most serious studies was conducted by the famous British psychologist, Professor H J Eysenck. The answer to personality and character, he said, is a lemon. Tests show you could tell an introvert from an extrovert by putting lemon juice on their tongue. The introvert produces more saliva. (In fact the introvert reacts more strongly to all kinds of stimuli: noise, pain, etc.)

For this foodology quiz I have divided eaters into five classes. Put a ring round the answers which best reflect your own feelings, then look up your scores at the end.

SECTION A

1 *You've had a good lunch, and suddenly you're asked out for a second big meal, dinner in a first-class restaurant the same evening. You feel:*

    a Pleased, but sorry you've already eaten.

    b Disgusted at the idea of overeating.

    c Very keen at the idea of going somewhere new and exciting.

2 *You're offered an item of unnerving food you've never tried, like snails. You:*

    a Taste them a little anxiously, feeling comforted because they have a good reputation.

    b Taste them quite unwillingly.

    c Turn them down – they might make you feel sick.

3 *You eat too much at a meal:*

    a Almost never.

    b Sometimes.

    c Quite often.

SECTION B

1 *You're taken to a restaurant and the waiter sits you near a nosiy serving hatch. You:*

    a Feel annoyed, but sit down there.

    b Ask him if there isn't a better table.

    c Refuse to take the table and ask to speak to the manager.

2 *Given a choice of three exciting-looking dishes you:*

    a Choose the one that looks the prettiest.

    b Ask how each one is made, then weigh the decision carefully.

    c Say you don't mind which one you have.

3 *At a friend's house you've finished a pleasant but unremark-able meal. You:*

    a Repeatedly thank the hostess to make her feel comfortable.

    b Smile silently to show appreciation.

    c Express enormous enjoyment and ask for the recipes.

SECTION C
1 *Your host at a meal tells you that the food is organic. You:*
   a Think, 'Good, it will taste better.'
   b Wonder, 'What the hell.'
   c Feel relieved.

2 *When buying tinned food in a supermarket, you read the label because:*
   a You're mildly curious.
   b You want to know the ingredients to see how nutritious the contents are.
   c You want to make sure it doesn't contain chemical additives.

3 *You think the Government's approach to food safety is:*
   a Very thorough, thanks to modern science.
   b Not nearly thorough and demanding enough.
   c Just about safe within current limits.

SECTION D
1 *When you go back to your family, the kind of meal that pleases you most is:*
   a A delicacy that you've never tried before.
   b An old childhood favourite.
   c Any meal in which you know extra effort has been taken.

2 *How important is it to you that milk, tea and sugar are put in the right order for you?*
   a Mildly prefer it in the right order.
   b Doesn't make a shred of difference.
   c Feel irritated if the order is wrong.

3 *The glass and cutlery are not gleaming. Would you:*
   a Discreetly clean it with a napkin.
   b Leave it – you can trust your hostess.
   c Check it, just to make sure it's OK.

SECTION E
1 *The sort of restaurant you feel is best for a night out if you aren't having to pay is*:
　a An informal, crowded, candle-lit bistro.
　b A celebrated restaurant with music, dancing, frequented by famous people.
　c The local Italian or Chinese restaurant where they know you.

2 *The kinds of waiter you prefer is:*
　a A charmer who can make the menu sound like a love poem, and makes you smile.
　b A frank waiter who tells you all about the menu and makes firm suggestions.
　c The one who leaves you alone, and doesn't try and influence your decision.

3 *The kind of cookery book you enjoy most is*:
　a A Marguerite Patten, who gives you masses of straightforward recipes.
　b A Robert Carrier or a Fanny Craddock, who generate a lot of excitement about style and the way food is presented.
　c An Elizabeth David, who concentrates on authenticity, capturing the spirit of the original dish.

SECTION A	SECTION B	SECTION C
1 a5 b0 c10	1 a10 b5 c0	1 a5 b0 c10
2 a5 b10 c0	2 a5 b0 c10	2 a0 b5 c10
3 a0 b5 c10	3 a5 b10 c0	3 a0 b10 c5

SECTION D	SECTION E
1 a0 b10 c5	1 a5 b10 c0
2 a5 b0 c10	2 a10 b5 c0
3 a10 b0 c5	3 a0 b10 c5

Add up the scores for section A, B, C, D, and E quite separately. Note which section rates the highest, then consult the key below. If you have equal scores in more than one section, you are combination of different types. If you have the same score in all five sections you are either very mixed up or, conversely, a model of the perfectly balanced eater. You will know which.

Section A You are an eager eater. You are greedy, uninhibited and prepared to try anything new, which goes for other aspects of your character. You have a tendency to overeat, though you are sometimes so eager for other experiences you have no time for food at all. Typical eager eaters are Robert Morley and Peter Ustinov.

Our psychiatrists say: 'Eager eaters have a feeling of emptiness inside. They may have had a good experience of the breast, but they are also filled with the envy of it.'

Section B You are a moody eater. You never think about food until pressed. You quite like food when you get it, but you are never demonstrative or demanding. Some moody eaters, out of a sense of emptiness, go to the extreme and overeat. Moody eaters include Emlyn Williams, Dame Sybil Thorndyke and Sir Terence Rattigan.

Our psychiatrists say: 'Moody eaters have feelings of emptiness inside. They are somewhat akin to eager eaters, but they feel that their hungry assault on the nipple will damage the breast, and this causes feeling of guilt. Hence their rather sulky, moody, approach to food.'

Section C You are an alarmed eater. You feel you are treading your path through a minefield of health hazards; you buy organically-grown, unsprayed apples, and read the small-print in stores to make sure there's no monosodium glutamate or sodium carbomethycellulose in your food. Alarmed eaters include Yehudi Menhuin, Pete Murray and Carol Channing.

Our psychiatrists say: 'It could be a fear of taint on the mother's milk. Could have been sparked off by a change in a predominantly good experience at the breast to a bad one. Bad weaning is the most obvious such crisis.'

Section D You are a fussy eater. You must always have your eggs boiled just so many and a half minutes, and you think tea tastes different if the milk is put in last, and you find it hard to make a change in your dietary habits. Lord Boothby is one of those fussy eaters.

Our psychiatrists view: 'They are orderly people with a sense of cleanliness which often comes from a parent or nanny's fussiness about their toilet.'

Section E You are a showy eater and you like excitement and drama with your food. You like eating in exotic places, especially places which reflect the grand life. You love cook books in which cookery writers dress up their food with travel excitement or history. Liberace is a showy eater; it's not what he eats , but how he eats it: 'Elegantly and beautifully prepared.'

Our psychiatrists say: 'Showy eaters had good eating experiences as a baby, when mother made every feed an occasion.'

Vanity Fare

This and the ensuing Vanity Fare articles appeared as monthly recipe strips in Vanity Fair *magazine.*

Herring and mackerel would surely be delicacies if they cost enough. As it is they are both cheap, and rich in all kinds of food value, and it's a pity not to take full advantage. Soused herring and soused mackerel are particularly delicious.

To prepare the fillets: Cut off the head and tail
Slit herring lengthwise, clean under tap
Place down on board, press flat with heel of hand
Turn over, pull out bone. Divide in two, trim neatly

Soused herring or mackerel. Put the fillets, one or two per person, into a buttered oven dish, cover with rings of sliced onion, with black peppers, allspice, chilli pepper, to taste. Cover with half vinegar, half water (though an old recipe gives beer instead of water). Bake in medium oven for 30 mins, then leave to cool in own liquid.

Pickled Herrings. Served as rollmops in smart restaurants, but simple to make at home. The Scandinavians don't only eat them on their own, but also chopped up, in salads – mixed, for example, with cold potatoes, pickled beetroot, pickled cucumber, raw chopped cooking apple, chopped onion.

Roll the fillets from wide end first, with a little piece of onion in the centre, securing them with halved cocktail sticks, or toothpicks. Prepare a mixture of 1oz mixed spice, 1oz sugar, salt, peppercorns, with garlic and chilli peppers to taste (just a little). Pack jar with layers of herrings and spices, filling it up with boiled vinegar which has been allowed to cool. They are ready to eat in a week, should keep a month or so.

Elizabeth David

There's only room for one at the top. And that place is occupied by Elizabeth David.

Her reputation stands on a comparatively small amount of work. Her first devastating *Mediterranean Cooking*, which burst like a firework on the post-war era of rationing. (She didn't even mention margarine in it.) Then her two French cookery books, *French Provincial Cooking*, and *French Country Cooking*. Then *Italian Food*, and *Summer Cooking*.

She appeals at three levels: to the romantic, in the way she evokes memories of the pleasure of food; to the scientist, in the way she is scholar and researcher, looking into the whys and wherefores of recipes; and to the ordinary cook, producing workable recipes explained step by step, with enormous patience, recipes tested and tested again.

She alone among cookery writers can be so aloof as to say of some classic dish, of French onion soup, for example, that she doesn't like it, and therefore won't give the recipe.

Her recipes stem from experience of cooking in many foreign kitchens, in France, Germany, Italy, India, Greece. And they also flow from her love of reading old cookery books, many of them in French. She has a large and fascinating library, though nothing like as comprehensive as André Simon's. In fact, she wishes she could give up the whole of the business of writing about cookery, just to get a chance to start reading all her cookery books.

She rose so sharply to the top that she seems to have been there longer than she has. For some years now, books have been coming out from other writers in which they acknowledge debt to her, one unsolicited testimony after another. Arabella Boxer, author of *First Slice Your Cookbook* acknowledges a debt to her, and her only. Katharine Whitehorn, in *Kitchen in a Corner*, says she is David-inspired. Jean Robertson, in T*he Sunday Telegraph Cookery Book* goes all the way. 'It was Elizabeth David with her scholarly integrity and magnetic style who first made me want to cook. Her influence will be manifest to anyone who uses this book.' And so on.

Elizabeth David, to meet, is a slender woman, looking younger than her early fifties, shy, graceful, feline. There's something of the goddess about her. A faint trace of the Sarah Bernhardt. Something of a Victorian engraver's study – this one called Diffidence. She is, in turns, sad, distracted, frail, then breaks into charming laughter, catches a mood of gaiety and pursues a gently mocking line about someone's unusual characteristics.

The archaic English of the English girls' boarding school breaks through. 'I was cross as two sticks', and 'Distraught', 'What a fag' and 'Ghastly disaster'. She seldom looks at the person she is speaking to and, like a cat, goes her own way. Sometimes she turns on you, and again like a cat, gives you her rare, fascinated attention. She doesn't like being questioned about herself. And she finds the search for answers a strain, forcing out names and dates and places. It's as if to say, what do names and dates and places matter – lost in the past among dreams and teeming memories of happinesses and unhappinesses? She makes you feel it's wrong to try to call back the past...

She was making bread when I went to see her. She lives in a quiet street in Chelsea, in a house where you wend your way down to the kitchen, the key room, of course, sunk deep down, right at the back. There's an impression of confusion, but only an impression. Everything has a deliberate place and Mrs David is constantly putting things back. You come in past her well-furnished study, lined with books, down a few steps, past a bookcase lined with files (for another recipe book? - she shrugs), past some wine-racks, a large refrigerator, and then down more steps into the kitchen.

She lives here summer and winter, a happy room which was once the backyard, but had this kitchen built into it. It looks out onto a whitewashed wall, but some strange, thick stemmed plant which is not a bamboo grows here in clusters and makes the window look like the back window in a stage set.

Nothing gets into the house that isn't individually cared for: lovely pots from Provence, every sort of earthenware jug and pot, kitchen fittings in pine. Three dressers of unvarnished pine, two pinewood cupboards with sliding doors, wooden plate racks, a pine table six feet long, specially made for her. On the wall she has made a feature of half a dozen metal, Spanish cake-racks. There are jars of spoons, wooden spoons of all shapes and sizes, round ones, short ones, pointed ones, square ones. 'It's very important for me to have the right spoon, and if I can't find the spoon I want, I get quite distraught.'

She was making bread and dressed in an attractive brown apron, made of linen. The bread was to be photographed for an advertising pamphlet. 'No, not advertising bread – advertising vodka, actually. But they pay on the nail, which is jolly. Unlike editors.'

It was a delicate operation, baking, because she was worrying about the gas. 'It keeps popping, and it goes out if it gets too low. I have to watch it. I'd like to have a real stove down here, but I can't because of ancient lights and all that, you know, smokeless zones and so on. The kitchen was built over the original yard. I have no heater, and as I live in the kitchen I keep the oven going all the time, in the winter, anyway.' She gave me one of her what-else-can-you-do looks.

On the table was a sweet-smelling arrangement of sweet peas and roses in an attractive brown earthenware pot. All round, signs of bread-making; bags of flour, 'Horsfields stoneground, containing the whole germ of the wheat. And Pride of Sussex made by Hodson, they're very nice and helpful. Harrod's use theirs, but under their own name. I use eighty-five per cent wholemeal with some white. All wholemeal gives too much flavour for the sort of thing I want.

'I can't believe American bread is worse than ours. If you're writing in papers and mention bread or sausages you start a controversy. Useful when things are dull. If you opened a bread shop, I mean with real bread, you'd be swamped. George and Cecilia Scurfield wrote a book for Faber, *Home Baked*. They did that, then opened a place for bread, but they soon had too many orders to carry on.

'The recipe for this bread (the one she was making) runs to eight typed pages. It's not a short recipe. The trouble with magazine articles is that you can't say anything in them because they want four to six recipes. I'd like to use all my space doing just one recipe and doing it properly.'

The loaves were ready now and Mrs David took them out carefully. She tapped them thoughtfully all round, like a builder listening for hollow floorboards. She put them back in the oven with the gas off. 'Slightly undercooked, but they will photograph better. I've been bashing away at this awful bread,' she said. But she didn't mean awful bread because a few minutes later she was saying, 'It's a pity it's got to be sent away. It's a shame I've got to send them.'

The boys from the agency came in and collected her bread; looked at it, sniffed at it, asked for props to photograph with it, and Mrs David obligingly handed over some treasured possessions, jugs and pots. She tied the bread in a white napkin, first by two opposite corners, then the other two corners over the top of the first knot. There was a hole in the cloth which made her smile. Very authentic. When the boys left, she said to me: 'Do you think they know what they are doing? I wonder.' Another sigh. 'Never mind, let's have a drink.' By this time another well-wisher had arrived, with an almond cake for her. The 'drink' was a fine wine. It was a Graves, Chateau Pontac Monplaisir, 'From Christopher's,' she said, 'A present I suppose.'

She talked about the bread she was making, then said she was now making her own cheese. Her visitor promptly said she'd started growing tomatoes on the roof. 'You'll be keeping a goat next,' laughed Elizabeth David. 'Oh, it's deplorable what things are coming to. I hope I don't have to grow my own wine. I still shop a bit at the Wholefood shop in Baker Street, but they've turned themselves into a self-service shop, nullified themselves. They serve cut cheese in cellophane wrappings. So I'm making my own cheese out of untreated milk. You can't make it out of pasteurised milk, the temperature has been raised too high and kills bacteria. Bacteria help make cheese.'

She smokes a lot, the strong-flavoured *Gauloise*. 'It's a fairly disgusting habit,' she says. 'I tried eating sweets instead, but all I managed to do was dislodge several very expensive fillings. And so I started again.'

Elizabeth David was one of the four daughters of Rupert Gwynne, who was conservative MP for Eastbourne until he died in 1952. They lived near Wilmington in Sussex. One of her sisters now lives with her in London.

It was a happy upper-middle-class childhood, in a home where children were not welcome in the kitchen.

'We had governesses, then I went to school at Godstow, near High Wycombe, until sixteen. The food was horrible, terrible boiled fish, awful meat. I wanted to be a painter. I couldn't paint at all, as you can see (*shrug*) but after school in Switzerland I was sent to Paris to study. I worked in a studio, but after six months I was not getting anywhere...' (She manages to convey a deep sense of gloom, of disappointment and failure.)

While she was at the Sorbonne studying, she lived with a French family who awoke her interest in food. Her encounter with this 'exceptionally greedy and well fed' family is humorously described in *French Provincial Cooking*:

'Their cook, a young woman called Leontine, was bullied from morning till night, and how she had the spirit left to produce such delicious dishes I cannot now imagine. Twice a week at dawn Madame, whose purple face was crowned with a magnificent mass of white hair, went off to do the marketing at Les Halles, the central markets, where she bought all the provisions, including flowers for the flat. I don't think any shopping at all was done locally, except for things like milk and bread. She would return at about ten o'clock, two bursting black shopping bags in each hand, puffing, panting, mopping her brow, and looking as if she was about to have a stroke. Indeed, poor Madame, after I had been in Paris about a year, her doctor told her that high blood pressure made it imperative for her to diet.

'Her diet consisted of cutting out meat once a week. With Friday a fish day anyway, this actually meant two days without meat. On Wednesdays, the day chosen, Madame would sit at table, the tears welling up in her eyes as she watched us helping ourselves to our *roti de veau* or *boeuf à la cuillère*. It was soon given up, that diet. Her grown-up children, two of whom were afflicted with a tragic eye disease and were probably going blind, simply could not bear to watch her sufferings – although, of course, they were not prepared to go so far as to share in her privations. Denise, the only able-bodied daughter, was the greediest girl I had ever seen. She worked as secretary to a world-famous Parisian surgeon, and came home every day to midday meal. Before she took off her hat and coat she would shout out to Leontine to know what was for lunch. Munching through two helpings of everything she would entertain us to gruesome details of the operations performed by her employer.'

Elizabeth David learned French and German.

'I did my time in Munich like everybody else. I was eighteen. It was a time when things were beginning to get rather hectic with decadent German barons sloshing about. It was delicious food but I'd never want to do a book about that.'

'I went on the stage then. To get away from home, partly. From 1932 to 1937 I was with the Oxford Rep as assistant stage manager. One week playing the lead, the next week sweeping the stage. I wasn't very good. I was a thundering bad actress. Then I worked in the Open-air Theatre, Regent's Park, pranced about the park in the amphitheatre. I enjoyed the life (she waved a wooden spoon) but I couldn't make a living at it. I was glad of the training, though.

'Then I went to Worth's, selling clothes. Not very long though. Under a year. I didn't like it, and I wasn't very good at it. I wouldn't be very good at selling any sort of clothes...

'Just before the beginning of the war, I went to Greece with a friend. We lived on the island of Syros, for about a year. It is the centre of the Cyclades, a port-of-call between Athens and Turkey. Very cheap, and the food was very poor, but you could live on such a very small income. For about £100 a year.'

And then?

'A curtain denotes the passing of time,' she said, dropping her eyes. 'The Germans were kind of charging about a bit. I went to Crete.' She fell to silence and offered no more information.

Then?

'I spent the rest of the war in the Middle East, Egypt. At the

Admiralty in Alexandria, and the Ministry of Information in Cairo. My French came in handy because I ran the reference library and the Free French were there. French has been useful in every job. I married in Egypt, an officer. He was posted to India and I joined him in 1946 in Delhi. It certainly was peculiar, very peculiar. I had always had a job and here I was in Delhi, doing nothing. Auchinleck wouldn't let anyone out of Delhi. Petrol was rationed so you couldn't travel. It was a garrison town and it was the end of the Raj. The British hated the Indians. The Indians hated the British. I was there seven months, then I got ill. Sinus. It was really disastrous. I don't know if you know anything about sinus, but I was told I would never get cured if I stayed. It was a complaint to be taken seriously. It meant a long leave. They could whip them home. I had killer headaches and got very depressed. I'd burst into tears for no reason at all if someone spoke sharply to me, or simply said, "Shut the window". You can't drink or if you do, immediately you get a headache. It cleared up and I've never had it again so badly. I was miserable, but one is miserable because one's ill. There's really no known cure for sinus. For bad sinus there's an operation, but they say if the operation doesn't succeed it may make you more vulnerable.

'We came back to rationing, and my husband bought this house. I needed a job and I had turned down an offer from the Council of Industrial Design. About this time I started writing cookery articles. Through a friend on *Harpers Bazaar*. I said, "Everyone writes such humbug." And she said, why didn't I try? I said, "I can't write, don't want to." Mrs David said this like a petulant girl, "Don't want to."

'But she forced me to. It was Anne Scott James who gave me the job of writing a cookery column.

'I was seven years on *Harpers Bazaar*. They paid eight guineas an article, it went up to ten guineas, finally to twenty-five guineas, a huge sum of money (*actress's ironic expression*).

'I started to write *Mediterranean Cooking* in the terrible winter of 1946-47. I had no gas or electricity, and I went to a hotel in Ross-on-Wye. The food was bleak, ghastly, and it was terrible weather. I just started to put recipes down, purely for my own pleasure. I got them into some kind of book-shape, but they were turned down by two or three publishers.

'Robin Chancellor showed it to John Lehmann, and John Lehmann sent for me: "I'm going to publish it," he said. I was flabbergasted. "I'll get John Minton to illustrate it," he told me eagerly. John Lehmann is an absolutely riveting person, an intellectual, one hundred per cent genuine, and what's more he's a poet, very good to authors. It was almost the first cookery book after the war.' This was cookery's El Alamein and the tide began to turn.

'It was a time really when they didn't have cookery articles. Why should they? They didn't have food. The person who really helped me was Audrey Withers, editor of *Vogue*. Audrey gave me the jobs on *Vogue* and *House and Garden*, and she was first to put the article in the middle of the magazine with a picture. She told me, "I want Anthony Denney to do the pictures." I was very much against it. You can't do colour pictures of food, I said. I think they're damned awful. We looked at them, and I said it can't be done in studios. She said, "Will you meet him?" I did and I liked him. I saw he knew what he was doing. We took all the pictures here. Audrey gave it a lovely lot of room and space.

'In 1958 we went around France photographing markets. Fish, cheese, butter markets. It was all rather terrifying, such hard work and anxiety. Well, I had to get lots of information. Maybe it was raining or you were late. I went with Anthony Denney, and maybe Anthony would say, when we were all finished and two hours away, "I took all those pictures with no film in my camera," or we'd get to another town and I'd say to Anthony, "Oh, I forgot to ask the people what variety those tomatoes were."

'It was a very nice series though and people liked it. One picture we took of a butter market looked very tranquil, someone told us later. We laughed. There had been a raging wind and I was hanging on to his coat so as not to blow away. A beautiful calm atmosphere!'

Her first book led to others; her first disappointment was when John Lehmann's publishing house was taken over by Macdonald. It wasn't a happy arrangement for Mrs David. Then her books appeared in paperback.

'One doesn't make much money on *Penguins*. I get fifty per cent with the publishers for *Penguin* rights. What John Lehmann did was to take my books just after the war – and publish them with understanding the way I wanted them done.' She wrote in the *Sunday Times*, the *Daily Telegraph, Sunday Dispatch, Daily Mail, Harpers Bazaar, Vogue* and more recently in *The Spectator* and *Nova*.

Her books are still building up. They go to America and one by one get translated for the European markets.

'*French Provincial Cooking* was a notable flop in the US. I had fan-*tas*-tic notices in the US, better than here, so it shows you that notices don't do anything for you. I just don't know the market. I think television matters there. *Italian Food* sold to the Swedes. The Norwegians bought *French Country Cooking*.'

As she was talking, she was moving about the kitchen and suddenly a knife and fork slid in front of me on to the table, napkins, plates, and without any fuss a marvellous and simple meal appeared. She appeared lost in thought, then seemed to remember: 'I've got these delicious new potatoes I cooked last night... do you like a potato omelette?'

She started talking about Spanish omelettes and the awful people who thought you just tipped everything in it.

'I think you should only use potatoes for Spanish omelette,' she said.

I said they usually used potatoes and some onions.

'They do. I like going to Spain. You hear the food isn't good, but perhaps that means the coast. Inland, the food is very good indeed. I like the very simple things, tomatoes, cheese, simple wine. I'm a Greek bore and a Provence bore, but I'm not going to be a Spanish bore.'

While she was preparing the omelette little things appeared on the table. Salami sausage for slicing, called *casalinga*. Chunky pieces of meat and fat matured for eighteen months at least, from her favourite shop in Soho. Black olives, which she keeps in a jar steeped in olive oil, only the best olive oil. 'Expensive,' she shrugs, as if to say, what else can you do. She drains the olives carefully and sprinkles them with lemon juice.

'Lemon juice – echoes of Greece. Greece is halfway to the Middle East and that's where they start to use lemon juice.'

She makes the omelette deliciously light. Serves lettuce salad separately in a dressing which is mainly oil.

'I use the least possible amount of vinegar.' She measures precisely eight times as much oil into a white salad bowl. Throws in a pinch of coarse salt, a pinch of sugar, a couple of turns on the pepper mill. Tarragon vinegar, she says. She doesn't make her own. She says it, as if it were a shortcoming.

'Can you open that case?' She points to a cardboard case. I opened the box to discover a wine called Gigondas, *La Cave du Vigneron*.

Now we are eating raspberries and redcurrants. She serves cream too, but not on top. She likes to eat hers separately. Everything seemed good. What was the butter? Oh, just Wheelbarrow Dutch unsalted. 'It's just that...' I began to say.

She laughed: 'Food seems better in other people's houses. Do you know Provence?'

'Mostly from your books... when I go through Provence I'm always thinking of one of your pink-washed kitchens in the Camargue.' (True; my wife and I living in Spain insisted on having a pink-washed kitchen in our Camargue.)

'Ah,' she sighed, 'Provence. Was it really like that? And if it was, is it still like that?'

I asked her about her writing. 'I don't like writing. Writing doesn't come easily to me. It gets more and more difficult. I do a lot of work – you should see what I don't use. I'm very interested in my new kitchen equipment shop. I've started it with two friends. I had the idea before I heard Madame Cadec was closing in Soho. You know what it is now? A strip club, her shop.' She said this with genuine shock, as if a church had been turned into a brothel. 'I miss it. I want to get out of writing. I have an article to do for *Nova*. It should have been in three days ago. I don't know what the editors will do. I do all the work. I can't do all the research I need to do for it. But I don't want to have to depend on writing. I don't want to be writing little bits about how to cook haddock when I'm seventy. Auntie Nellie's cookery corners are not for me.

'When I write I find I can say what I please. You're restricted by time really. There's so much you want to find out. You're not really qualified to write about things unless you see them from the start. I mean, milk the cows, see the wheat being ground.

'I don't copy recipes without trying them out. I don't reprint without trying them again. It's the sort of trap people fall into. The sort of thing that happens when people translate, other people copy it, and it didn't occur to them to give some detail that seems obvious to them. When it says sausagemeat they don't mean English sausagemeat which is half bread and rusk. In France and Italy it is pure pork. An awful lot of people think it's easy to lift recipes out.'

When she speaks her mind, she's liable to get into trouble. 'I once said it was better not to use soup cubes, and Oxo took it as personal. Would I withdraw, the editor asked me? I said no. I don't believe you can. Stock cubes, I don't know. I think it's a few chicken bones and lots of monosodium glutamate.' Being shown over a factory didn't alter her strong views.

Her books speak her philosophy and her prejudices. In *Summer Cooking* you find them frequently. She condemns over-refrigerated, lifeless food. She says that throwing away stale herbs is preferable to throwing them into the food. And salads! She says in *Summer Cooking*:

'How one learns to dread the season for salads in England. What becomes of the hearts of the lettuces? What makes an English cook think that beetroot spreading its hideous purple dye over a sardine and a spoonful of tinned baked beans constitutes an *hors d'oeuvres*? Why make the cold salmon, woolly enough anyhow by midsummer, look even less appetising than it is by serving it on a bed of lettuce leaves apparently rescued from the dustbin? What is the object of spending so much money on cucumbers, tomatoes and lettuces because of their valuable vitamins, and then drowning them in vinegar and chemical salad dressings?'

As for soup, she says, English soups appear to be exactly the same in summer and winter. Consommé is the exception, but is not sufficiently clarified, or if it is, it's a depressing colour.

Indeed the only other thing any other cookery writer has against her is the fact that she is so critical of English food so often. She defends herself, says it's not true, and that she's writing a book of English cookery.

Take this description of hers on going picnicking:

'The less heroic, lacking the organising ability and resolution of the outdoor cooking enthusiast, will settle for the car-borne picnic bought in a market, or in Sunday morning shops of small French towns. A bottle of wine from a café, a baguette or two of freshly-baked bread (it would be sad if English travellers new to the Continent were all to emulate the lady from the Midlands who wrote to a Leicester newspaper two years ago declaring that she had taken half a dozen large English loaves to France and so had made her family independent of French bread and French bakers), a little parcel of butter, a variety of ready-made salads, olives, slices of sausage and mountain-cured ham from the cooked-food shops; some creamy ewe's milk, Banon cheese wrapped in chestnut leaves, a hard, salty grey-coated Valenay, or a long neat little log of Sainte-Maure; a bag of cherries or fresh peaches – all these are crammed into your shopping bag. A last stop to buy a slab of chocolate and a packet of *Petit Beurre* and you're off. Does it matter very much that by the time you have driven fifty miles and settled on your picnic spot your parcels are a little crumpled, your wine a trifle warm (too late, you remember that had you taken the precaution of wrapping the bottle in several sheets of dampened newspaper it would have been as cool as cucumber), your chocolate beginning to melt? After all, it is summer. You are on holiday. You are in company of your own choosing. The air is clean. You can smell wild fennel and thyme, dry resinous pine needles, the sea. For my part, I ask no greater luxury. Indeed I can think of none.'

She makes her own bread, her own cheese, not her own vinegar. 'You must have a Mother of Vinegar. Robert Carrier got me some. It died. It's slippery, slimy stuff and you put it in a keg, and pour in your odds and ends of wine. I used to get my vinegar from Madame Cadec. She made her own tarragon vinegar, put the tarragon in it, leaves and all.'

One thinks of Elizabeth David as the pinnacle of perfection, never going wrong.

'No. Of course I make mistakes. I make mistakes all the time. But what goes wrong really when you're putting a meal together? Panic. You should have raspberries. There aren't any. You don't want cream, but what about the guests? Won't they think you're mean if you don't offer cream? Somebody's husband is not going to be happy without potatoes. Put some French beans in. Already you are overloaded. It destroys you, it destroys the meal. And don't forget, you're a cookery writer, and for a cookery writer giving someone a meal is pretty nightmarish. I don't care, but if someone goes away and says, all I got was a pork chop ... so what do you do if they don't enjoy a pork chop and a salad?

'I'm not against tinned food. I don't make rules about these things. I like sardines, anchovies, chick peas. I don't make rules, I don't have the necessity. Tinned vine leaves, stuffed with rice. And Kit-E-Kat of course.' (Next time I saw her she said her cat wouldn't eat it any more.)

'I don't have any hard and fast attitude. There are an awful lot of ways of doing things with almost the same results. A lot of people with chef's training get there faster, but chefs are inclined to know only one way of doing things, They've either forgotten, or else they've had no chance to find out ... They don't know how to do things where there is a romantic appreciation. It's a historical thing, too. I'm terribly interested to know all about chocolate, how the Spaniards changed flavouring it with cinnamon to vanilla. Chefs say this is how you do it and nobody goes any further than that, and it seems bad to me. A chef is in command in a kitchen like a colonel is in charge of a platoon or a brigade or whatever it is.

'Of course, they have got to have rules or else ... They say it's right because Escoffier did it. He was eighty-nine when he died, and what he did was good, but if he had lived now I am sure he would have found a better way. His knowledge and skill was always developing, and it would be today. Naturally, I've read his books. I think they're marvellous, only I have reservations. They are not good for the present day.'

The books which are good for the present day are in fact – Elizabeth David's. And long may they last.

Good English Grub

We Britons are pretty generous about foreign food and you'd think foreigners would be decent about us in return. But they're not. They're absolutely rotten about our food. They think we live on fish and chips and egg and chips. I suppose that's because there are translation difficulties when it comes to explaining about kippers and smoked haddock, black pudding and jellied eels, Cornish pasties and Stargazy pies (the fishes' heads stick out of the pastry), and such regional oddities as frumenty (crushed wheat, soaked overnight in milk and water, baked with honey and cinnamon).

Here are some truly British recipes.

Cheese-and-ale from Gloucestershire. Cut cheese, Gloucestershire for preference, into thin slices, and place in a fireproof oven dish. Spread with made mustard, pour enough beer on to cover, and bake till cheese melts. Wet some slices of toast made with brown bread in beer, pour on the hot cheese and serve at once.

Jugged hare. Joint the pieces, dust in seasoned flour and put in a jug or casserole; cover with 1½ pints good stock (something better than a stock cube if you can manage it). Hare is sweet, so put in a sliced lemon for tartness, a halved onion, a dozen peppercorns. Stand the jug in a big saucepan of water and bring to the boil, leaving to simmer for 3 to 4 hours. Now mix the blood of the hare with a glass of red wine, port if possible, and four generous tablespoons of redcurrant jelly. Stir into the stock with hare and heat up till sauce thickens, not letting it boil. Then serve.

Bakewell tart (from Derbyshire). Make (or buy a packet of) puff pastry and line an oven dish, then cover with a mighty layer of jam. Up to ½ lb. In a separate bowl, beat 2 eggs and 4 oz. melted butter, adding ½ lb sugar, mixing well. Put this in a thick layer over the jam, and bake in a moderate oven till light brown, 30 mins or so.

Parkin from Lancashire. Mix 1½ lb oatmeal with ½ lb brown sugar, 1 teaspoon allspice, 1 teaspoon ground ginger. Heat together separately 1 lb treacle and ½ lb butter, add it to the other ingredients, and leave the mixture to stand overnight. Bake in a shallow, well-greased baking tin, in a moderate oven for two hours. It's done if it's springy when you pull at it.

A Roman Banquet

Wanted to entertain a dozen people, but didn't want to give a buffet party because this do-it-yourself attitude makes people feel they haven't been properly entertained. Main problem: how to cope in a not-very-big room with a not-very-big table, and not-very-much cutlery, crockery and so on. My answer was a Roman banquet. It beats the table problem because you sit on the floor. It beats the cutlery problem because you eat with your fingers, and you can give the whole thing a sense of occasion by camouflaging the room. I invited people to dress up in togas, promising in return to do the whole banquet as authentically as possible.

Organisation I did some thorough research (a new book, *The French at Table* by Raymond Oliver, published by the Wine and Food Society was helpful). Main differences: no sugar, no pasta, no potatoes, no tomatoes in Roman times. They would start a meal with fruit, carry on with shellfish. Pork was highly prized. I picked this menu: oysters, mussels, roast belly of pork, pot-roast hare, followed by cheese.

I made low couches by unscrewing the legs of a studio couch and two divan beds. For a table I used a work-bench top on bricks, an old door would have done. Because my carpet is so grotty I laid down tough washable tile-patterned wallpaper covered with polythene sheeting. Out went the electric light, and on to the centre of the table went about 15s worth of heavy church candles, (they sell them by the pound at Mowbrays, the church bookshop at 38 Margaret Street, W.1 great value). No cutlery was put out, but I provided masses of orange paper napkins. I also cheated with a dozen cocotte type bowls from Merchant Chandler in the New Kings Road.

Food For swank I filled up a basket with screwed-up newspaper, surrounded the top with napkins, then topped it with fruit to fake a vast cornucopia (or anyway, to make a few expensive figs look like a lot). I put out six violently tough knives with stubby blades for the oysters, so that the men could open them for the women. It's a knack, opening oysters, you dig the blade into the slit in the pointed end, cut the muscle which locks it shut, lever open, then sever the mollusc from the shell and serve with slices of lemon.

The mussels were served, moules marinières style in a huge soup tureen. They were washed, scrubbed, beards tugged off, then popped into a big pan with a glass of white wine, a glass of water, a chopped onion, sliced lemon, two crushed garlic cloves, a table-spoonful of oil and handful of broken parsley. Boil them for five minutes and they are ready. Serve them in a tureen in half-shells, pour back on top the strained liquid warmed up with half a cup of cream.

The belly of pork was a big piece. Score the skin with a knife and rub in salt. Half an hour before cooking rub the meaty side with a mixture of red wine, honey, salt, pepper and herbs. Roast in a very hot oven for 20-30 minutes, depending on size, then slowly, with the heat right down for another 30 minutes. The hare, ideally goes underneath the pork so the fat drips on top, basting it. A dressed hare costs 12s :6d which is incredibly good value. Boil up the heart and giblets with some chopped onion to make about a pint of liquid stock. Put the hare casserole under the pork, turning at intervals in its own liquid. If you're cooking the hare on its own, cover with fatty bacon rashers to prevent drying out. It has a nice pheasant-like taste and cooks well in a medium oven in an hour. Keep it moist by turn-ing it fairly regularly.

Drink Parmigiani Figlio of Frith Street, Soho, recommended a medium sweet red wine as the nearest to the Roman Falernian. For white they suggested Retsina, the Greek wine flavoured with pine resin which the Romans also used. It's an acquired taste, but some people acquire it with great and alarming suddenness!

Banquet? It was practically an orgy!

Len Deighton

The scene at the Deighton home is one of intense activity. Work, work, work and more work. He's working on films and novels, besides his cookstrip. His accountant is in and out. His wife is fetch-ing and carrying and cooking in between doing her own design work. There is a demand for him to go to America that he is trying to put off.

'If I go for three days, that means a whole week's work wasted. Three days there, two days travelling, and then you've got the weekend. A whole week.'

The strange thing about Len Deighton is that in spite of his enormous impact in one circle, only a small number of people in the country know about his cooking activities. Len Deighton is the author of *The Ipcress File*, the only successful film rival to the Bond films. A creator of a nameless, classless secret service anti-hero who is nothing that Bond is, everything that he isn't.

But it was through cooking that Deighton first made a name for himself with the exciting innovation of a cookstrip that did something more than showing drawings of the ingredients.

Len Deighton is a humorous, unassuming man in his thirties, a man you can identify with Michael Caine, who plays the bespectacled hero of *The Ipcress File*. The same glasses, the same air of what? A sort of dumb insolence to authority. Tracking him down is like embarking on one of his own books.

You find a telephone number for him, if you're lucky, from T*he Observer*, where his cookstrips appear. You find you are ringing an answering service. They have obviously had some stick from him. They are as cagey as a zoo.

They won't give a clue, not a clue to his whereabouts. They will only say that they will ask him to ring you. Today? Tomorrow? Next week? They can't say. Is he in the country? Is he overseas? All this questioning, they don't like it. They get you off the phone. You try again for a few more days, you become persistent. They say they will pass you on to his accountant. No you can't ring him, he'll ring you. More calls, more persistence. How time is flying, weeks have passed already. Ah, you get his accountant. No, Mr. Deighton is very busy, you can't see him. But if there are any questions, he'd be glad to answer them. Of course, a lot has been written about him. One could look at the cuttings. More persistence, another call. Very well, you can see him just for an hour. That must be understood – a promise – only an hour. Very well. The address? The address is given reluctantly.

This is going to be tough, you reckon. But no. It's the very opposite. He lives in a quiet square off the Elephant and Castle, in a charming row of tall, terraced houses. His wife, Shirley, answers the door, a very attractive woman. It's light and bright inside, bursting with paintings and colourful furnishings. Some are Deighton's drawings, some are by his friends of art school days. There are two styles: the dramatic way-out fancies of Len Deighton and the meticulous, beautifully painted, engraving-like works that his wife collects. A Japanese-looking fish painting on the wall isn't a painting at all. It's a rubbing made with ink pressed out on an actual fish. There's a Persian carpet hanging on the wall – a gift from his accountant. There's something that looks very like a Russian icon, but it's an authentic Deighton fake. A drawing by a friend, of Deighton with a moustache comes as a surprise. A Peter Blake. Burmese temple rubbings.

His study is upstairs, an organised clutter of books and papers and new wood shelves; a tape recorder prominent on a table. An electric typewriter.

Against one wall is a board with a stick-up of pictures. He explained it was part of his technique for preparing material for his books. He researches heavily for them. To write *Horse under Water* he spent months diving. For *Funeral in Berlin* he went to Germany and collected *bric-a-brac*. For his latest he had this stick-up board, pasted with items from the German occupation of Paris, bus tickets, photographs, civilian passes.

He talked about his writing at first, the difficulties he had because he wasn't really a writer at all. He may run to eight current drafts, working patiently, doing enormous research. The current book was set in France, and all the characters were French. He was travelling backwards and forwards for research.

'Why French characters? Because it's more difficult, more fun to do. I enjoy the research more than the writing.' His recipe? First of all the research. He takes the tape-recorder, and records conversations. (He did try putting tape-recorded conversations into his books as they were, but it didn't work.) He had just recorded a BBC talk on life in Paris by a doctor. He plays it back and goes over it. Then he uses his cine-camera. He finds the actual house where one of the characters will live, and films it. He films likely characters in the street. 'I have to do it this way. I have no imagination,' he insists.

Then he types out the story, and again. When it's coming right, he cuts it up with scissors and pastes pieces into different orders. Then he gives it to a typist. After that he has to push characters up or down, because some may be too similar.

'The trouble is, I have to do it this way because I don't know how to write a book. I still don't know. I try other methods but they don't work. I've tried dictating into the machine. I tried that for my cookery book (*Action Cookbook*) but it sounded too twee and arch.'

Even when it's written and published, he's still dissatisfied, feeling that there were things he could put right.

He talked extremely freely and modestly, and it was difficult to believe it was the same man who had been so difficult to hunt down. Ah, he said, that was because he was so easily seduced by friends. Sometimes he works in a car fitted out as a studio – with its own radio telephone. But the calls don't go straight through to him. He collects them when he's ready.

'It's fatal to try to write in London. The telephone always goes, there's a great wave of social things. I don't know where I am.' When he gives a dinner and plans to ask four or six, he usually manages to come back with about a dozen friends. His wife, Shirley, nodded with resignation. 'He asks back everyone he meets in the day.'

He's a friendly, gregarious person, but by no means easy-going. He makes the same demands on others that he makes on himself. He likes the company of people like Clive Irving, the magazine boss of the International Publishing Company – the man who set Deighton off on his cookstrip. Why? 'Because he's a ball of energy.'

He was born in Marylebone, the son of a chauffeur. His mother was a cook in a hotel – though Deighton prefers to boast that she was an oxyacetylene welder, which she was in a factory in the war.

'I started cooking very young. My mother let me fool around. I'm no good with my hands, can't fix taps, can't mend windows. I'm hopelessly bad. But everyone's good at one thing, carpentry, cooking, something. There was a boy at school called MacDonald who once came up to me and said, "It's funny how everybody is either good at games or work, and you are no good at either, Deighton." I didn't take offence because you never take offence as a schoolboy where none is intended. So I said "No, that's true".'

'The day of triumph was the first day I cooked the Sunday lunch. It was roast beef and Yorkshire. Then I used to take up playing with dough. It would go grey, then it would have to be put in the oven and cooked, and it would come out a hard lump and I would eat it. I think parents should encourage their children to fool around. It's a pity they discourage children who want to become interested in it; a shame. Frightened, they may become queer.

'In the war I went into the Air Force. I was always interested in airplanes. Afterwards I became a BOAC steward. From the Air Force I got a training grant for three years to art college, then I got a scholarship for another three years. (He was at the Royal College of Art.) In my spare time I did a lot of things. I started a glossy camera magazine, on the principle that you sell them because of the smaller ads. I still say that's right. We gave our small ads away free, but it was unpopular in the trade. If you're a dealer you say it's another bloody expense. A big distributor refused to handle it as a result of pressure because camera people are always exchanging bits and pieces. They collect photographic equipment more than they take pictures. They like collecting all the shiny bits.

'Restaurants – I've worked in a few. It's a nice, soft job in the winter. You're working in the warm. I'd watch what people did, try to make myself useful. I was a waiter and a pastry cook. That was in the Festival Hall restaurant. I was called assistant pastry cook. It was a very good way to learn cooking, and anyone who has an interest is helped along. It's nonsense to say that cooks are secretive. They'll always show you how to make a dish. I never thought of cooking as a way of living, but I did buy some interesting cookery books.

'I helped run a gown factory with a friend in Aldgate. Then I was a freelance artist, and worked in agencies here and in New York.

'I had a six-month contract as art director of an agency. But London isn't a good place to be an artist in. It's a place to write. The artist is considered a lower form of life. You can't study art in Latin or Greek – though I suppose you could study the history of art in Latin and Greek.' He smiled with his eyes, an amiable blink.

'In the ad' agency the artist is only called in as an unpleasant afterthought. They say, oh, we'll have to get that bloody artist. I've got the scars to prove it. In New York it's much better. But you can't serve commerce and art. People say, oh, look at the Seagram build-ing (in New York), but I say it just shows that they've got enough money to buy a work of art.'

The cookstrip happened purely by chance. He had his proud col-lection of recipe books which he didn't want to spoil, so he copied the recipes out when he was preparing for a meal.

'The easy way for me to do it was by means of drawings. Very simple stuff. I used to draw the saucepan as a square. I just found it easy in diagrammatic form. I could get three recipes on a sheet of paper, and that was easier than using three cookery books. One day Clive Irving and Ray Hawkeye (Raymond Hawkeye, the designer) came to see me and saw the cookstrip hanging on the wall. Clive said he liked it, so I did it in ink for him. Ray suggested I put num-bers in for each stage, and make a grid of it. Put a surrounding to it, like a grid. Clive Irving was on the *Express* and took it to them, and it appeared twice. And that was all. Then Clive joined *The Observer* and took me on.'

Typical of his thoroughness, he had prepared a typed sheet for me with details of the work he did in preparing his cookstrip. He emphasised that cooking was not necessarily an art. It wasn't a creative art except perhaps once or twice in a decade.

He thought that what was bad in British and American cooking came from a desire to invent instead of a desire to work to tested rules and recipes – which was what made French cooking good.

His idea of what is worst in cookery was summed up by a piece of pineapple taken from a tin and balanced on a piece of square ham, and called Hawaii on the menu.

'The recipes I select, are for the most part, classics. I read what the master cookbooks, *Pellaprat, Larousse, Savarin*, etcetera, say. When I have six to eight authentic recipes I compare them on paper. I look for, one, logical procedure, two, scientific accuracy, three, sim-plicity and four, does it work? I try it out, watching for pitfalls that an inexperienced cook might fall into. At this stage I have roughed out a cookstrip with tracing paper and fountain pen. I then give the rough to someone else to see if there is something not quite clear in my text. When I finally okay it, it goes to a lettering expert, and returns to me for the final drawing to be done.'

His first book of cookstrips came out simultaneously with the première of *The Ipcress File*, with a picture of a revolver on the front sprouting a piece of parsley. The publishers wanted to identify the little-known cookery writer with the well-known thriller writer. It was more than a book of cookstrips from *The Observer*, however, and was packed with succinctly written information about all stages of cooking, from choosing meat, to bachelor quickie meals, and on to world classics.

'What I'd really like to do,' he admitted, 'is to draw it as it is, but with almost no words. Just draw two eggs, and don't write two eggs beside them. If there is a lot of heat, illustrate it by means of big arrows, little heat by small arrows. There is a lot duplicated, otherwise. The trouble is, you have to allow for new readers.'

He's quite modest in his claims. If people know better than him, then they won't need his book he says.

The cookstrip is only the top of his cookery iceberg. Delve into his *Action Cookbook* and you find it packed with interesting facts and items he has discovered in his researching.

What sort of thing? In his chapter on nutrition the strange fact emerges that iron necessary for the diet is to be found in liver, kidney, black pudding, cocoa and lentils to a large extent, but to the highest degree in curry powder. Twenty-three milligrams to the ounce. (Of course, he says, an ounce of curry powder goes a long way.)

He expounds a personal view that the fridge is something you can do without. The opening and shutting of the door causes fluctuations in the food temperature, one of the quickest ways of turning food bad. The best thing it can do is provide ice, and what is a tray of ice cubes compared with a large slab from your fishmonger? He is against meat and poultry being put away in the fridge, and would rather hang them for a day or more in a draughty, cool place. He won't put cheese in the fridge, or eggs, or even cucumber. And a shop-bought ice-cream melts in the refrigerator.

His wry humour creeps in when he's talking about diet – 'Remember, most of the world have diet problems of a different sort: they are hungry.'

No pompousness either. For a sauce to go with *quenelles*, he says it's not the *Sauce Normande* it pretends to be – 'but it will pass in a crowd.'

Talking about utensils, he lists the important ones: three sharp knives, two-handled saucepans that will go in the oven, asbestos mats for cooking in earthenware pots on the stove, a cast-iron casserole (another source of iron he says), a double boiler, egg whisk, wooden spoon with a square corner, heavy chopping board – and skewers. Skewers for meat, skewers for kebab, because the heat radiates to the centre. If you haven't got skewers, he suggests, run long nails into potatoes before baking them.

On the subject of vegetables and fruit he says that those which win prizes in displays are no friend to the cook. Choose tiny, flavourful vegetables. His favourite vegetable? Mangetout peas, small peas which you eat pod and all, cooked, of course, with lettuce and butter. And why do shops only stock King Edwards, a dreary potato which dissolves into slush at the first sight of warm water? Why not waxy potatoes that the French have – they call them Dutch potatoes?

Cooking pulses (haricots, lentils and so on) the Deighton way is novel too. No need to soak them overnight, he says. Put them for two hours in cold water, then put into boiling water with ham bone, or a piece of bacon, or a piece of salt pork, a piece of fresh pork skin, or a pork knuckle – any of them, or all. Cook till tender, depending on the degree of softness wanted. Mix into pulses a vinaigrette dressing, sour cream, crispy fried onion, chopped herbs and butter, crisp streaky bacon broken up, or chopped almonds.

He sometimes picks up American ideas, as in his salads. Orange pieces with celery, apples and raisins; cranberries, banana and water melon slices together.

And although he works from classical ideas he doesn't worship at the altar of *haute cuisine*. Tins? Why not? He suggests an enchanting lobster *bisque* for bachelors. A tin of condensed chicken soup and a tin of lobster. Mash the lobster into soup, add butter, milk and a sprinkle of paprika. I suppose if you really wanted to fool your friends you'd add a dash of brandy. Time – two minutes.

And twelve minutes to cook his 'Phoney Chinese Dish'. Twenty minutes to cook his *Sukiyaki* (pretty phoney).

But his idea about grilling comes straight from the top restaurants. Light the grill *half an hour* before using it. It must be really very hot indeed. Which explains why some people ruin every steak they attempt.

You make some delightful discoveries talking to Deighton: that South Americans use ginger with their beef; that coriander seed is good in milk puddings; aniseed is fine for flavouring shellfish; rosemary is an ideal flavouring in jams and jelly; that you can pickle your own nasturtium seeds, and in eight weeks you have something very close to a caper; that you can spread chopped mint on a grapefruit, and add chicken feet to a soup to make it more glutinous.

As a pastry cook himself, he is especially interesting on the subject of pastry – an art, he says, which goes back to the Greeks. Experts classify pastry-making into ten distinct categories: puffpastry, flaky pastry, short pastry, and so on. He gives a recipe for a simple short pastry which is basic.

'The notion behind the recipe is the combining of fat and flour into crumbs so that air expands into the tiny cavities formed by the crumbs. Since the air here isn't so tightly trapped the pastry doesn't rise as high as flaky pastry. Heavy hands tend to knock the air out of the pastry instead of knocking it in – subtle difference.

'All I can say to reassure you is that if you understand the principle involved you are probably handling it right. Because the action of expanding air is involved it is best to keep everything as cool as possible. Furthermore, cold fat is more manageable. The optional beaten yolks make the pastry rather tougher and less likely to soak up the subsequent filling. Similarly egg white on the surface also proofs the pastry against moist fillings.

'Mix four ounces of fat (butter gives the best flavour) chopped small; eight ounces of flour, and a pinch of salt. Using the tops of thumbs and fingers rub fat into smaller and smaller pieces until it is the size of breadcrumbs. Add two beaten yolks, gently but thoroughly. You may need no cold water to make a firm pastry that holds together. Beware of too much water, add it just a sprinkle at a time. When it needs just a little more water it has had enough. Roll the pastry out and use it to line the tin.' Note – keep all utensils cold.

He makes it all very clear, but still it's no substitute for practical experience. 'If people have the opportunity to watch someone cooking, then it's better than reading, and they won't need my book,' he says.

'A woman once wrote to me on *The Observer*, saying what a terrible thing my strip was, what an awful thing. I wrote back and said, "I'm sure you don't like it but it's the only thing I have to keep my widowed mother."'

'I've been very lucky about the people who have helped me. My letterer is very good. He thinks up lots of ideas. He thought up the idea of writing the words upside-down actually upside-down.'

Errors? He laughed. 'I offered to do a Christmas message in *The Observer*. I'm sorry for all the mistakes I've made, and I will try to make fewer in the coming year. But *The Observer* refused to print it. I try to avoid answering letters, and I get other people to test my recipes.'

He said he didn't know many cookery writers. 'I find cookery writers as a breed are sometimes unpleasant and rude. They are more gratuitously rude to each other than any other kind of person I know.' He reflected for a moment, with a humorous blink or two. 'And I suppose I'm hostile, too. But I don't read their things – I haven't time to see what other people are doing.'

Were there any special privileges in being a cookery writer, I asked him.

'Perks? I once got a Danish butter dish. I suppose if I phoned the dairies I'd get a gallon of yoghourt. But I don't feel right doing this sort of thing.'

Already Len Deighton had exceeded the permitted hour by a long way, and his accountant had arrived. There was just time for him to show me his kitchen.

We left his study and he told me how he rang up a friend, and an unfamiliar voice answered the phone.

'Where is he? Tell him to shift his bum.'

'His bum sir? As in bottom?'

He realised he had said too much. 'Yes, his bum. But not as in bottom. As in British United Metals.' A piece of quick thinking, he said. 'I hope they thought I was telling him to make a move on the stock exchange.'

His kitchen is geared to quick thinking, too. His most important items, he said, were a pressure cooker and an electric blender. It was a pleasant open place on the basement floor, opening out onto a bare plot of grass at the back. It had a wooden ceiling, a room divider of shelves, and the dinner table was his father's old work-bench, with the top planed off. ('There was one like it in Liberty's the other day for £25,' he said.) There were four gas taps, which he said should ideally be in the centre of the room with working surfaces all round.

His wife took over as he retired for a conference with his accountant. And their two cats appeared, one called Beetle-ink, and one without a name, usually called Tiddles.

She pointed out Len's £5 ice-cream machine, and his meat grinder. They make their own sausages with pork and plenty of pepper, she said. 'I use the Kenwood. Len's more gadget-minded. He does the meat dishes, I do the desserts.'

They have an omelette pan and always begin by saying 'it will only be used for omelettes, but it never works out that way.'

She does a lot of the cooking but has to admit, 'I don't read cooking for pleasure. I cook because I have to.' But the Deighton influence is there, and she works from *Pellaprat*. 'Well, it has 3,500 recipes.'

They were about to go to dinner with Clement Freud, *The Observer's* colour supplement cookery man. He had suggested they should dress up. She raised her eyebrows. 'Can you imagine us here, dressing up? We never have dressed up. We sit down to dinner, usually about fifteen of us. We produce terrible folding chairs, and we haven't enough glasses. Len invites everyone he sees in the day. It's more like being in a farmhouse kitchen.'

Any follower of the Deighton cookstrip can have a pretty good idea of his special tastes. I asked him his favourite foods.

They didn't come as a surprise. Ham and cheese, salt beef, steak and kidney pudding.

Cooking may or may not be an art, he said. But the difference between cookery and writing was that cookery had a beginning and an end.

'Writing can always be tickled up. Cooking, when it comes, you eat it.'

A practical observation from a superbly practical man.

Vanity Fare

Bread is pretty basic food, so you'd think by our day and age bakers could do better than some of the pap that appears in the shops. If you feel strongly about it, try baking your own. It's more fun than you might think.

You need *flour*. Any old flour *will* do, but bakers get all the best flour, so it's best to go and beg from them. You don't want the stuff they sell on the shelves, you want 3lb dug out of a sack at the back. Strong flour. Strong flour has more gluten, which gives greater elasticity to the dough. You need *yeast*. Only 1oz for four loaves, and they will let you have this. If you can't get fresh yeast, use dried yeast from a grocer or chemist, and half the amount is sufficient. Costs a few pence. You also need *salt*, *water*, a little *fat*, and *–heat*. Get the oven really hot to start with, and gradually let the heat down. Reason – high heat expands the gas bubbles created by the yeast; then medium heat solidifies the bubbles; the low heat dries the bread out gently.

Here is a basic recipe. For four loaves put 2½lb flour in a large bowl, sprinkle with 2 tspns salt, and make a well. Dissolve 1oz fresh yeast (½ oz dry yeast) in a little warm water, pour into well, stir in. Then add 2oz melted fat, liquid but not hot. Butter, lard, margarine will do. Mix together, and add enough warm water to make a good dough. With white flour, up to 1½pts. With wholemeal flour, up to 2pts. The next bit is the bit which explains why more people don't make bread. Pound, beat, bash, twist, tug and pull the dough for about 20 mins, till you've developed the elasticity of the gluten in the dough. There's a moment when it goes all stringy and you know you're there. Put in a bowl, cover with damp cloth and let the dough rise in a warmish place. In about two hours it will have doubled. Cut into shapes (you've got four loaves here) and put them back in a warm place to prove for another 45 mins or so. They go puffy. Pop them into a hot oven, on flat baking sheets, lowering the heat to moderate after 30 mins, and lowering it again after another 20 mins, finally to low heat for 10 -15 mins. Cool on a wire rack.

Use the same quantity of dough to make rolls. The same method, but they're smaller, and don't need to prove so long. Give them 20 mins before baking. Then bake them in a hot oven for 15 mins only.

Slice Out of Life

The Schofield way: Breakfast of fresh fruit and dried fruit. Lunch, egg or cheese, for protein, with salad. Evening meal, a chop or piece of steak with green vegetables. No tea or coffee, no white sugar, no white bread. Because the system is calling out for sweetness, provide it in Nature's way, with fruit or dried fruit, where sugar comes in the right balance with other nutrients. She recommends (unsprayed, naturally) dried dates, date chips, sultanas, raisins, dried pears, figs, and apricots for snacks in the day. If you want any bread, try a crusty piece of wholemeal occasionally, or crispbread, or pumpernickel.

If you are going to be eating a lot of salad it's worth taking that extra trouble to make it tasty. No Frenchman will accept an ordinary English green salad. Their secret is infinite care, in choice of a lettuce with a good firm heart, in washing it leaf by leaf, in shaking it dry in a cloth, and then in painstakingly drying each single leaf, patting it with a cloth so lightly that you don't crush the leaves' fragile structure. Put the leaves in a bowl well rubbed with cut garlic. Make the dressing to taste, with olive oil and wine vinegar in the proportions of five to one, plus a little salt and pepper, and moments before serving, mix the dressing so that there's a little on each leaf. Leave it longer, and the leaves go limp. It's so simple, and well worth the considerable trouble.

Vanity Fare

Greengrocers never seem to have the herbs you want at the right time, so why not invest a few shillings and a lot of loving care on growing your own? You don't even need a garden, herbs flourish in window boxes. Use soil mixed in equal parts with leaf mould and sand, and buy or beg seed, seedlings or cuttings. Here are a few suggestions.

Parsley. The most popular English herb which shows how canny we are. It's packed with vitamins and so it's not only attractive as a garnish, it's healthy too. Parsley butter is tasty on grilled meat and fish. Mix 4oz butter with 2 tbspns chopped parsley and work in a few drops of lemon juice. Chill in the fridge, then cut into shapes before use.

Mint. Grows in profusion. Problem isn't to grow it, but stop it spreading. Mint with potatoes, mint with peas, mint sauce with lamb. Also dried mint sprinkled on lamb in cooking. Mint is an aid to digestion, so are other mint family herbs, the peppermint, and the pennyroyal which you can pot at home. Make mint jelly instead of mint sauce, by boiling up $1/2$ pint white wine vinegar with 6oz sugar. Take it off the boil after a few minutes, dissolve $1/$ oz gelatine in a $1/2$ pint of hot water. Add 3 heaped tbspns freshly chopped mint, and briefly bring the whole lot to the boil again. Pour into a container to chill. Keeps well in a fridge.

Sage. Trad' English herb which is supposed to be very healthy. Dried sage is better than fresh. Sage can be used in sausages, in sage and onion stuffing, as sage wine, sage tea, and sage cheese in Derby. Make your own sage cheese spread, mixing 2 tspns into a carton of cream cheese, with a few drops of lemon juice.

Bay leaves. They won't grow on the windowsill but they look nice in a tub at the door. Use them fresh or dried, in curries, casseroles, kebab or tied in a *bouquet garni* with dried thyme, marjoram and parsley. The bouquet should be removed before serving.

Rosemary. Grow this from a cutting. A strong flavoured pungent herb. Put a sprig on lamb or pork chops when you're grilling, and get the delicious scent of the burning leaves.

Thyme. Take cuttings or roots. Nostalgic herb to Mediterranean-lovers, and belongs to Provençal dishes where tomatoes and garlic and wine are used in slow casseroles. Use it in stuffings, too.

Chives. They thrive on being cut. Scissors do the job. Tasty and pretty with a salad of tomatoes, delicious in plain omelettes, mixed in cream cheese, sprinkled on new potatoes.

Basil. Seed. A herb which is lovely sprinkled on fresh or cooked tomatoes. Basil is used in Italy to make Pesto. Three tbspns of fresh chopped basil are pounded together with 2 or 3 chopped cloves of garlic, 2 tbspns Parmesan cheese, and enough olive oil to make it into a smooth paste. Pesto is served on plain spaghetti or pasta. In France it is called Pistou, and stirred into vegetable soup.

Tarragon. You need cuttings or roots. Tarragon has a dry, haunting taste which gives mysterious depth to chicken. It is also an essential ingredient of Béarnaise Sauce. The classic method is to make an essence by reducing, boiling fiercely 4 tbspns each of dry white wine and white wine vinegar, with a tbspn of chopped shallot, a tbspn chopped tarragon, a little thyme and half a bay leaf. Reduce by half, strain and add 1 tbspn cold water. In a double saucepan over gentle heat put 2 egg yolks, whisk in the essence, adding 4oz butter piece by piece, beating quickly. Strain again, and add another pinch chopped tarragon, and serve with grilled meat or fish.

Fish 'n' Chips

Accountants do it. Gourmets do it. Pretty girls out with nice-young-men-in-Rolls-Royces do it. Even Dr Magnus Pyke does it. Let's do it. Let's ask for fish and chips!

Next to arriving at a party with your hostess's ex-husband, the surest way to be a social outcast is to come to a genteel gathering bearing a bag of fish and chips; especially if it's been maturing on the seat of your car in a sweaty wrapping for half an hour.

Not without reason have fish and chips been the butt of vulgar comedians for well over a century. Even today, in spite of fresher frozen fish, deodorised cooking oils and fats, and better ventilation, the visit to a nasty fish and chip shop can be an experience. The shop will be as welcoming as a white-tiled public lavatory. There will be the standard unit, a massive metallic frying range and greasy high counter. There will be a few shelves holding assorted bottles of fizzy sweet red ink, and tins of sickly brown cola. Also some jars of gherkins and onions pickled in some kind of acid which strips the tooth down to the nerve. The air will make you choke, as you inhale the volatile elements released by the burning fat.

You'll sprinkle your fish and chips with salt, and douse them with malt vinegar, wrap them again, and take them home. In the car the wrapping will colour as the fat seeps out, and, before you know it, the smell has contaminated your car seat, and will remain there for some months. At home when you unwrap the fish and chips, they are not what you thought you took away. Unaccountably, the crisp chips have gone soggy; the steam in the hot chips has turned to water; the vinegar has wet them. The fish has a mysterious smell of curdling ammonia which chokes even the appalling smell of the vinegar.

And yet, the world's most disgusting dish can as easily be the world's finest. In another shop you've been lucky enough to have a proud and honourable fryer. He's taken the best fillet of fish, lightly floured it, dipped it in a light newly made batter, plunged it into the hottest fat for seven minutes, turning it after two; the instant heat of the oil has cooked the batter, creating a sealing envelope around the fish; in it, the fish cooks in its own steam. The fish is removed, and allowed to drain for a few minutes, and it's ready. Eat it, not with vinegar, but a wedge of lemon.

The same with the chips. Freshly peeled potatoes, dried and sliced (not too thin or you get French fries which are all crunch and no potato) plunged into very hot fat, or else the potato just absorbs the oil like blotting paper; removed, and again allowed to drain for a few minutes. Put these in a bag, salt them (but don't cover with wrapping paper) and you have the finest take-away food in the world. And one of the most nourishing.

However, you'd better make the most of this experience while
you can. In the last ten years almost incredibly, this traditional food
of the poor has swung from rags to middle-class respectability;
and, conceivably, our grandchildren will not have fish and chip
shops to go into. The great fish and chips industry is on a sad
decline. Why? Because fish is no longer a cheap food. First we over-
fished our own waters, then Iceland decided to extend its fishing
limits which blew up into the Cod War. Depending on the outcome,
if we have to buy on the market, we'll discover Iceland, Denmark
and Norway are selling to the Americans who are offering better
prices.

Poor old fish fryers. And just after the war there were 25,000 fish
and chip shops in Britain. A shop for every 2,000 people. Ten years
ago there were only 17,000 shops. Now there may be less than
13,000. They are closing at a steady rate. At the lowest level, they are
losing ground to the new 'fast food' industry, convenience foods like
burgers. (Convenient only to the franchise-holders, not to the paying customer.) Fish is fish is fish. A burger can be almost anything
from bull-hides to cows' tails, and there's no indication of the level
of extenders – soya bean protein, cereal and so on; no indication –
apart from the flavour of reconstituted cornflakes packets.

Fish and chip shops have also taken a battering from the battery
chicken boom. This highly efficient, but hardly humane industry
yields profitable margins to the franchise-holders of the Kentucky
Fried Chicken chains, under the goatee-bearded scrutiny of the
American Colonel Sanders. (He wouldn't be a colonel in the British
Army, and that's a fact.)

The contrasting advertising on Capital Radio of Kentucky Fried
Chicken and the fish and chip people illustrates the social swing as
fish and chips go soaring above the pocket of the traditional customer. Kentucky Fried Chicken's voice-over is smacked out hard
and fast, in the accents of young Metropolitan London, with grinding consonants. Fish and chips is drawn-out Kensington vowel-
power; 'Dah—ling, I feel the *uuuuuuurge!*" The *uuuuuuurge*,dahling?" Yes, dahling, the *uuuuuuurge* to buy some fish and
chips.' Then there's the rise of the Chinese take-away trade, taking
away the fish and chip shops' trade. 'We are going middle class,' says

the National Fish Fryer's Federation president, Alan Crisfield. 'Before the war, it was all working class, but now we're definitely moving into the middle classes.' In Crisfield's shops at Rochester and Gillingham in Kent, not only are the sailors and the dockers coming in; so are doctors, solicitors, accountants. 'At least three clergymen are regular customers.'

But as the little corner shop bows out, the bigger, better-class shops are booming. Yorkshire's pride and joy is Harry Ramsden's in Guiseley, on the road between Otley and Leeds; the biggest fish and chip shop in the world, created by Ramsden, but bought up by a fish and chip franchise chain called Seafarer, owned by Associated Fisheries: a star in the firmament like Harrod's in Hugh Fraser's clothing shop chain, Fortnum and Mason in Garfield Weston's bakery empire, *The Times* in Lord Thomson of Fleet's local newspaper chain.

Ramsden's was built up from a wooden shack in 1928 to the shrine to fish and chips it is today, with 150 staff, a car park for 400 cars, carpeted restaurant, decked out with 100 seats, and hung with chandeliers. In keeping with their flair for publicity, Ramsden's are ready to furnish you with all the statistics you can swallow: in a year the customers consume 170 tons of fish, 380 tons of potatoes, twenty-eight tons of flour for batter, sixty-eight tons of dripping (Yorkshiremen won't have chips fried in oil); a ton of salt, 1100 gallons of vinegar, 18,000 bottles of tomato sauce, 4,500 bottles of HP Sauce. That's the recipe for a £300,000 a year turnover.

Another sign of fish and chips' new class-consciousness is the respect now shown by the gourmets. Food writer Derek Cooper thinks it's a splendid dish, and names his favourite fish and chip restaurant as Bryan's in Leeds, (I'll give Bryan's frying secrets at the end.) Fish and chip shops have also made it into the food guides. Christopher Driver, editor of *The Good Food Guide*, was first to single out and honour a fish and chip restaurant in this way. He thinks the best fish and chips make a first-class dish. But for every good fryer, he's sorry to say there are hundreds of bad ones. 'It's amazing that we British never get it quite right. But we took a smart step back when newspaper was outlawed as a fish and chip wrapping. Newspaper has the perfect degree of absorbency. The essential quality of fish and chips is the crispness of the chip, and the crisp coating which seals the juice in the fish. So when you've finished cooking them, it's important to drain them quickly. What you *don't* do is to seal the fish and chips hermetically, which is what those modern little greaseproof cartons do. That sort of wrapping means the steam instantly softens the batter and makes the chips soggy. When Parliament banned newspaper wrapping they were being truly anti-gastronomic.'

Driver is surprised that with our experience we've never been able to emulate the French who produce crisper fried potatoes, *pommes frites*. 'They cut them thinner, so they cook more crisply. We cut them larger, and they are inclined to go soggy. What you should do is have a man in the restaurant cooking nothing but chips. Cooking them in small batches, so the temperature of the fat doesn't drop. In our fish and chip shops we often cook them in too large batches.'

The gourmet view; but the British working classes voted with their pockets. They like chips bigger. Chips are certainly more nutritious when they are larger; in *pommes frites* the vitamin C is almost all destroyed by the cooking, as in potato crisps (a crisp contains more fat than potato).

In the opinion of Dr Magnus Pyke, a nutritionist who makes no claim to be a gourmet, the British have been very lucky to have a staple dish for so long like fish and chips; it's the perfectly balanced meal, give or take a trace mineral or two. The fish has the B vitamins – vital for growth and repairing body tissue. Fish is pure protein, with a good balance of amino acids. The chip is a good source of carbohydrate for energy, and contains vitamin C; very little is lost, because it's sealed in by the deep-frying process (unlike peeled boiled potatoes which leak the vitamin into the water). The oil is a source of fat, of course, which gives you calories which don't do you any harm on a cold winter's night.

Weight for weight, ounce for ounce, chips have less than half the calories of fried pork or lamb chops, fried bacon, milk chocolate, cream crackers and chocolate cake. Chips have a good deal fewer calories than boiled ham, roast beef, pork sausages, steak and kidney pie, fried onions, Dundee cake and treacle tart. Chips have even fewer calories than sardines, liver and fried eggs. And although a chip is fried in fat, it has fewer calories than *unbuttered* bread.

Dr Pyke is another who believes we are seeing the end of the golden era of cheap fish and chips. 'They are fast becoming upmarket. They are becoming to us what oysters were to Dickens. Soon it will be Chips Without Anything, not Chips with Everything. Let me refer you to Pyke's Principle of Poverty and Style. We'll come to eat less and less fish with our chips, until we're like those impoverished Italians who have a plate of spaghetti and grate some Parmesan cheese on top, thus adding beneficial protein. We may also have to eat enormous amounts of carbohydrates – in our case, chips – and perhaps we'll sprinkle a little nutritional powdered fish on top.'

No one is quite sure when fish became wed to chips, but it's a toss-up between London's East End, and Lancashire's Mossley. In 1968 the National Fish Fryer's Federation felt it was time to celebrate their centenary, based on the claims of Malin's of Bow, a fish and chip business which is believed to have opened in 1868. No sooner had they awarded the plaque, than Lancashire exploded in fury; Lees' of Mossley had been selling fish and chips since 1862. The federation declined to withdraw the award from Malin's, so Mossley's British Legion indignantly made their own award, pre-dating the London shop by six years. Malin's, alas, has since gone the way of many similar premises – falling foul of the redeveloper's bulldozer.

The fish and chip trade is lucky to have a distinguished historian, or at least a historian at all. Until a few years ago nothing had been written about the country's most famous dish. Then on the centenary out came a gourmet guide to fish and chip shops, by Pierre Picton. A few years later, Gerald Priestland wrote *Frying Tonight*, a lovingly detailed, and amusingly chronicled history of fish and chips. Both books are now sadly out of print. (I was warmed to learn from his book that one of the important frying ranges is called Bateman's Carousel; Priestland says this is a vast horseshoe-shaped console whose 553,552 square-inch trapezoidal pan was proclaimed the breakthrough of the century.)

Priestland was the BBC's man in America for fifteen years, quite frankly the product of your English upper-middle class family. 'I never tasted fish and chips as a boy. There was no question of us children eating such a vulgar food. It was forbidden. Then along came the war, and fish and chips were OK all of a sudden. Instead of being the noxious food of the lower classes, fish and chips became a Good Idea.' And so it is: much nicer than hamburgers, his staple snack food when he worked in the States. He had written one book in the States on politics, so when he returned to England his colleagues expected some intellectual light to be thrown on vital issues: 'Whither Vietnam', or 'The Nixon I Knew and Loved'. Instead he announced that he was going to travel Britain interviewing fish and chip fryers. 'When you're abroad,' says Priestland, 'you develop such a nostalgia for fish and chips. It's something you really feel you need to eat. When you do get a smell of them, then there's a trace of anxiety. *Will they disappoint?*'

He had many disappointments, but he reassured himself that even our worst fish and chips are quite delightful compared with the imitations offered abroad, 'The World's Worst Fish and Chips,' says Priestland, 'are undoubtedly cooked in Sydney, Australia. The fish is shark; the cooks are Serbo-Croat, in whose culinary tradition fish and chips is not. It comes in a plastic cocoon, and cringing in the middle is a shark finger, grey and rubbery. Its taste is faintly like rock salmon.'

Fish fryers, he discovered, were not a great fund of information about the trade. 'In fact, I've seldom come across people who are less talkative. They were terribly suspicious and I'm sure they all thought I was from the taxman. A lot of them were obviously doing very well, in spite of the modest façades. If you managed to look out into the back yard, you'd often find a Jensen.'

The trade press was a great source of information, luckily, and Priestland even found a novel written about a fish and chip fryer, called *Johnny Higginbottom and His Experiences in the Fish Trade* by William Loftas. And a ghost story called *The Lock*, more horrific than ghostly: the adulterer meets his death when a pan of dripping hits flash-point and consumes him in the fire.

Priestland has his own theories about the birth of fish and chips. He thinks the chip left Liverpool, travelling across the country in an easterly direction, until it bumped into fried fish, travelling westwards, having come from the fish fryers in the Yorkshire fishing ports. 'As far as I can tell, they met somewhere in the middle. On Ilkely Moor probably.'

Fried fish and fried chips have their own separate histories. In the sixteenth and seventeenth centuries hawkers took trays of rather smelly cold fried fish round the pubs, where you'd stand your friends a round of fish instead of a round of ale. Frying the fish was one way of slowing down the decomposition, but by all accounts not always effective. The hawkers led a dreadful life. Mayhew, the great social commentator of the nineteenth century, wrote about the fish sellers with their trays spread with newspaper, and 'the shapeless brown lumps' of fish. The fish fryer was avoided by his fellow men, for these were days long before we'd learnt to control the smell of the cooking fats. Cottonseed oil was particularly disgusting. An East-ender told Mayhew the fish fryers lived in back alleys and attics: 'A gin-drinking neighbourhood suits them best. For people haven't their sense of smell so correct there.'

Chips, on the other hand, are a relatively modern invention. French chefs, who'd been rather slow to recognise the potato, sud-denly turned their skills to transforming this humble object, and a stream of creations poured out of their kitchens: *pommes Anna, Dauphine, fondants, soufflées, Lyonnaise, noisette*, matchstick-shaped *allumettes*, and their bigger brothers, the *pommes frites*.

Chips arrived in Britain around the middle of the last century, and were at first rejected by Londoners, where street-vendors had a monopoly in baked potatoes which they sold from contraptions like small fire engines. The baked-potato vendors were no more willing to let the newcomer in than the modern London cabbie will make room for the mini-cab drivers.

But chip shops opened in the North, notably in Scotland (where the French cookery influence has always been strong) and in Liverpool which was geographically well sited to cater for the new craze. This was the port which landed the bulk of the Irish potatoes, and alongside the potatoes came cottonseed oil, a by-product of the cotton which went to the Lancashire cotton mills.

It's no accident that Liverpudlians Ken Dodd and Paul McCartney have spread the fame of the Liverpool chip butty – Ken

Dodd on the music hall stage; the ex-Beatle in Paris, when he caused panic in the prestigious Georges V hotel by ordering one of these unlikely sandwiches.

It was unthinkable that the middle classes would ever embrace either fish or chips. The early history of the trade is smothered with a smelly black fog, and the nearest the middle classes got to fish and chips was always too near. They made sure that fish and chip shops stayed under strict control of the public health authorities, and until 1911 it was classed as a noxious trade, along with rag-and-bone dealers, tripe boilers and tallow melters.

The kindest thing ever said about fish and chips is by Gerald Priestland: 'If it wasn't for fish and chips there would have been a revolution in the 1930s. It saved thousands of the Victorian poor from malnutrition, and then, when the Depression came no one could starve as long as there were fish and chips. People could get cheap hot meals.'

By the Second World War, the darkest days had passed. There was Sir Winston Churchill himself, a man who'd surely never got his fingers greasy scoffing fish and chips, praising the dish: 'The Good Companions,' he said, borrowing the title of J B Priestley's novel. The Government made allowances of extra oil for fish and chip shops.

Since the war, the 'perfect marriage' of fish to chips has had more than its share of buffetings. Fish could hardly have chosen a more promiscuous partner than the flirty chip which familiarises itself with every newcomer to the 'fast food' trade.

Arnold Wesker, the playwright, saw the way things were going, when he entitled his play *Chips With Everything*. But it is more of a comment on our way of life than our gastronomic tastes. He must have touched a nerve: none of his plays has been so successful; *Chips* ran for over a year, and when it was revived last October on TV, some thirteen years later, the message was still as direct.

Why chips? Arnold Wesker says it wasn't even his own idea. 'Lindsay Anderson (the gifted stage and film director who created *If* and *O Lucky Man*) had just come back from the Continent to find the country in a mood of resignation. Bus conductors were rude to you. In a café you were presented with a stained menu offering chips with everything. The thought stuck in my mind. It seemed to sum up how the working class in this country accepts the simplest, easiest way out without questioning it. There's no desire to look for alternatives, or variations, nuances. We settle for chips. There's no feeling. . . that life might have more to offer.'

But Wesker's not against chips in their proper place, tumbling out of a bag of freshly fried crispy fish.

However, it is wrong to assume that the North Americans cannot affect our national dish. North American technology has taken over chipping. The biggest company selling pre-processed chips in this country is actually Canadian, McCain's.

Lyons, the British caterers, have been in this pre-processing, blanching business for some time, too. Only very few, small, family shops now buy their own potatoes, peel, wash, dry and cut them for frying. 'If you're eating chips in any restaurant, hotel, institution, hospital or factory of any size, the odds are that you're eating pre-processed chips,' says the Lyons man. 'People just can't afford the labour to do this job any more.'

In the factory potatoes go into huge baths of alkali solution, the same caustic soda you sometimes use to budge a difficult drain. Potatoes are softened in this process, so the skin rubs off easily. Then the potatoes are washed in a neutralising bath, sliced, dried, and dropped into hot fat for ninety seconds to seal them. They are usually sold within twenty-four hours.

The technologists have even tried to reduce costs by producing a potato flour and water paste, which you extrude through a chip-shaped ejector, dropping the chip-length pieces straight into hot fat. It has been a ghastly flop, happily.

Experiments with fish have been more successful, and sometimes you may find you've been served a square of fish sawn from a laminated slab of mixed frozen, flaky, rather wet fish. The manufacturers will tell you that you can't tell the difference, except for the uniformity of the shape, but that's an insult to most people's simple but sure sense of taste; as big an insult as the Can't-tell-Margarine-from-Butter ads. Some fryers, who won't use the stuff, say the danger is getting one piece of fish – what they call a stinker – sliced up and pressed into service with the rest of the fish. 'It may not be bad fish. Just a fish which ate something which didn't agree with it.'

As standards drop, the most faithful clients are bound to look elsewhere for satisfaction; so, surely these economies are stupid in the long-term. As stupid as the practice of many fish and chip shops who stock not malt vinegar, but coloured acetic acid, or the non-brewed condiment, as they call it. British Vinegars Ltd are very sour about this trend. They make Sarsons, a passable malt vinegar if you are a malt vinegar person. The vinegar manufacturers say that many more shops use the cheap, non-brewed stuff: 'We've bashed the drum and I think we're making inroads. We're a completely superior product. Our product is brewed, it takes time and money. It's the same process as making beer, actually, except that you don't add the hops. We use proper barley, not any old corn or maize.' When the brew is made, a special bacterium is added to turn it sour and it takes about three months to mature.

'Malt vinegar stimulates the palate,' the British Vinegars spokesman said. 'Non-brewed condiment is absolutely ghastly. You don't catch the full smell until you actually pour it on the chips; then it comes at you, like the smell of rotten eggs.' (Silvino Trompetto, the Savoy chef, says he couldn't use even malt vinegar. 'I just couldn't eat fish with malt vinegar on it,' he says in a pained voice. 'It would burn the throat.')

Fads in fish-frying vary. Yorkshiremen want haddock. Lancashire calls for hake, a longer, slimmer fish which cuts nicely into smaller portions. Lancastrians are 'snackers', they don't treat fish and chips as a main meal the way Londoners do. Londoners are scorned by the North because they will eat *any* fish. They are certainly not squeamish about eating the wings of the rather horrendous-looking skate (a member of the ray family) with its gelatinous texture; nor the coley or saithe, with its darker, greyer flesh; nor even pieces of sea-eel; nor the monk-fish, though this delicate-flavoured fish is becoming more difficult to find, and few people will have seen one with its amazing and monstrous black head. Unlike the French, we do not have a bizarre fascination about the appearance of the creatures we are about to eat.

What does not vary is the very rigid standard of perfection in frying, which every fryer can attain if he's prepared to use the best ingredients, and take the proper amount of care. Earlier, I mentioned that Derek Cooper's favourite fish and chip was Bryan's in Leeds. Albert Bryan is a fryer in his fifties and the son of the man who founded this shop-cum-restaurant as Bryan's Modern Fisheries back in 1934. 'We're called modern fisheries, but I'd say we're old fashioned,' says Bryan junior. 'We buy only quality fish, and we have to pay more, so does the customer.'

Albert Bryan is keeping a worried eye on the Icelandic extension of fishing limits. He knows that fish is going to get dearer. He's wondering how long the clientele will remain loyal as prices go up – and up. He hopes the answer will continue to be quality – if not, he's been wasting his time.

Here, then, are some tips from Albert Bryan, Britain's best:

'*Fish*. Buy only best-quality fish, fillet it yourself. I think there's a lot of satisfaction in handling good fish. Now I cook it with the skin on; I think it adds something. There's a little bit of oil between the flesh and the skin which has a lot of flavour. Get your fat hot, till a faint, almost invisible blue smoke begins to come off. We don't flour the fish here, we haven't the time, and I don't think there's a need. Just coat the fish thinly in batter, lower into the fat, skin side down. After a minute, when the batter's set, turn it over, and cook another five minutes or so. Remove fish and leave to drain for a couple of minutes. Then serve at once with a slice of lemon and a sprig of fresh parsley.

'*Batter*. People like to make out there's some secret to making batter and that's bunkum. You mix flour and water to a paste, adding just enough water to get the consistency of thick cream. Add salt to taste and some baking powder. We used to make our own, two parts tartaric acid, and one part bicarbonate of soda. Leave batter to stand for forty-five minutes. You can use the batter without letting it stand, but, if you do, the batter comes out pale in colour and the fish doesn't look cooked. If you leave the batter too long, for more than an hour, the baking powder stops working and the mixture will be spent; that's what happens when you get a batter which is gluey. You may have to thin down your batter after it's ready. Otherwise you'll get too thick a coating.

'*Chips*. Don't buy in pre-processed chips. I've tried them all, frozen chips, blanched chips, and all, and they don't taste the same to me. There's nothing like the ordinary potato. We do use a preparation called Driwite which means you can keep the cut potato fresh, without discolouring, but that's all. At home, all you need to do is cut up the potatoes just before frying, dry them on a cloth and put them into smoking fat in small batches. Don't leave chips to soak in water, because this drains the starch out, and you want some starch in so they'll puff up nicely. (If you wanted to make crisps you'd do the opposite; soak slices in water to get the starch out, then fry in deep fat.) As the potato season goes on, potatoes get more starchy; when you cook them, the starch turns to sugar, and they caramelise quicker; that's why they go brown in colour. Then they need less cooking time, or a lower temperature, or you can cook them in larger batches.'

Albert Bryan ended on a line from the Fish Fryer's Creed:

'Frying is a hard life, sometimes it's been a very hard life, but you know there have been few experiences so deeply satisfying in my life as cooking a really nice piece of fish.'

To that we say: Amen.

Vanity Fare

It must be the fault of our elder Indian army generation that curry is specifically regarded as 'hot'. Curry is a way of life. It's just as much a cool scene as a hot scene. The fragrance and aroma of Eastern cooking have made spices prized through the centuries, and it has nothing to do with the addition of a few hot chilli peppers. Where to start? If you're serious about it, don't buy tins of curry powder, the Indians don't. Make your own. Either pound the spices in a mortar with a pestle, or use an old coffee grinder. Warm the spices before use, which will release fragrance and odour. Commercial curry powder employs the cheaper spices like coriander, turmeric, ground ginger, white cumin seed. Here are two excellent mixtures which don't.

	Garam Masala	Special masala
Cardamom	$^3/_4$ oz	1 oz
Cinnamon	$^3/_4$ oz	$^1/_4$ oz
Cloves	$^1/_4$ oz	$^1/_4$ oz
Black Cumin Seeds	$^1/_2$ oz	$^1/_4$ oz
Mace	Pinch	3 blades
Nutmeg	Pinch	$^1/_4$ oz

A few **dos** and **don'ts** when making a curry. **Do** use ghee or puri-fied butter for frying. (Heat up some butter to a froth, let it cool in fridge, and water and impurities fall to bottom.) **Do** grate onions to get them fine. Or mince. **Do** sieve spices after grinding them. **Don't** let onions brown in pan. **Don't** let spices burn, or you lose flavour.

Here are some basic recipes. **Chicken curry**. Fry one onion, grated, till soft, with chopped clove of garlic. Then simmer with 1 large tbspn mixed curry spices as above. (If you have them to hand, the following make a good chicken blend – 2 cloves, 2 cardamoms, 1 tbspn coriander, 1 tspn turmeric, $^1/_2$ tspn ground ginger, $^1/_2$ tspn ground chillies.) Cook spices into onion for 5 mins, then add joint-ed chicken, and pint stock or water; cook 5 mins more, then cover and simmer till done, adding juice of lemon just before serving. Time, 30 mins at least, but all curries improve with long slow cook-ing, say, 2 hours, well-covered. **Madras Beef curry**. Fry one chopped onion with one clove garlic, blend 1 tbspn curry powder when soft, then after 5 mins, add chopped 1 lb beef, stirring anoth-er 5 mins. Add $^1/_2$ pint stock, cover well, simmer till done, adding lemon juice at end. **Prawn curry**. Same thing, but if you have coconut milk, add that instead of stock. Alternative spices for prawns – 1 tbspn coriander, 1 tspn turmeric, 1 tspn mustard, $^1/_2$ tspn cumin seed, $^1/_2$ tspn ground chillies. Add prawns last, just long enough to warm through. Don't overcook.

Vanity Fare

Some picnickers pack everything including the kitchen stove in the car and cook Cordon Bleu stuff the other end. The radio personality, Jack de Manio, for example, has a roadside meal of Borsch, lemon sole with shrimps, pork chops with barbecue sauce, fondue. It's not obligatory to try to be brilliant out-of-doors, though, and one of the top cookery writers, Elizabeth David, likes to buy her picnic ingredients on the spot. Sample menu: anchovies, salami sausages, pâtés, smoked fish, fruit and cheese, with crisp local bread, local wine.

You can have fun cooking out of doors if you've got a Girl Guide mentality (in the nicest possible way, I mean). Do you enjoy making fires? If so, go ahead. Build a basic oven of bricks or stones, use skewers if you haven't got a grid to balance on the top, use plenty of dry brushwood, and start cooking only when you've got to the embers stage. Ideal for chops, sausages, bacon, steak. Make a mixture of four parts oil, one part vinegar, one part soy sauce, with salt and freshly ground pepper, put it in a bottle, and bring it along for basting the meat. Scrubbed potatoes weighing ½lb each you can cook in the ashes, and aubergines too. Grill tomatoes on top. Don't forget the butter for the potatoes. It may rain, it may blow, but to addicts of outdoor eating, an underdone potato with a piece of burnt meat is the height of *haute cuisine*. If anyone criticises, let them try and do better.

But the real picnic, with a hint of *tête-à-tête*, takes place on a dreamy summer day by a stream, under the willows, a-buzz to the mumble of lazy bees. (If they are wasps, you've had it.) If the bloke's got a car, make sure you go with masses of cutlery, plates, cups, glasses. You'd better provide the tablecloth and napkins. Pack tin-opener, bottle-opener, salt in that order. Now your basic ingredients. Buy crisp french bread on the spot if possible. Also fresh lettuce, celery, watercress, tomatoes. There's nothing like a selection of good cheeses on a picnic. English Lancashire and Wensleydale cut off a large wheel for preference. French goats' cheese, which you wash down with a rough red wine.

Now, your tins of things. Sardines, anchovies, tuna or salmon,

pâté, are useful bets. Hard-boiled eggs, if you like them, are nice to
have around. A tin of potatoes, drained and sliced, with mayonnaise
make a ready potato salad. Spring onions, of course, or even a mild
Spanish onion, rather than no onion at all. Ham, cooked sausages,
veal escalops pre-cooked, cold fried fish (the Jewish delicacy), cold
chicken legs, deep-fried that morning before you set out, tongue,
salami. As a real treat you might, for your *tête-à-tête*, manage to
produce lobster mayonnaise, or salmon. Salmon must be poached
gently, 10 mins to the pound, then lifted out and drained, and that's
all. But no fast cooking or you ruin rather an expensive delicacy. I
personally think picnics are a time for picking at things with your
fingers, and I welcome things like prawns. A bottle of wine com-
pletes the pleasure but not if it gets hot with the sun. Red or white,
I like picnic wine to be cool. If you can find a stream I suggest you
fasten a string lightly round the neck of the bottle, anchoring it of
course to the shore, and submerge it till you are ready to eat. One
last tip: just for once, forget sticky, sweet foods. Why should insects
bother getting nectar from flowers when they've got picnickers like

Vanity Fare

Chinese Philosopher, he say: 'One Ox Take Five Days to boil, Ten
Thousand Pieces One Minute Each'*. There you have the secret of
Chinese cooking – timing. The French beat a big gong about *haute
cuisine* but Chinese cooking is a philosophy of its own – philosophy, poetry, economics, history, the lot. And recipe books in China
turn out to be written by artists, doctors, poets. It's a country which
gives names to its dishes like pigeon of the five fragrances, cinnamon blossom, eight valuables (for a dish we would dismiss as offal),
chicken in snow white clothes, noodles crossing the bridge.

Many dishes are made with familiar ingredients used in different ways, but considerable use is made of soy sauce, which is easy to
buy, cornflour, rice wine (use dry sherry), Ve-Tsin (monosodium
glutamate), garlic. In frying they often cook chopped ginger and
garlic in oil then remove it. In preparing the small pieces of chopped
pork or chicken or beef, they steep them for an hour or two in sher-

ry, soy sauce and seasoned cornflour. Vegetables cooked the Chinese way are a revelation. The basic principle is to fry the vegetables briskly for one minute in oil or lard, then add a little water or stock, and continue cooking, and stirring for another three to six minutes. Spinach is an eye-opener cooked the Chinese way. Wash and drain it, then toss it into a hot pan with two tablespoons of oil, teaspoon of salt and cook three minutes only, stirring all the time.

Cabbage: cut it into shreds, fry one minute while stirring, then add half a cup of water or stock and cook three minutes, stirring. For runner beans: break into inch-long pieces, stir-fry in oil for one minute, add half a cup water, cover three minutes; take lid off and cook another five minutes, stirring constantly.

Easiest and most famous Chinese dish is Chow Fan (it means 'eat rice'). It is the bringing-together of cooked rice and separately fried ingredients, blended with an egg. For four, boil $1/2$ lb rice (cooking Chinese rice is a book in itself), wash, drain. Fry lightly a selection of pieces of chicken, pork or prawns and cubes of tinned meat, seasoned in soy sauce, cornflour and sherry; and some select-ed pieces of vegetable, e.g. a few slivers of carrot, cauliflower florets, sliced green peppers, bean shoots, bamboo shoots. Now fry rice for a few minutes, then add the pre-cooked ingredients, heat them; then break two eggs on top. Let the eggs cook for 2 minutes, then break them up and let them set in the heat of the pan, till it makes pleasing blobs of yellow and white in the rice. Warning: do not on any account overcook the rice. The pre-cooking can be done ages before, but the last stage only takes a few minutes of heating up. (It is a delicious dish, but secretly it's a marvellous way with left-overs.)

  * Philosopher BA TE MAN

Vanity Fare – August

No month yields so much for the kitchen. The problem is what to do with it all?

Apples, pears, plums, blackcurrants, peaches, blackberries ... bottle them, turn them into jam, make them into wine, make tasty tarts.

The gooseberry makes an ideal tart. Fill an oven dish with gooseberries, sugar to taste, half a cup of water. Stand an inverted egg-cup (not plastic) in the middle to support the crust. For the pastry, 8 oz flour, 4 oz diced butter, mixed into crumbs lightly with fingertips. Add only enough water to make it moist enough to roll out into a $\frac{1}{4}$ in thick crust on a floured board. Prick with a fork, to let steam out, bake 50 mins at Gas 4 (moderate oven). Or try blackberry and apple tart, plum tart, all the same way. Delicious with vanilla ice cream. (Mix in glacé cherries and nuts and peel for your own special blend of ice-cream.)

Fruits are delicious turned into fools, eg gooseberry fool. Slowly stew 1 lb for 20 mins, till it pulps, then let it cool. Boil a cup of milk with a cup of cream, and let this cool. Mix pulp and cream with sugar, and serve chilled in glasses.

All fruits convert to wine, but some say this gooseberry wine is as good as champagne. Well... But you don't need any special equipment to try it, and it's fun. Bruise and crush 3 lb gooseberries, pour on 6 pints water, leave for three days, stirring occasionally. Now strain, and stir in 3 lb sugar till dissolved. Pour into a gallon jar, adding 1 oz isinglass (any chemist) and a miniature bottle of brandy. Bung tightly, and in six months' time, bung out, and bung-ho. Longer you keep it, the better. Transfer to bottles after six months, though.

Collier's Cuppa

People who deal in drugs (legally, of course) find the current fuss about pot pretty funny. It's just another jar on the shelf to them.

To Dr Harry Collier, chief of pharmacological research for one of Britain's biggest drug houses, the pot problem is academic. 'Civilised man cannot live without a mechanical crutch,' he told me. 'I've met only two people all my life who haven't taken caffeine, or alcohol, or nicotine.' His garden in South Kensington has its own drug corner—all native stock. 'That meadowsweet came from Sussex. Its real name is *spiraea*, which gives its name to aspirin. It provides salicylic acid. That's hellebore next to it, and lily of the valley. They give cardio-tonic drugs. Then there's foxglove which gives us digitalis from the leaves.'

In his drawing room he has a big drinks tray, but hardly touches the stuff himself. 'I find you can't think if you drink. I shouldn't say this, but I'm really very sceptical about drugs. I've invented a few myself, but I don't use them. I don't think you should use drugs without having a very powerful reason.' He even regulates his intake of tea and coffee. 'I never take caffeine after 4 p.m. That gives the body time to work out the caffeine by about 11 p.m. when I feel drowsy and go to bed. I get up between 5 a.m. and 7 a.m. and start the day with a powerful caffeine intake, two large cups of tea. Then two cups of coffee at breakfast. Then I have less. You see the pattern? I tried giving up tea and coffee, but after three weeks I gave up the attempt.' If people want drugs he thinks they should choose substances which don't interfere with work or damage health. Alcohol and pot both interfere with work. 'And that's bad. Work is very important, isn't it? I can't think of anything better for us than work.'

As a drugs man he's worried about hallucinogens, LSD especially. 'There's a hallucinatory mushroom that grows in England which the Vikings used to eat before going into battle. It also happens to be the chosen inebriant of a Siberian race in Kamchatka. They eat it, and because the hallucinogenic element is preserved in the system, they save their urine. I think it must be the mushroom in Lewis Carroll's Alice. But I don't think we should help people to find it.'

Dr Collier used to collect mushrooms himself, but no longer. One day he cooked and ate his gleanings only to discover that part of the batch was poisonous. 'I had a stomach ache. But the worst thing was waiting all day in case it was something more serious.' A man who knows about drugs can get really scared.

Atticus

The Danish bacon people in London have a trade relations man called Mr R. Haddock which sounds fishy enough, but they also have another one called Mr W. E. R. Tongue. That's offal.

Badger Gammon is Off – may we recommend the hedgehog?

Until a few weeks ago, any hedgehog that managed to escape the hurtling traffic at the intersections of the M3 and A30 at Bagshot, Surrey, could scramble into the safety of the herbaceous borders of Pennyhill Park, those beautifully landscaped grounds around a mock-Tudor pile where the inventor of sandpaper, Colin Heywood, used to live.

Not any more. The house is now a hotel and restaurant, and hedgehogs that stray in are likely to end up in the kitchens, where the German chef makes them into pâté. This is proudly presented to guests as pâté from the hotel's very own garden. The manager, 30-year-old Michael Garbutt, says it is a novelty for overseas visitors.

It doesn't amuse the locals, who are reacting in a predictably prickly fashion. 'It makes a mockery of our attempts to conserve wild life,' says Mrs Marjorie Chapman, a member of the Camberley Society. 'They'll be eating badger steaks and fox chops next.' (No. They discussed gammon of badger, a delicious course, but found that Lord Arran had just pushed through a Bill to protect badgers.)

Hedgehogs have long been eaten by gypsies; they used to wrap them in wet clay and cook them over wood fires. But this seems to be the first time they have been raised to *haute cuisine* level in this country. The Savoy, the Dorchester and the Ritz say they've never prepared hedgehog.

The German chef, Mr Pfeifer, makes his pâté (price 80p) by blending the rather strong-flavoured, scanty pieces of hedgehog flesh with veal, folding in cream and white of egg, and baking in a mould. Now he is working on a more elaborate two-day recipe in which the hedgehogs are marinated in sheep's milk.

Dr Maurice Burton, the leading British authority on the hedgehog, is a vegetarian of 75. He was saddened to hear of his little favourites going to table – though he recalls that the Romans used to fatten them up as a delicacy. They also used to be buried under buildings to ward off evil spells, and the hindquarters, burnt to ashes and mixed with resin were supposed to be a cure for baldness,

Mr Garbutt is not inclined to bow to the critics. 'We are full of contradictions about animal life,' he says. 'What is more ludicrous than hand-rearing a young cock pheasant, a beautiful creature, and then expecting it to be good sport?'

Then a thought makes him smile; 'We discussed how we should present the hedgehog dish. I thought we ought to call it the dish with the built-in tooth-picks.'

What Makes One Run, Stops the Other

Are there special foods and diets which give one sportsman an edge over the next? Did David Bedford, the extrovert middle-distance runner, smash the 10,000 metres nine days ago because he'd been training on Nutrament?

Could the burly Peterborough policeman, Geoff Capes, who broke the British shot-putting record during the AAA Championships, put it down to his newly increased meat diet?

Certainly Oxford United must have thought they had stumbled on a secret elixir the day they ran on to the field last season and drubbed Sunderland 5-1, straight after their first taste of a new energy drink, Dynamo.

No group of people on earth are so fussy and faddy about food as sportsmen, and no people seem to contradict each other so completely. What's ordered by one coach is often forbidden by another. British professional boxers step out into the ring stoked up with steak and salad, while the coach of our Olympic boxing team won't let his boys near a steak before a fight.

Who is right? Our chief coaches do agree there are two classes of diet. If you're training for the power events, like tennis, sprinting, putting the shot, you'll need a different diet from the athletes training for events involving stamina, like the marathon, football, canoeing.

Tom McNab, a leading national athletics coach, advocates the high protein diet for power events, and a controlled use of liquid carbohydrate diet for the stamina events. But who can afford a high protein diet today?

One champion shot-putter, Geoff Capes, couldn't. His policeman's salary wasn't enough, so his wife has been working to help sustain the 23-stone champion as well as their small children. Then the Meat Trades Journal offered to pay his butcher's bill for a month, and others chipped in too.

Cape's butcher is Arthur Johnson in Peterborough: 'Geoff came in and we discussed his diet. He said he needed a pound to a pound and a half of rump steak a day, not well hung. It must have done him some good. The day after I gave him the first piece he went off and broke the British record.'

The power events breed huge men, and they eat hugely. Angelo Parisi, one of our most promising judo hopes at the age of 20, weighs 15 stone, eats a gallon of ice cream every day in his father's ice cream factory, as well as grand helpings of steak, chips, and eight pints of milk.

That's a protein diet all right. And the ice cream? 'There's a lot of protein in it: not like the commercial leaders which is all air whipped into it,' says Angelo loyally.

Jim Aukett, 23, is one of our 400 metres hopes of the future, and although he's a dentist he consumes up to four Mars bars and two or three Cokes a day. It might not do much for his teeth, but his coach Charles Taylor says it doesn't seem to hurt his running.

'What food he eats is irrelevant as long as he enjoys it,' says Taylor. It's a nice endorsement for Mars and their advertised claim: Work, Rest, Play.

But it doesn't amuse Professor John Yudkin, the nutritionist dedicated to a life-long fight against sugar. 'With regular training the sugar would probably be burnt up,' says the professor, who blames sugar for killing more people than cancer by bringing on coronaries.

'But I'm not so sure about the long-term effects. He may be laying up trouble for himself. It's not natural. The Almighty didn't intend us to eat such large amounts.'

But the carbohydrate diet is very much part of the training diets of our long-distance runners, and sugar, in the form of glucose, is taken in extremely high concentrations.

Ron Hill, and other long-distance runners who represented

Britain at the last Olympics, followed a 'depletion' regimen evolved by the Swedes some years ago. The runner trains himself to zero, eating only protein for seven to ten days, taking no carbohydrates. Thus he uses up all the glycogen in the muscles, the substance which he needs to fight mid-race fatigue and depression.

Then he rests for three days before his race, switches to a carbohydrate diet, with masses of glucose and sugars. The body, desperate to restore its glycogen reserves, takes in double the requirement, and this is what he can spend in a long race which would usually exhaust the body's glycogen.

Beecham, the drug firm, are considering marketing a powerful energy drink called Dynamo, which would suit footballers and other sportsmen who depend on stamina. They have raced two teams of canoeists against each other, one fed on Dynamo and one on a placebo, and found that the Dynamists improved on lap times while the placebists dropped back.

Oxford United tried it, beat Sunderland soundly in their first Dynamo match, and as manager Gerry Summers puts it: 'The lads wouldn't leave it alone after that.' Oxford finished seventh in the Second Division and no one would say they weren't fit. They also take enough vitamin C a day to equal 50 oranges.

David James, our Olympic boxing coach, recommends a carbohydrate meal before a fight. This is sharply different from accepted practice. You'll sometimes see the pros eating at Isow's in Soho before a fight, consuming huge steaks and salad.

James says they've got it all wrong. 'It's a very old idea; you take a bull, chop off the horns and hooves, and tuck in. It's the one thing you don't want to have before a fight. The blood doesn't want to be coping with digestion when it should be oxygenating the muscles.'

How do you get protein if you don't eat steak and fish and chicken? The manufacturers of Nutrament say the answer to that is Nutrament. If Bedford wasn't forbidden by amateur status to say so, he might admit that he trained for his 10,000 metres record on this liquid meal-in-a-tin.

It's a Canadian product which has been in use in Britain for about two years, and there's no great secret formula. Each can gives you 397 calories and contains a mixture of milk solids and soya flour, fat from milk, and carbohydrates, mostly sugar and corn syrup. It comes in lovely flavours and tastes like a milk shake.

Claim can be made for any kind of food. Rice pudding just happens to suit Kevin Murphy, our long-distance swimmer who has done the Channel both ways without stopping, and was the first man to swim the North Channel of the Irish Sea as well as the 66 miles round the Isle of Wight. But in Murphy's case rice pudding isn't so much a source of power as a means of combating seasickness.

Ron Franklin, a British runner who's nearly 46, and still competing with the Thames Valley Harriers amazes his colleagues with his non-meat diet which includes handfuls of muesli, raisins and nuts, fruit juices and nut steaks. He fasts before a marathon. His mother, in her seventies, doesn't really approve. 'Well, I think he's eccentric,' she says.

Herb Elliot, the Australian miler who shattered the world record, sometimes ran on such items as raw rolled oats, walnuts and carrots, and many Australian swimmers swear by wheatgerm, the nutritious centre of wheat which gets lost from flour in the milling.

Tennis players are not usually as careful about diet as they should be. One exception is Julie Heldman, the American, whose sister is a bit of a hippy in California. She's interested in the whole-food movement, prefers organically-grown food, and knows the vocabulary of Yin and Yang. (Sounds mysterious, but Yin – acid – should balance – Yang – alkali. The blood is fractionally more alkali than acid.)

No-one is more diet conscious than the Russians, but athletes might hesitate before imitating them. Currently they are shouting about their vitamin E discovery; vitamin E, say they, inhibits the production of lactic acid in the blood, and it's lactic acid which burns up the oxygen which supplies stamina.

The South Africans are working on a similar theory because the Masai tribesmen of East Africa are remarkable athletes, and fermented milk is important item their diet; they think the milk acts like an inoculation, counteracts the effect of lactic acid in the blood.

Professor Yudkin is suspicious. 'I don't believe a word of it. The Russians in particular have a very peculiar idea about nutrition.

They are really a little backward.'

The Masai may simply be good athletes, because they've evolved that way. And no one in the world can equal the long-distance runners of North Mexico, the Tarahumaras, who have been studied by Bruce Tulloh, our own long-distance runner who ran across the United States.

These amazing runners compete in two- and three-day races covering distances of 160 miles, or more. But American dieticians, who examined them, found that they subsisted on half the nutritional requirements of the average American sportsman.

One class of sportsman who neglects the dietary aspect of food is the racing driver. In fact, he may not eat for quite a long period before a race, so that his stomach will be empty just in case he's required to put in an appearance on the operating table.

Racing driver Jackie Stewart gives another reason for not eating. 'When I'm switched on, food makes me uncomfortable. I have to be hungry... I have to feel hunger in order to succeed.'

Stewart adds that love-making has just the same effect on him as food. But that's quite another story.

The Bland Leaders

A new Lifespan series that investigates the Great British Convenience foods, the fish fingers, corn flakes, sliced bread and flavoured yoghurts that are the staples of our national diet.

Heinz

BEANZ MEANZ HEINZ, saith the advertisement. But like all advertisements, this is a dangerously sweeping assertion. For the Heinz bean, a small specimen shipped to Britain from Michigan via the Great Lakes, is actually a very unimportant bean in world terms.

Beanz meanz soybeanz if it meanz any beanz at all in terms of global consumption. The soybean is a workmanlike little fellow who divides neatly into fine protein and oil, can be handled as flour, fermented into a tasty soy sauce or made into bean curd. The nutritious oil can be refined and homogenated to make margarine, or the soybeanz can be processed into fibres, spun and woven into imitation chicken and steak and sold to vegetarians under brand names like Kesp. That's a bean for you.

BEANZ also meanz black beanz, brown beanz, black eye beanz, and green beanz such as broad beanz, French beanz and juicy runner beanz.

Start again, with this qualification: HEINZ MEANZ BAKED BEANZ. But what a pale and insipid child of their great American Mother, the Boston baked bean, a smouldering, simmering thickness of haricots, molasses, and mustard! And it compares in no way with the world's great baked bean dishes, like Cassoulet, a casserole from the South of France enriched with salt pork and preserved goose; or Feijoada, the Brazilian national dish of black beans eaten with hot sauce, or Chilli con carne, that shuddering taste sensation of red Mexican beans, chilli sauce and beef. Just imagine putting the oomph of a national advertising budget behind dishes like these.

Start again. HEINZ actually means an excellent brand of tinned, steam-cooked beans in tomato sauce; a convenient, cheap, nourishing snack which is a godsend to the housewife with the clamouring children at her skirts.

The housewife votes for Heinz with her purse. She buys 1,250,000 tins a day. Heinz sell nearly £30 million worth a year. They easily out-sell their rivals, Crosse and Blackwell and HP, because they are better, Heinz will explain blandly.

They are also blander. In common with most of the brand leaders in other fields, market research has shown that the nation's taste buds are about as receptive as those of a three-month-old baby.

Quote: Mr Nick Cutcliffe, head of public relations with Heinz (he's been there 34 years): 'Our bean has a slightly blander taste. Other beans are more highly spiced, children in particular seem to like our taste.'

Blandness is one key selling point. Nutritional value is another. As far back as 1910, this grand old market leader was claiming: 'Builds up brain, body and muscle.' Another early advertising claim: 'Children like them as much as men.' Then they realised children liked them more, and the flavours were duly modified. Before the war Heinz went along with the slogan 'Joy of Living'; after the war they improved it to 'So Good to Grow Up With.' Today's advertising is directed to children, and it's fun – kids' poetry and drawings.

Do they help you grow up? Yes, they do. A large tin of baked beans, say Heinz, contains as much protein as ¼lb of meat or three eggs. You could live off baked beans, and Melvin Roberts, aged 15, of Ashby-de-la-Launde Lancs eats nothing else. He has beans on toast twice a day. And he's 5ft 10in tall.

Beans on toast have the blessing of vegetarians like Dr Alan Long, a chemical analyst with one of the top drug firms: 'The protein in the beans equals 40, the toast equals 50, but it's an odd case of two and two making five. Add some fresh tomato for Vitamin C and you've got a nicely balanced meal.'

They find favour too with non-vegetarians like Clement Freud, MP, gourmet and gourmand: 'I cook them for my children. They are excellent things, the nicest things. You can make them sophisticated by adding dry sherry, crisp bacon, Tabasco sauce. I like baked beans cold with Dijon mustard and vinegar.'

Sourgrapes: Silvino Trompetto, Savoy master-chef: 'Beans on toast. What a terrible idea! Two stodgy things together.' Christopher Driver, editor of the *Good Food Guide*: 'I can't stand them. It's a piece of brainwashing. Why buy them in a tin? There are few cheaper, easier foods to prepare for oneself.'

Heinz baked beans did not do Roger Daltry of the Who any good. He posed for a publicity picture sitting in a bath of baked beans and caught pneumonia.

The Heinz fortune is solidly embedded in baked beans, by far the most successful of its many lines – which number many more than the famous 57 varieties, about 200 in Britain, and 1,250 around the world.

They are made in an exciting factory set in Neasdeniana west of London; it's a children's paradise of whirling, shining cans hauled up clanking to overhead canways, from which they come spinning down into Z-bend curves for filling, crimping, labelling, packing.

The factory manager is a jinking rugby three-quarter called John Stagg who still plays the game at 46. All the Heinz men have an easy, confident way with them, which comes of being brand leaders for 35 years.

He proudly shows me the process: the cold mix of tomato purée, spice and cornflour, into which is pumped salt water and sugar syrup. Steam is pumped in to gel the starch, but done quickly to retain colour. Artificial colouring is something Heinz shun; so to get a tomato red enough to give the natural colouring the housewife demands, they've produced their own strain; this they sell to farmers in Portugal and Turkey to grow.

Beans are also politics: Mr David Coode, of purchasing, says they used to get tomatoes from Italy and Spain. They like to buy beans from a third world country like Tanzania. But they are affected by attitudes in the City where it's felt that Tanzania raises uncomfortable questions about white and black.

Then sauce meets bean: the bean has been on a mighty journey, it's sorted, washed, blown dry, cleaned, sized, passed over magnets, through colour discriminators which reject coloured immigrant beans, and then it's launched into a 4,000ft trough of hot water which rushes it over vibrators to shake out stones.

Then it is passed through what they call their infra-red oven, thus entitling them to claim on the tins: oven-baked. This is a small gas-heated frame. The beans come out the other side a little drier, but not markedly different. 'You call this oven baking?'

They exchange glances: 'We've got a right one here!'

Then the cans are half-filled with beans, topped up with some sauce, and helter skelter they're carried away, to be cooked in the three 40ft hydrostatic sterilisers which rise like Daleks above the factoryscape.

Back at Hayes' Park, in the Heinz HQ set in lovely parkland you can meet the backroom boys, the Heinz chefs, the purchasers, the researchers, fine interesting, intelligent people. With your know how, you cannot help asking, couldn't you do a bit more for flavour here and there? 'The public is our palate,' says the Heinz PR man, Mr. Cutcliffe.

More sayings of a PR: 'People are very surprised if a can of beans is not perfect,' says Mr Cutcliffe, ' but they aren't surprised if a £1,500 car isn't perfect.' And again: 'We are perfectionists. There's the story that our first manager here, Charles Hellen, was looking at artwork for a huge poster, when he suddenly pointed with his finger: "I don't like that bean."

One more thing I said I'd like to know - how do they suppress the unglamorous fact that beans cause wind?

Mr Cutcliffe: 'Well don't all foods have that effect?'

No.

Dick Barre, product develop menu manager: 'Well, of course it used to be considered quite proper to belch and make wind after a meal, a compliment to the host.'

Mr Heinz: our compliments to your chefs.

> *You can a tell a person's income*
> *By his intake of baked beans.*
> *It's a sort of meanz test.*

Wall's

Every packet of Wall's pork sausages you buy is endorsed by the royal warrant. But this is not an allusion to the fact that one of their directors is about to become Princess Anne's father-in-law. It derives from royal patronage which goes back to Queen Victoria's happy association with the Jermyn Street pork butcher, Thomas Wall.

It's the image of such a wise, knowing old Jermyn Street butcher that Wall's promote in their TV ads. Wall's product group manager Peter Humphreys says: 'It's a difficult piece of advertising to get across. We looked for the embodiment of a pork butcher with expertise.'

So advertising gives the product what it lacks: personality.

A much bigger complaint: Wall's are surely deceiving us by implying that their sausages are made to traditional recipes by an old-fashioned pork butcher?

The modern Wall's sausage has barely a superficial resemblance to the porkies before the war. Peter Humphreys recognises this. 'In the 1930s,' he agrees, 'the pork sausage had distinction. They were 80 per cent lean pork. They were very serious up to the Second

World War. Then they were made of ersatz materials; there was too much water in them and they spluttered in the pan. They literally went bang, so the name 'Bangers' was born.

'By the 1960s the sausage was competing against fun foods, like fish fingers and the Vesta quick frozen range. Yet we held our own very well.'

But how? They held their own with a sausage-style meat-and-cereal-type product. Not with a sausage. The whole standard has gone down so completely that our sausage isn't even rated as a sausage in Europe.

This is the composition of a Wall's sausage: one-third lean meat of pig, one-third pig fat, one third cereal filler with brine, preservatives, flavouring, colour.

Question: from reader Mrs WTA of Abingdon, Berks: 'Is it true that every bit of the pig is used in making sausages?'

Answer: No, Mrs WTA of Abingdon, it is not true. The back goes into bacon, the fore and rear legs are prepared as joints, meat from the head is used in pork loaf, blood goes into blood sausage, liver to liver pâté, bones for pork jelly and bone meal, surplus fat is used for lard for pie crusts and soap-making, the bristles for brushes. It's what's left over that goes into sausages, together with rusk and water.

But, Mrs WTA, do not be down-hearted. The royal sausage has just gone decimal.

How did Wall's achieve the breakthrough? By using a principle of co-extrusion which Unilever pioneered to put the stripe in Signal toothpaste. Sausages have traditionally been made by the Dickensian method of stuffing meat into casings, the large and small intestines of cows and sheep. Unless you make the sausages so short and stubby as to be laughable, there's no way of stuffing sausage skin to get 10 to the pound.

So Wall's have found a way to dispense with clumsy old casings, and by co-extrusion, spin a web of liquid skin round a long pipe line of sausage meat. This skin is made from a substance which the casings contain, collagen. They take it from the underskin of the hides of animals, and it comes to their Southall factory in huge white lumps like wash-leather, where it's sliced into chips, mixed with glue called methycellulose.

I've tried the sausage, and frankly, I find it quite disappointing in colour, flavour and texture. They are pink because Wall's says the housewife doesn't like white sausages. (Pork, unfortunately, happens to be white.)

But for Wall's it's one huge success story, an impressive tale of business acumen from the efficient network of distribution, to the housewives working part-time at point of sales in supermarkets; and back to the factory and the farm, where their chief pig buyer, Peter Phillips, Mark Phillips's father, is purchasing 750,000 pigs a year. They are bred from sows which are a cross between Landrace White and Saddleback. These are sold to farmers along with test tube sperm from their own champion hogs. The cross produces a heavier, fatter pig, but that suits Wall's. They can use all the fat on a pig.

Humphreys says the housewife gets exactly the product she can afford. And with the dramatic rise in carcass meats soon she won't be able to afford even this.

Even now, Wall's say they are phasing out the pork sausage in favour of the cheaper pork-and-beef products. (Humphreys: 'A housewife, blindfolded, can't tell the difference.')

Well, so much for your Royal warrant, Mr Walls! Humphreys: 'I'd definitely like to see a return to the pre-war distinctive pork sausage. One you really could be proud to take down on your bike to Buckingham Palace.'

Harp Lager
The best-selling fizz in Britain isn't champagne, but Harp lager.

We asked Harp: 'What special characteristics make Harp the brandleader?' One of their brewers said: 'It's not so much what you can say for it. It's just that there's not much you can say against it.' This remarkable taste for nothing-in-particular, therefore, scores over rivals like Carlsberg, Skol, Heinekin, Tuborg, and strong, costly Lowenbrau.

Harp is the most modern of modern beers, the concept on which all today's keg beers are established. Keg beers are the bright, sterile, highly-carbonated beers, advertised widely on TV.

By tradition beer is a drink with body. This can make it murky. It's strongly flavoured with hops, which can make it too bitter for many. It goes on fermenting in the barrel, which means it may go off in the pub; turn sour. And those breweries who still make it the traditional way are closing at a rapid rate.

About 10 years ago, the beer marketing people stumbled on the curious fact that not so many people liked beer as liked the idea of it – the promise in a tankard, the message of merriment, sociability, loosening of restraints.

So they set to work to make a beer which wasn't beer, and Harp is a monument to this scientific and technological breakthrough. Clarity replaced body. Fizz replaced flatness. Gold replaced the dull brown colour, thanks to added maize flakes and caramel – two ingredients never allowed in lager's fatherland. (No risk of offending the Trade Descriptions Act: lager is German for storage, and Harp is duly cold-stored from six weeks to three months.)

Harp is the work of scientists rather than craftsmen. Lab. chemists ensure that the bib of foam on your lager stays stiff with alginates from seaweed. They make sure it sparkles by injecting carbon dioxide. And although Harp's Alton factory is set in the heart of Hampshire hop country, they rule out local hops because they lack the necessary stability a scientist calls for.

The beer trade today looks for its recruits among a new breed of technologists, like John, who runs the biggest of their breweries. He's a university graduate, a chemical engineer with a smattering of microbiology. He has a certain nostalgia for the old days, but it's balanced by the chemist's pride in his skills. 'We make the brews the marketing people call for. They must be right, because we're the best-selling lager.'

Harp's retort: *(Following the* Sunday Times *Bland Leader above, Harp's retort was printed a week later)*

Harp is a monument to this scientific and technological breakthrough (in beer). Clarity replaced body. Fizz replaced flatness. Gold replaced the dull brown colour...

A Song of Abject Penitence
Sorry I drank that Harp, Mr Bateman, didn't know it was wrong.
I supposed, from the first,
It was good for my thirst,
Now I'm singing a different song.

I'm ashamed to admit that I thought it was nice.
Before you showed me the light.
I assumed, like a fool,
That I wanted it cool,
And I thought it was right to be bright.

Believe me, until I had studied your piece,
I did not understand,
The evil that's traced,
To a lager whose taste
Is the same in all parts of the land.

I'm an idiot, sir, and I freely confess
My mind was an echoing void.
To imagine that men,
When they said, 'Same again',
Were buying a brew they enjoyed.

Published by the brewers of Harp, who until quite recently misinter-
preted the annual purchase of 400 million pints of their lager as
some kind of evidence that people liked it.

Coca-Cola
The man from Coke was full of pep. It was as if he wanted to teach
the Whole World to sing.
　　Did he drink a lot of Coke?
　　Well, on a hot summer's day, up to ten.
　　Who wouldn't want to teach the world to sing? Ten jets of caf-

feine in a day, plus the usual quota of coffee and tea.

It's the caffeine in Coke which keeps you buzzing just as the caffeine in tea and coffee is a pick-me-up.

How do you ever wind down?

Well, you don't, unless you search out the solace of a depressant – like alcohol!

But children can't balance the effects of the two. *Oh,* say Coke, piously, *children don't drink a lot of Coke.* In Britain, apparently the consumption of Coke is less than a bottle per person per week.

Coke have an answer to the criticism about its pep. 'It's equal to the caffeine in a third of a cup of coffee and we don't sell it as a pep drink ... it's a refreshment.' They're not about to take the caffeine out, though.

And what about the sugar level? Children bathe their teeth daily in quite enough confectionary to risk dental decay without the addition of sugar sweet Coke. There's a legend of an extracted tooth being left in Coke and getting eaten away.

'It's been shown,' say Coke, 'that the drink passes through the mouth very rapidly. The teeth have saliva round them, and you can't hold a carbonated product in the mouth for more than five seconds because it is so gassy. Yes, that tooth would show some "weight loss" over a week or month – but so it would in a glass of apple or orange or lemon juice.'

Coke is the real thing. But what precisely is that? Just 1 per cent flavour and caramel colouring, topped up with sugar and water, chilled carbon dioxide fizz, and a massive, sparkling bubbling dose of image and advertising message. You drink your fantasies – and very refreshing they can be.

The history of Coca-Colanisation is also the history of America's rise to world supremacy in advertising and marketing. Even before a country seeks election to the United Nations, they take out a subscription to civilisation by paying Coca Cola dues. Coke provide a minute quantity of the flavouring essence, send in advertising men to propagate the word, and brief advisers who tell local franchises how to build the product up. Along go Ford and Co. with their lorries, freezer firms to keep the Coke cool, and suddenly – civilisation has come.

Coke's inventor, John S. Pemberton, first sold it as a cure-all – a brain tonic to relieve physical and mental lethargy (which is just what caffeine does). Why *Coca Cola*? Because the essence was thought to contain extract of cola seeds (which contain caffeine) and coca leaves, the Peruvian shrub which yields the stimulant cocaine. But Coca Cola say that Coke has never contained cocaine. They got it wrong in 1886.

Coke is one of those 'secrets' known only to two men. But arguably, it wouldn't matter if it was two million. Pepsi Cola will never catch up Coke any more than *Penthouse* will catch *Playboy*.

Nor does it matter that you can make cheaper, better, tastier summer drinks with mint and wine and fruit juices and ice if you're prepared to take just a little time and trouble.

The Coke spokesman: 'I'd rather read a book.'

Libby's

Lovely, lovely Libby's who've reared us healthily from childhood with authentic canned fruit and fruit juices. Now they're promising still more for our health – more orange and lemon drinks with Triple Vitamin C.

This product has been a staggering success since it was added to Libby's 'C' range just over six months ago. It comes in dimpled glass jars like other fruit juices, tastes nice and sweet like a good juice should, and costs around what a juice usually costs, which is quite expensive (up to 22p a bottle).

But this is the thing. Read the legal definition on the labels and you'll see that it's not juice but ORANGE DRINK and LEMON DRINK. Like a strong squash.

Don't Libby's feel they might be misleading the customer? Phil Barton, at the London offices of this American firm, 'It could be confusing. I'll be quite honest with you. This is a tricky one. People still think it's a juice. *But we've never tried to pass it off as a juice.*'

Oh, no?

Libby's orange drinks are very nice. Their researchers in Westmorland find the average British housewife actually doesn't like the pure juice. It's too strong, too acid, too sour. So they've come up with a drink more like an orange than an orange. Sweeter, weaker, better coloured.

This drink is made from concentrate 'comminute'. This is a concentrate which includes the whole skin, juice, essential oils, pips.

The mixture is then diluted with five parts of water – thus relieving the housewife of the tedious chore of turning on the tap to dilute the essence.

Anyone can play the tripling games, so why not try diluting a 21p bottle of comminute, Sunquick? It gives about two and a half the quantity for the same price, if tasting slightly more bitter.

It won't have so much Vitamin C but how much does this matter? Vitamin C is not very expensive, and we get plenty if we eat fresh fruit, vegetables, boiled potatoes. Unlike 17th-century sailors with rotting gums, we don't need it desperately to ward off scurvy.

Libby's says its market tests show that the British housewife does want the stuff. This could be the influence of Dr Linus Pauling, the Nobel Prizewinnner, who claims that Vitamin C wards off the common cold. The Government doesn't yet agree with his findings, so it's illegal to make claims for Vitamin C in ads.

So the Libby's men have on their hands this dilemma. Rocketing sales of a drink which the public think is a juice and it isn't. Should they tell all?

We offer this solution. Instead of showing on their label succulent slices of cut orange, shouldn't they show a jug measured with one part concentrate and five parts water?

For this, surely, should be the next challenge presented to Libby's admirable marketing department. To do for water what they've done for crushed pips, oils, pith, skin and orange pulp.

Stuffed Sweet Aubergine
Imam Bayildi

The popularity of this dish may have much to do with its name in Turkish which means 'fainting prince', the Imam having apparently swooned when this sweet delicacy was presented to him.

Serves 4
4 long, medium sized aubergines
4 tablespoons olive oil
2 onions, finely sliced
2 green peppers, seeded and finely sliced
4 cloves garlic (or less), finely chopped
3 medium-sized tomatoes, peeled, seeded and chopped
3 tablespoons parsley, finely chopped (keep 1 spoonful for garnish)
1 teaspoon allspice
2 oz sultanas
salt and freshly ground black pepper
juice 1 lemon and $\frac{1}{4}$ pint water

Cut a deep slit lengthways down each aubergine, stopping short of the top and base, and place them in a bowl of very salty water for 30 minutes.

Meanwhile prepare the filling. In a heavy pan heat 2 tablespoons olive oil.

Gently fry the onions with the green peppers and garlic until soft and melting.

Then combine them with the tomatoes, parsley, allspice, salt and black pepper, to taste.

Drain the aubergines, gently squeeze out the moisture with your hands, and dry with paper towels.

Put the rest of the olive oil in the pan and fry the aubergines, gently turning several times (take care not to spoil the shape) until they begin to soften.

Transfer the aubergines to an ovenproof dish, the slits facing upwards. Force as much filling as possible into the slits and put any that is left on top. Pour on the lemon juice and water.

Bake in a preheated oven at 325F, 160C, gas 3 for 45 minutes. Leave to cool at room temperature, then chill if you like.

To make the dish as a starter for 8, halve the aubergines after soaking. Scoop out the flesh and chop and fry in oil before blending with the other ingredients. Drizzle filled halves with oil and bake in a hot oven for 30 minutes.

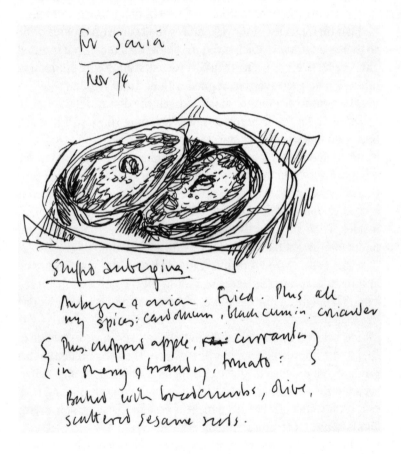

for Sania

Nov 74

Stuffed aubergines.

Aubergine & onion. Fried. Plus all my spices: cardamum, black cumin. coriander
{ Plus chopped apple, ~~the~~ currants }
{ in sherry & brandy, tomato : }
Baked with breadcrumbs, olive, scattered sesame seeds.

Goodbye Fish Fingers...

Fresh cod became more expensive than beef this week – and this heralds, among other things, the end of the pedigree fish finger as we know It. Bland it may seem but we are currently blessed with a vintage we shall never see again. So lay down a few cases of North Sea '74 in your deep freeze while you've still got the chance.

Fish is a prime source of protein. It builds muscle, it contains iron, calcium and phosphorous so enriches blood, bone and brain.

Fish thrive freely in the Seven Seas. They aren't tampered with, so there's no nasty suspicion you may have with meat, that in a previous existence, has been artificially forced, stuffed with antibiotics, injected with preservatives, stained with harmful colour.

The housewife knows fish is good. But she doesn't like buying it. It lies there on the fishmonger's slab dripping slimy scales, wide-open and bloodshot eyes staring accusingly. It's handled by a man in white overalls which are wet, bloodstained, and smelly, and the odour lingers on in the wrapped package she buries in her shopping basket. Back home, she has to handle the slimy flesh, chop off heads and tails, maybe slit the guts and rinse out the stinking black insides. Then she's got to cook it, a scientific operation calling for understanding of temperatures, texture and flavour.

Fish goes soggy and disintegrates, fish goes dry and loses taste and texture. It takes a degree of skill to hit the nail exactly on the head. The slightest hint of failure, and a small child is saying: 'I don't like fish, mummy.'

For nearly a century the fish-and-chip makers have been able to exploit the housewife's nervous fear of fish, They've produced a fish product in a hideous disguise of brilliant yellow and orange batter, served with glistening chips, soaked in malt vinegar, tingling with salt; yet it's a happily balanced meal of protein (fish), carbohydrates and Vitamin C (potatoes) and fats (frying oil).

How could fish and chips be improved? They have almost every advantage of the modern convenience foods – cheapness, blandness and, in common with the sausage, they bear little resemblance to their origins. They lack only one thing. When the housewife wants to eat it, she has to go out and buy it. So much trouble.

And so it came to pass that the crispy brown fish finger quickly jumped into the lazy vacuum. British manufacturers did not have far to look. They found the answer sitting top of the American hit parade, under the name of a fish stick. It was the product of a Mr Birdseye's freezing company. Today Mr Bird has become separated from his Eye, but Birds Eye (alias Unilever) are the British freezing-giants.

At their Grimsby plant they freeze more fingers and more peas than any other plant in the world. Britons consume more than 1,000 million fish fingers a year.

The name 'Finger' is a peculiarly British bit of fun; and more effective than the name they originally chose for their new Cod Fries. They were about to launch them as Cod Pieces when someone pointed out the fifth century allusion. In the hilarity which followed a voice was heard saying: 'Well, couldn't we call them Fish Balls.'

The fish finger is an adman's dream. It's addressed to the children's market. The creative head of one of our biggest advertising agencies explains: "Here's a wonderful way for mum to get some fish into her child. It's fish in a palatable form. They'll eat small things and it's good for them.' The adman doesn't need to stress the convenience, the cheapness, the blandness. Just provide absolution for mum's latent guilt.

The fish finger is a highly successful commercial answer to the housewife's problem – but it's hardly a gourmet's delight. It has in common with so many other items on the nation's shopping list this prime quality of tastelessness, a lack of both flavour and texture. This is not surprising as it's made from cod, which must be quite the dullest fish in the kitchen, begging for special treatment – added cheese, curry, lemon, tomato, onion, garlic.

Be that as it may the price of cod is far from bland these days and it is getting spicier every week. So the British fish industry is looking desperately for cheaper alternative fillings for its fingers. Recent technical developments have made it possible to trawl at deeper levels than previously and up from 500 fathoms have been dredged goggle-eyed monsters to take the place of the fish we know and love. No less than 100 Hull fish merchants have gathered this month to taste these creatures and what they nibble today the nation may devour tomorrow.

The **rat tail** – which the fishmongers anxiously insist on calling by its less colloquial title, the grenadier – has been dubbed 'the most cod-like' of these newcomers, while the **black scabbard** is compared to plaice.

The **rabbitfish** is a bitter disappointment – literally – while the **smooth-head**, on which great hopes were at first pinned because of its easy availability and large numbers, turns out to taste like a fish-flavoured junket.

More promising is the learned-sounding *gephyoberix darwinii*, pronounced 'extremely good eating, with a nutty flavour a bit like coconut and the texture of lobster.'

Any one or more of these deep sea delicacies could be put into our fish fingers in the not too-distant future and Birds Eye chairman Ken Webb told me (I'd like to think jokingly) that they'd happily include ground fishheads if they could get the law changed.

Most fish landed at Grimsby, where fish fingers are made, are not acceptable to the housewife in fish fingers, or on the fishmonger's slab – yet – so they go to the friers: coley or saithe, with its grey flesh, which gets sold as 'rock salmon'; catfish which fish friers sell as rock salmon; dogfish also known as husk, which they sell as rock salmon. We eat a lot of rock salmon, huh?

The Birds Eye cod is sliced, flattened into trays, frozen for $1\frac{1}{2}$ hours. Then it's taken out in beautiful slabs textured like white marble. **Fact**: Fish in tray weighs 9lb 12oz i.e. 156oz. Each tray yields 200 fish fingers weighing 1oz each. By logic then, the breadcrumbs and batter must add 44oz to each batch of fingers, thus making up a quarter of the weight.

From the cold half of the factory, with its attendant stench of chlorine, the fish moves to the warm half, with its sweet and pungent smell of cooking oil. Machines with diamond saws rotating at 7,000 revs a minute slice the blocks into fingers, and off they go through a waterfall of flour-and-water batter into a snow of breadcrumbs. They pass through a frier to seal the batter (one minute at 170 degrees F), and into the hands of the packers.

The fish finger is very much a product which reflects our times, but in spite of its huge popularity, it could become extinct in only a matter of years. By political act, for example, if we lost the cod war. By commercial greed, if countries continue to overfish the cod (as the whale has been depleted). By trade union acts, even ... workers holding out for wages which cut into the shareholders' pockets. By scientific discovery, perhaps, if a huge publication and advertising campaign was to boost an acceptable protein alternative (so you'd have Soy Bean Crunchies, or maybe Yeast Crackers).

It seems certain that the 100 per cent cod product that we are currently offered will have to be blended with cheaper fish, not to mention potato, rice or rusk in the style of the mass-produced sausage. So this could be the golden age of the fish finger today. Enjoy them now.

Self-Sufficiency

Our confidence in the consumer society has taken a nasty battering these last weeks. And even when the current crisis has been manipulated away by the politicians, we shall have to learn to live with more leisure (three-day weeks or otherwise), higher prices and infuriating shortages of everything from apples to rawlplugs.

Worst of all, we will have to battle even harder against erosions of quality in workmanship, service, value – and taste in particular. When did you last enjoy some really fruity jam, sharp cheese or hearty beer? We think the answer lies in relying far more on our own resourcefulness – smoking our own fish, making our own wine and beer, raising our own livestock even learning to enjoy the free food that the hedges, countryside and sea shore have to offer.

I like Pyke. Dr Magnus Pyke is this year secretary of the British Association for the Advancement of Science. He is author of nearly a score of books on nutrition, food science and technology. The most instructive and witty of these are *Food and Society* (subtitled *Facts, Fallacy, Religion and Folklore, the Background to Scientific Nutrition*) and *Technological Eating* – or *Where*

Does The Fish Finger Point? (published by John Murray).

Why do I like Pyke? He's saying what food is really all about – food as fuel, food as social custom. Before you go seeking self-sufficiency Dr Pike may help you define what you mean by it. Better nutrition? And to achieve what? Dr Pyke quotes the proud achievements of American scientists who were able to show that children from the same family reared on American diets grew faster than their cousins in Japan.

Some people might say this is significant nutritional achievement, but Dr Pyke wonders what real social benefits accrue to a Japanese whose legs are 4.1 cm longer than his relatives in Japan and whose nose is 2.3 mm longer?

And in what sort of food fuel are we seeking self-sufficiency? Dr Pyke is amused at the random way in which Western man selects the animals which go on the table or sit beside the table. In different cultures, different times, roles of dog and cow, for example, are reversible. The Hindu holds the cow sacred, while earlier civilisations cultivated the dog for the table.

The historical view is one which certainly adjusts my attitudes towards self-sufficiency. I'd recommend a racy new one, called *Food in History* by Reay Tannahill (Eyre and Methuen). Also the standard work, *The Englishman's Food* (Cape) by Sir Jack Drummond and Anne Wilbrahim, an educative and scholarly but by no means dry book: it describes five centuries of this island's struggle against shortage of many dietary needs.

Self-sufficiency is also prompted by accounts of making-do in other cultures. None are more exciting than Elizabeth David's evocation of sunnier life-styles (all in Penguin), Her special insistence on excellent fresh raw materials has inspired many English housewives to grow their own Mediterranean foods simply enough in English gardens.

The sumptuous coffee table books of the Wine and Food Society (David and Charles) are inspiring in a different way, and open up new possibilities for self-sufficiency in every subject they treat. I'd recommend Tom Stobart's *Complete Book of Herbs and Spices*. Stobart, an Everest adventurer, has made an encyclopaedic collection which gives you plenty of ideas for your own garden.

On the subject of encyclopaedias, I'd recommend that fat bible of food knowledge, the *Larousse Gastronomique* (Paul Hamlyn). Packed with recipes, as well as masses of lore about all that's edible.

Currently, the soundest practical books are those from Her Majesty's Stationery Office. They cover everything from husbandry and cheese making to beekeeping and growing vegetables.

And the Ministry of Agriculture's own book of Common Prayer, the *Manual of Nutrition*. It has absolutely everything you need to know about diet and is the basis of every other book on the subject written in this country.

Finally, with supermarket standardisation chasing away our options there is a series of country cookery books produced by the Federation of Women's Institutes. Some have a wider range of practical advice than others. But they all charmingly keep alive country traditions, and that's where self-sufficiency really lies.

Self-Sufficiency – Living off the Land

John and Sally Seymour live life as if the seventies hadn't been invented. Or the Sixties for that matter, or the Fifties.

For the self-sufficient Seymours don't depend on the decisions of top politicians, union leaders or Arab sheiks. There's no fuel crisis so great which can't be solved by John shouldering an axe and spending an afternoon down in the coppice by the stream.

John is the author of a delightful new book called *Self-Sufficiency* (Faber and Faber). It gives you a practical breakdown of all the ways you can cope for yourself, from farming and husbandry, dairying, beekeeping and gardening, to plundering sea, river, wood and field, and exercising kitchen skills, like baking, brewing, preserving.

They live in a beautiful stretch of Pembrokeshire, in a farmhouse they've rebuilt by themselves, and manage there to provide fully for their needs – everything except tea and shoes they reckon. Sugar? 'Honey's better.' Salt? 'Have a bit of fun on the seashore this summer with the kids. Collect wood, light a fire and boil up sea water all day. You'll get enough salt to last a year.'

He says he doesn't care if we have bought it, but it's where he keeps
his goats.

The Seymours will even grow their own corn and mill it in an antiquated plate mill. They naturally bake their own bread. They have a cow called Buttercup which provides milk, and enough over for butter and cheese. They have pigs for ham, bacon, pork, and keep sheep for meat and wool. They have chickens for eggs. They grow their own vegetables and fruit, and two miles away, at the sea's edge, keep a boat for occasional sorties after mackerel and herring.

For anyone wanting to achieve total self-sufficiency John's wife, Sally, warns: 'It's hard work physically, I never did one-eighth of the physical work I do now. But this is the better life for me. It's more relaxing mentally.'

The Seymours are not so self-sufficient that they spurn extra sources of income – he from writing and TV, she from pottery. And they do think they'd be able to make some more money by manufacturing soft cheese here. 'It's absurd that the British have never made a cheese like Brie or Camembert or Port Salut,' says Sally. 'We have the milk. It's only a matter of care.'

Self-sufficiency developed logically for John and Sally when they were living in Orford on the bleak Suffolk marshes.

Says John: 'We decided we'd better keep a cow because it was the only way to get fresh milk. You get all this surplus milk so we decided to keep a pig to use it up. We had to grow a bit more food to feed the pig and the cow. You've got all this dung. And as digging gets hard work you need a plough and you've got to have a horse for that.

'We couldn't get eggs because the village was a long way away and we didn't have a car, so we kept chickens.'

Other things came naturally too. Like poaching. 'Fabers asked me to cut out most of the references to poaching in my book.' In his day John's eaten swan and other birds. Man's law says he mustn't, but John's inclined to follow Nature's law. He doesn't believe this is immoral. What is immoral to him is broiler farming, and he's sickened by the cruelty he sees. 'I think of the effect on the people who do it. They have to dehumanise themselves.'

Sally's typical day wouldn't serve as a model for a town housewife or even many a farmer's wife today. Wind the clock back 50 years. She gets up at 6.30 am, puts on a cup of tea, wakes the children at 7 am. (Jane, her eldest daughter, is at art school in Bristol.

Anne, 16, Kate, 13, and Dafydd, 7, go to good local schools.)

She gives the children breakfast, then throws some food to her 40 chickens, four pigs, three geese, two dogs and sundry cats and kittens. She also milks Buttercup if she happens to have wandered up to the house.

Lunch is bread and cheese. Bread she's baked herself, crisp and tasty. Cheese she's made herself, flavoury and crumbly. And butter she makes twice a week. (She invited Caroline [Conran] and myself to make it. We took the week's cream which had been standing in a cool place, and beat it and beat it and beat it, till our muscles were tearing. It took 20 or 30 minutes. You drain off the buttermilk and drink it, which is delicious. Then you wash the butter in cold water, beat it in salty water, to salt it, and pat it into a shape with wooden bats.)

The children start coming back at 4 pm. They have supper at 6 pm. Sally helps the children with their homework, or mends or knits. She spins her own wool, 3lb of thickish two-ply per sheep.

The self-sufficient life is a busy one but sounds a lonely one. It needn't be so lonely. In his book John suggests ways in which groups of people could live in the same area, dividing roles for the community. But he doesn't. 'People here don't want to, in fact,' says John. They're climbing out of the hole just as John and Sally are climbing in. 'It's a pity. The local farmers are losing their old skills. They don't even give their children the benefit of buttermilk because they don't make their own butter any more. Every last pint goes for cash to buy modern plastic furniture.'

The Skinny Side of Sausages

The sausage skin industry is in a crisis. For, as revealed in the Look! Bland Leaders series a few weeks ago, Wall's, the biggest sausage-makers in the country, stopped using natural casings this year, and turned over to a process invented by its parent company Unilever, which puts the stripe in Signal toothpaste. The Wall's men pioneered a new kind of casing which is spun on to extruded sausage-meat. It's made of the same stuff as sausage skins, collagen, but it's obtained in great sheets from the underside of cowhides, then cut, sliced, chipped, mashed and pulped into a sort of fibrous glue.

This means a drastic drop in demand for natural skins which the big butchery firms and about 50 small operators buy from British abattoirs. They use pigs' intestines for the big bangers, the sheeps' intestines for chippolatas, and bulls' guts for blood sausage.

The Natural Sausage-Skin Casings Association wrote to Look! about our article which criticised the new Wall's sausage. 'The fact that the sausage you tasted did not have succulent flavour,' it points out, 'would be due primarily to the lack of skin.'

So what has natural skin got that the imitation hasn't? 'A unique combination of texture, tensile strength and porosity which give the sausage the optimum shape and optimum taste,' says the association. And the ability of the skin to withstand 'the stresses of stuffing and frying, grilling and even boiling.'

The association obviously has an uphill struggle against the cost-conscious boys of Unilever's marketing division, but it is hitting out strongly with advertisements in the trade press, and it has produced an impressive 38-page booklet on the case for casings.

If you presume that animals' guts are not a particularly sexy subject to promote, you could be wrong. Some advertisements are as tasty as anything in *Playboy* or *Penthouse*. One shows a huge cleavage, in which nestles a Victorian locket with a straw-hatted butcher smiling, and the slogan: 'have you got the hidden qualities women go for?' (Lucas's natural casings). While the lady from Hueck's Natural Casings has a plunging neckline captioned: 'Has your product the natural curve it deserves?'

Natural Curve? How does that apply to a sausage? Well explains the association, that's the point of the whole campaign. Natural skins come from intestines that curve in the animal's tummy. So that's how you can tell a naturally-skinned banger from an imitation. It bends in the pan.

A Hot Little Number

Mustard is a killer. Dose your meat with mustard, and you're committing bacteriocide on the contents of your tummy, killing all the bugs.

A good thing too, if you were living in days before the freezer; or in hot countries where meat soon went bad. John Hemingway, who grows the mustard crops for Colman's in Norwich, says he has a friend who passes mustard through his system to kill unfriendly bacteria, then takes a yoghurt to replace them with friendly bacteria.

You'd think Colman's would want to exploit a hot property like mustard: but their new approach is distinctly bland and cool. Current slogans: *do a pork pie proud: stir up a steak pie: make a sausage sizzle.*

Nothing there to remind you of the fiery qualities of Britain's greatest spice. Britain's only spice, in fact. It's enough to bring tears to your eyes. But mustard does not only get up your nose, and burn your tongue. It's useful as a preservative in food, and it's an emulsifying agent. That's why it's so good with fatty bacon, sausages, hams and pork pies. 'It helps the digestion of fats,' explains John Hemingway, 'the mustard holds the chewed-up fat in suspension until the bile attacks it and breaks it down. Otherwise it clings in blobs of fat.'

In the old days mustard was considered more of a policeman than a killer, maintaining law and order within the body. It was often applied in a mustard plaster. From its nineteenth century advertising: 'It purges the body of toxic products, relieving pain, giving a feeling of warmth and well-being, and an increased flow of blood: it stimulates capillary circulation, relieves rheumatism, cold, flu', bronchitis, coughs on the chest, aches in the nape of the neck, neuralgia in the side of the face, and toothache.'

None of this in Colman's 1975 image. 'According to the history books, Colman's mustard should have outgrown its cycle,' says marketing manager Ken Tweedie. 'But in the last three years mustard has been selling better and better, a seven per cent growth rate each year.'

Tweedie puts it down to their 'aggressive' marketing approach. But much of it is due to the success of prepared mustard which now takes up 55 per cent of the market, compared with 25 per cent for the tins of dry mustard. And the growth of new varieties of milder mustard, French, German and American.

'English mustard is the hottest,' says John Hemingway, 'but it's not as hot as it was.'

Hemingway is the man to blame. English mustard has been made with a combination of black and white seeds ever since the Romans introduced it. The black gives the pungency, the white is for sweetness. But after the war we set out to make mustard an up-to-date crop,' says Hemingway. 'It used to grow 10ft to 11ft high, and when it was dry the stalks were cut down by hand with small scythes, and many of the seeds were shaken out on to the ground. Now it's 5ft high, and we cut it with a combine harvester.'

To make this possible, Hemingway introduced the more manageable brown seed, *juncea*, instead of the fiery black, *negra*.

It's worth visiting the Colman's mustard shop, if you're in Norwich. They keep it like a museum, and it's a fascinating record of a marvellous paternalistic socially-conscious Victorian family firm. It's run by Ben Cook, one of their ex-salesmen, togged up in striped trousers, stiff white collar, Dickensian manner, and he knows the faded family groups by heart. It was one of the Colman's wives, Mary Burlingham, who really deserved the credit, though. Due to her efforts Colman's became the first firm to have its own school (1864) and works canteen (1868).

Oh, mustard isn't what it was, sigh, sigh. Mr Cook: 'When I was a boy, my mother always used to give me a mustard bath when I got back from school. It was the old-fashioned heat treatment, made you feel really good. We sell mustard bath packs in the shop, you should try one. You don't get out of the bath yellow. You don't get out smelling of mustard. But if you take a ham sandwich in with you, you can dip it in the water.'

Fat Chance These Ads Give You

How's this for a slimming diet? Eat plenty of bread, thickly spread with butter, all the cream you can manage, pints and pints of milk, and Guinness with every meal.

If you've ever tried to slim, you'll know this is rubbish. But there may be a nagging doubt in your mind. Haven't you read somewhere that perhaps bread's OK, but not butter and cream? Or didn't they say you could eat plenty of cream if you didn't eat something else? And surely Guinness is good for you?

If you do have these nagging doubts, they were almost certainly placed there by the bread people, the dairy people and the Guinness people; in the last six months they have spent hundreds of thousands of pounds between them to bamboozle you into thinking they are in the slimming business. They are determined to make you believe you can slim without dropping their products from your diet.

The National Dairy Council puts on the boldest front; they headline their full page ad in the *Daily Express*: SLIM THE SENSIBLE WAY. A sub-heading underlines the point: A painless way to slim.

Guinness are the cheekiest; they place a whole page in the colour magazines to promote 'The Guinness Diet'. Quote: 'Just imagine, for lunch, you tuck into Veau en Paillotte. You wash it down with a lightly-chilled bottle of Guinness. Then, in the evening, it's down to the pub for another leisurely half-pint, a chat with your friends and even a game of low-calorie darts or two...'

The Flour Advisory Bureau are the newcomers; they headline their ad with a straightforward 'SLIMMING WITH BREAD,' and back it up with a convincing selling line: 'Some typical slimmers' questions answered by Derek Miller, Lecturer in Nutrition at London University.'

In the big print, how to slim. In the small print, an invitation to write away for their slimming booklets. If you don't send away, you could be forgiven for thinking that bread and dairy food and Guinness aren't as fattening as you'd been led to believe. If you read the artful little booklets, the wool could be pulled completely over your eyes. For these booklets, admirable in every other way, just

happen to omit the most important piece of information the slimmer needs to know: the number of calories in the products. Fancy
them all forgetting to say.

How do you get in on the act when it's obvious that you're marketing foods that are very fattening indeed? You hold back the actual facts about their calorie content, and present your foods as part
of a 'calorie-controlled diet'.

So how much truth do these ads contain? Derek Miller, the
nutritionist quoted in the bread ads, gives a novel reason to keep
bread in your slimming diet: 'It's good training for maintaining
weight after your target weight is achieved, because one learns the
calorie value of ordinary foods, rather than knowing the value of
so-called slimming foods.' He adds: 'For many people it's easier to
cut down on fats rather than bread. They contain, incidentally, three
times the number of calories in bread, on an ounce to ounce basis.'

But who eats fats in the same volume? What Derek Miller does
not state is the calorie content of bread. Six slices a day, the average
consumption in the UK, contributes 400-600 calories to the diet.
The average office worker uses up between 2,000 and 3,000 calories
a day, so you can see that 'bread calories' count a lot, especially if
you're aiming at a calorie-controlled diet of 1,000-1,200 a day.

But the hidden secret of bread eating isn't just the bread, but
what you put on it – butter or margarine (with three times the calories of bread ounce for ounce) and jam, with its high sugar content.
The Technology Assessment Consumerism Centre estimates that
bread and what you put on it accounts for 40 per cent of our average dietary intake.

If you're going to slim on a pint a day, you really must get the
National Dairy Council booklet. You could balloon in size by liber-
ally interpreting the advice of the council's ad to slim 'by eating the
right foods'.

For example: a pint of milk contains 380 calories. Four ounces of
butter 828 calories. A quarter pint of cream 640 calories. Four
ounces of cream cheese contains 520 calories. Even a three ounce
fruit-flavoured yoghurt has 60 calories. Half a dozen eggs are 480
calories. Nearly 3,000 calories already, before you've tasted a mouth-
ful of bread, meat, vegetables, or fruit.

How do they work it? The National Dairy Council have been very shrewd. They invited Professor John Yudkin to devise the diet, conscious of his reputation as an author of many books on slimming, and particularly of his attacks on sugar and carbohydrates. Frances Kohn, an American nutritionist with the council, explains: 'If you follow the professor's instructions, you'll find that your consumption of dairy foods is self-limiting.'

But the pamphlet says you can eat as many dairy foods as you like; if you consumed the amount I quoted in a day, wouldn't that be fattening? Miss Kahn: 'I don't want to give you a straight answer. I know his thinking. He's giving you free rein, but I doubt if you would eat too much.'

Guinness's leaflet is the most colourfully presented of the three and doesn't bore you with any facts about food values and calories. It's just such fun the Guinness way. Fun to eat French-sounding dishes. Fun to be slim and bronzed like the Guinness girl on their cover. If you had the prescribed half-pint at lunch, and you did manage to limit yourself to a single unsociable half-pint in the evening, you'd have contributed 200 calories to your diet. Anyone who gets the wrong idea from the original colour ads, and takes draught Guinness as a slimming cure will have a rude shock. Six pints of draught Guinness and your whole day's dieting quota is used up, without a single crumb of food. A careful reading of the seven-day fun diet shows you what provides the bulk of your week's calories. To make room for the Guinness, out go potatoes (only two permitted in the whole week), out goes bread (only two slices in the week) and out goes even crispbread (two slices in the week).

Guinness have sent out 11,000 leaflets for their diet, and are indignant that people might not think it's serious. They say they didn't quote Guinness's calorie count because they didn't quote the counts of any of the foods in their diet. There was no need to. 'Everyone thinks that Guinness is fattening, but it's not. Not in the right quantities.'

The National Dairy Council sent out 17,000 leaflets after their last campaign. They seemed quite surprised when it was pointed out that they don't give a calorie count for milk, and they didn't know why not. 'But we never make the claim quite boldly that milk is slimming on its own.'

The Flour Advisory Bureau have only just launched their campaign, and they've had 4,000 requests for leaflets so far. They too seemed surprised to find they hadn't given a calorie count for bread. David Dodds, who handles the campaign, said: 'Isn't it in the ad? . . . No. You're right. There isn't anything sinister about this. It's just the way it came. We don't actually spell out the number of calories.' He says the object of the ad is to counter the message given in every slimming club in the country: 'We think the anti-bread advice they give is very wrong. You're encouraging people not to eat an important food.'

(When it serves their purpose they do give a calorie count for bread. Another bread ad – not directed at slimmers – gives a table which shows it has a flourishingly high calorie content compared with many other foods.)

The editor of *Slimming Magazine*, Audrey Eyton, takes an impartial view of the conflict, although she agrees the ads could be misleading if not read very carefully: 'Any advertisement is like that, they only tell part of the story.'

Bernice Weston, director and founder of Weight Watchers, the country's biggest slimming organisation (it's attracted 900,000 members since it began eight years ago) thinks the advertisements are designed to be confusing.

'I think the Milk Marketing Board are acting irresponsibly; Guinness are perhaps tongue-in-cheek. Bread's all right up to a point but they don't tell the whole story.

'I tell my people they can have bread, dairy products and Guinness, but not to excess.

'The Government haven't been helpful. As long as advertisers use the expression "part of a calorie-controlled diet" they can put out any kind of tommy-rot.

'With all the money they have to spend on advertisements I think these big firms should act more responsibly. The Government should make them form a body, and see to it they vet their own ads. They should stop playing games with the public.'

The Strange New Taste of Tomorrow

Britain may be heading for a food crisis but don't blame the scientists. They have many of the answers to providing us with more, cheap food. The real problem is you and your conservative habits and taste.

Scientific research is the goose which lays our golden eggs; let us say it has doubled farming efficiency in the past 20 years and there is no reason to see why performance should falter now, unless its funds are cut back. But successive Governments have not been content with stealing the highly-saleable eggs; they have started hacking at the legs the golden goose walks on.

In the six years since 1967 the Agricultural Research Council's share of the Science Budget has dropped from 12.2% to 4%. How much is that? This year £25m out of about £550m – that's how important our Government thinks food planning is.

As the Council's budget goes down, so inflation pushes it down further. *The New Scientist* estimates that agricultural research will have lost 200 of its 2,000 top men by the end of March because of a cutback in recruitment, and at a time, you might think, when we need them most. With chronic shortages looming, surely investment in research is the best investment?

If we do not meet this challenge, then we may have to tighten our belts. We could even go back to a war-time diet as Professor Kenneth Mellanby has already suggested. Professor Mellanby, former director of Monks Wood Experimental Station, also thinks it could be quite good for us too (we eat far too much sugar and animal fats for the good of our hearts). But mainly, the rising prices of imports will soon place too high a burden on our balance of payments. So we must try to be more self-supporting.

How? For a start he says, we could reallocate our farming land and use British-grown wheat for bread instead of imported strong wheat from overseas. It would not make the same spongy sliced wrapped loaves we all know and love, but a tastier loaf.

Indeed, we could make ourselves self-sufficient for a basic 1,700 calories daily on this diet: 1lb of potatoes, 1lb of cereal, 1oz of sugar, and 2oz fat.

That is what happens when you put the clock back. But can we put it forward? *The New Scientist* says we may well have to change our eating habits. But for the better or worse? It rather depends how we respond to the research being done on our behalf.

Food science, unfortunately, is not always dealing with what is acceptable to the public. The word 'new', such an exciting concept in other areas of advertising, causes only apprehension when applied to food. A new food? For science can open up exciting worlds of novel proteins, new methods of animal husbandry and feeding-stuffs, new crops and new meat and fish to eat. But the food trade can say no, and that is that. They know the extent to which the public attitude to food is guided by social and religious taboos, childhood conditioning, simple prejudice and preference.

Take fish. Put yourself to the test. Imagine yourself in a restaurant and offered the following fish. Which would you choose with pleasant anticipation. Which would you firmly reject?

Puddler, pughie, glashan and glassock? Green pollack, black cod, sea salmon and rock hake? Billiard and bluffin? Parson, nigger and goat?

If you have not already guessed, it is the same fish. These are some of the 40 names by which the British fisherman knows the third most plentiful white fish in our waters, coley. Under the food labelling regulations it is also permitted to be called coalfish and saithe. As it happens the British public has never really taken to it under any name.

We spend the best part of £40m a year researching into farming and fishing and growing, and the range of discoveries is extensive and fascinating. Indeed we have our own poultry people feeding chickens their own waste droppings (a great saving on expensive imported animal feeds); we grow apples like raspberries and harvest them with machines after two years: we are learning to trick cows into having twins and sheep into lambing twice a year by fiddling with their summertime. We're marvellously equipped to utilise everything from sea weeds to weed seeds.

But research is split among 40 or more establishments, and it's difficult for them to speak with one voice. Their work is tentative.

The men at the Ministry of Agriculture Food & Fisheries (MAFF) have been alarmed by the over-fishing of international waters – we can expect a 20% drop in catches soon. So they have been making sorties to discover possible new species of fish. With an eye on the rash of unilateral fishing limit claims they picked on the deep Atlantic shelf which hugs the West coast of Ireland, and they came up with a number of curious-looking deepwater fish. The best in quality were black scabbard and the grenadier.

What happened? The MAFF told Birds Eye and the big fish finger producers that they had discovered a fish which lent itself to the same treatment as cod, which is the basis of fish finger production.

At this point Graham Kemp, head of Birds Eye press, consumer and information services, started to sound out the Press, mentioning that Birds Eye was thinking of incorporating a new range of fish in fish fingers. His boss, Birds Eye chairman Kenneth Webb awaited reactions. Privately, he said: 'We'd put ground-up cod's head in our products if we thought the housewife would accept it.' But what was she going to say about what Kemp would call the new 'exciting' range of fish.

It was eventually John Waterman, long serving Head of Information at Torry Research Station, Aberdeen, who announced the 'exciting' news at a Press conference. Now, Waterman, much-respected by the Press for his patient briefings, also happens to be one of the world's most knowledgeable people on the subject of fish names. His lifetime hobby has been the collection of the very wide variety of names used by seamen from every European port.

Waterman knew that the grenadier fish was best-known as the rats-tail. He also knew that a name like rats-tail was bound to offend the aesthetic taste of the British housewife. So he judiciously chose one of the fish's more pleasant names. Thus the grenadier went on display with the five others; the rabbitfish, the black scabbard, the smoothhead, the hideously ugly *gephyroberyx*, and the *deania calcea* (a shark).

Asked by the Press at the conference if the grenadier was not better known as the rats-tail, John Waterman replied truthfully that it was, but they wished it to be known as the grenadier.

WOULD YOU EAT RATS-TAIL? asked the headlines in the

papers and TV. Big joke. But Waterman was not laughing because the thousands of pounds spent on the sea search was down the drain; Birds Eye, noting the public reaction, said it had no intention of using rats-tail in fish fingers. What a thought. And in a sudden panic it stopped labelling its fish fingers 'white fish' and put them out as pure 'cod'. Perhaps you've noticed, too, that Cap'n Birds Eye is back on TV extolling that fish fingers are made from cod – and no other fish.

Are we being irrational? But can we afford to be? We live in the affluent society. It may not always continue to be so. How will we cope? Are we always to ignore the rich possibilities on our doorstep – cultivating Highland deer herds, intense rabbit breeding, fish farming.

This is a theme enthusiastically supported by Dr Kenneth Blaxter, head of one of our most important stations, the Rowett Research Institute.

'Look back to the first animals man domesticated for food. The dog was probably the first, as a scavenger, the pig another. In Manchuria, now, there are quite extensive dog farms. The pariah dog of Northern China is kept specifically for meat and killed at about three or four months.'

Blaxter has a particular interest in boar and deer. We do not breed boar for meat because it is believed people are put off by the boar taint. So the boar are castrated. But if the boar were kept entire we would have the advantage that it grows more quickly and efficiently and you'd be able to market them within a year.

Boar taint is held by the trade however to be a limiting factor. But Blaxter says experiments done at the Agricultural Research Council Meat Research Institute, Bristol, found that only about 2% of people can smell it. And oddly, of those only 1% find it noxious. Says Blaxter, 'The other 1% are likely to say: "It's delightful".

Let's go back to fish again. At Torry, John Waterman can think of many examples where science has provided initiatives for the trade which have not been taken up. For example, they could save 20% of fish from the bones if the industry could find a use for fish mince. And if they could, on any decent scale, they could then encourage catching the blue whiting, an abundant North Sea fish which lends itself to machine stripping.

At the Food Research Institute, Norwich, Liaison Officer Arnold Tomalin says research can only go so far: it provides the information but we live in a society where it is left to the entrepreneur to decide whether or not to take it further. 'The entrepreneur is in advance of the field. They told Turnip Townsend he'd go bust, but he didn't. It's left to them to risk public acceptance.'

Of course, Tomalin is right. When people vote with their pay packets in High Street shops each week they make peculiarly conservative choices.

D.Elliston Allen, an anthropologist-turned-marketing man, pointed out in his entertaining book, *British Tastes*, that there is no question of accepting the foods of tomorrow; Britons have not yet accepted the foods of yesterday. In Yorkshire they are still suspicious of self-raising flour, that invention of the devil. The Scots, after centuries of distaste still can't bring themselves to eat pig products to any degree (least of all offal, despite the fame of the offal national dish, haggis). In the North-West they are still slow to accept tomato sauce and those new-fangled baked bean things.

There is no doubt that scientists can find new food alternatives, but who will find it worth their while to present them to a reluctant public?

Big Business – Unilever can do it, for one. Unilever's research covers everything from salmon fishing in Scottish lochs to putting Textured Vegetable Protein in meat pies; from sucking the last scraps of flesh off a cod's backbone to turning the world's cheap oils into hydrogenated butter-gold. It cost Unilever £250,000 in gas chromotography and allied research to identify and synthesise the 22 separate unique flavour components to get the butter taste into Stork.

It is obvious that a product like hydrogenated palm and coconut and herring oil could not have achieved world-wide acceptance without a boost from the persuaders. Perhaps it is there the whole key to food acceptance lies.

If it had not been for the last decade or so of brilliant advertising campaigning how could margarine have climbed out of the hole it found itself in at the end of the war? If Unilever can get people to eat their marge surely there can be no limits to the possibilities of brilliant research allied to clever advertising.

Few people know more about the pitfalls of food advertising than J. Walter Thompson, Britain's biggest advertising agents. It has the largest number of food accounts, Kraft and Kelloggs and Oxo. What Katie Did for Oxo is legendary in advertising.

JWT's creative director is Jeremy Bullmore. He has no illusion about what food acceptance is. 'We sell the myth about food, rather than the reality.'

Bullmore is the co-author of an interesting book designed for the food industry. With a colleague, Stephen King, he examined public response to packaged foods, and they did a sum. In Britain we spend 75% more on food than we actually need.

So, the advertiser is concerned with generating this excitement in products. He has to confess you can't do this in food by proclaiming it's novelty. But it's a challenge which will come, if we have to eat lower on the food chain, when beef becomes too expensive to produce. What about selling a soya bean product – textured vegetable protein, for example?

'Lots of people believe the meat myth. Only meat is real. It will be thought of as dishonest advertising to suggest that this protein is as good as meat. People are apprehensive about new things, which are by definition untried and unknown. It's one thing to say New Oxo, which means the same old Oxo only slightly different. But if you're talking about the Batemanburger, made out of soya beans, that's different.'

'We're talking about foods that haven't evolved. They'll need to be marketed in shapes which are familiar, like marge. They could have had a product which was clear, a kind of jelly, or a blue margarine, but it wouldn't have been acceptable. So they made it look like butter.'

The truth is, says Bullmore, that times change. 'It's really a matter of what's acceptable and what's not. Who's right and who's wrong about snails and eels and so on. A friend of mine, a great ornithologist, bought a book in France, and opened it at the Robin. It began: 'This charming little songster is best served...'

Secret Super-Crop Down on the Marsh

Like a matted blanket, knotted along the shores of Southampton Water where yachtsmen sail their dinghies, grows a humble grass called *Spartina Townsendii*. Now it is thought that the roots which hold the shore steady against tidal erosion might hold the secret of a great breakthrough in British agriculture.

Just imagine if we could grow crops and grasses which would shoot up like tropical sugar cane and elephant grass. We cannot, because the plants in our temperate climate are C3 plants. Sugar cane and elephant grass are C4.

C4 plants are those which are capable of taking up a continual supply of the carbon dioxide in the air around them, which they convert by photosynthesis into plant sugars for speedy growth. The humble British C4 plants pant and puff, and can only take in about half as much stop-go, stop-go. The scientists are arguing: if only we could breed a plant which kept on growing and growing, like Topsy, who was obviously a C4 girl.

Now some geneticists think you could simply transfer the genes, like a Dr Barnard heart transplant, from the scruffy *Spartina Townsendii*, to one of our natives. And then, even under the mild conditions of an English summer, you could start to think of monster yields for grass, hay, cereals.

We do have a C4 cereal which we grow in Britain and that is maize, an overgrown grain crop if ever you saw one. A fine photosynthesiser, too. But it is not a native, and not hardened to our climate; so it is a crop risk in spite of its amazing 100-day growth rate from seed to harvesting.

What is so good about *Spartina Townsendii* is that it has been growing in our temperate climate for 100 years; if it can take the sou'westers of Southampton Water, the bleakness of the Essex and Inverness mud flats, its two other habitats, it should be able to cope with warmer inland pastures.

This kind of research is a comparatively new area, and it has been made more urgent by the oil crisis. If it is true that the world will run out of its fossil fuel resources in our lifetime, we should be investing in research vigorously now. Scientific discovery is not made one day, and in commercial use the next.

The Agricultural Research Council has some 3,000 project units alone, working away at the research stations in the country. To justify further investigation, *Spartina Townsendii* must go before a series of committees. Now the ARC has some 86 members on its Joint Consultative Organisation and another 175 on their various committees.

So *Spartina Townsendii* must be led forward like a new member to a club, with its sponsors, letters of recommendation, references supplied. And there is always the danger, because of the stringent requirements of the club, that the grass, like a member, will be blackballed.

Spartina Townsendii has its sponsors in Dr Kenneth Blaxter, director of the Rowett Research Institute, Aberdeen, and Professor Harold Woolhouse at Leeds University. Dr Blaxter had a hunch this grass might have the C4 characteristic; Professor Woolhouse has proved it so.

The next step is some preliminary work. Dr Blaxter reckons you would need two or three men working for about 18 months to establish the real possibilities. It is not work you can hurry. Nature takes its time. It also costs money; three men, their equipment, materials and so on, would cost between £10,000 and £20,000 at least. Not a large sum, but these days research directors are cutting back. The rate of growth of the ARC budget has fallen since 1967 from 12.2% to 4%.

Let us say the three men find there is definitely a possibility genes could be transferred. Then you would want to put say, 50 men on to it. The Americans did this when they thought the soya bean might have a C4 characteristic. The chance of increasing the yield of this important world bean by 20% or 30% justified the cost of several hundred thousand pounds. They did not find what they were looking for, so the money was wasted.

But suppose your 50 men do achieve a breakthrough. That is only the beginning. Now you have to decide to invest on a really big scale, so you are soon playing the Concorde-Maplin-Chunnel game. Because these men are going to have to work over a 12- to 15-year stretch to build up the stock you need to launch a successful new strain.

So *Spartina Townsendii* has a long long way to go. But there is a modest start, an acorn planted. The ARC has just this month approved a grant of about £2,000 a year for three years to Professor Harold Woolhouse.

The ARC has rather ominously labelled its priorities in its annual report which came out last month, spelling out its criteria, rather as an adjutant might pin orders on the regimental notice board. What's the *significance* of *Spartina Townsendii*, they have to ask themselves, the *probability of success, timeliness, feasibility*; the *criticality, urgency, likelihood of implementation, cost and so on.*

There are, of course, many more important front-runners to pay for before our grass.

Take nitrogen-fixing. They've spent nearly £1m already on work which is not likely to produce results until 1990. That is if it is successful, and after 12 years work so far they still cannot be sure it will be.

If fossil fuels do run out in our lifetime, then the effect on crops will be staggering. Heavy multiple cropping all over the world depends on a heavy dosage of nitrogen and nitrates, which are made from a process using oil.

In Britain last year we made 920,000 tons of nitrogen – using about five times as many tons of oil in the process. So our own nitrates cost us about £150m. Very soon they'll be costing more like £200m. So our scientists feel it's vital now to try to find how to transfer nitrogen to higher plants. In 1963, therefore, they set up a Unit of Nitrogen Fixation at Brighton, attached to the University of Sussex.

What they have achieved is this: they can stimulate part of the process by which nitrogen-fixing bacteria can take nitrogen from the atmosphere, to produce ammonia at ambient temperatures and pressures. This is a big breakthrough, scientifically, but it's costing over £100,000 a year, with no very likely decrease in costs for the next 15 years.

Money is at the heart of all the ARC priorities, and it has to be. While the importance of nitrogen fixation is realised, it is not always easy to say how much should be put into the many other rival claims.

In poultry, perhaps the most efficient arm of agriculture, things run very much on a cost-efficiency basis. Dr Toby Carter, head of the Poultry Research Centre in Edinburgh, revels in the figures, which certainly seem to justify the £700,000 they spend each year.

Last year's research alone produced a discovery which will save the broiler industry £1m a year. They found that the thousands of chickens who were dying of the so-called Fatty Liver and Kidney Syndrome did so because their diet was simply the result of low-fat, low-protein diets, based mainly on wheat and barley. So they've designed a new diet with more fat and added vitamins with splendid results.

Not all research has to be expensive; for the cost of only a few hundred pounds they also developed a novel electronic egg which they can run through packaging stations to test machinery. Breakages cause an annual loss of 1,000m eggs a year. They can put the electronic egg on the conveyor belts and watch it on its journey. Every time it gets a jolt which would be enough to crack an egg, it lights up. You've isolated your trouble spot.

Research which reaps such ready rewards is easy to justify on the budget. Look at the appeal, for example, of new research to produce twinning in cows. No farmer's going to complain about money spent to give him two calves where there was one before.

This area is one of the best financed in agriculture. Both the Rowett Research Institute, in Aberdeen, and the Cambridge Unit of Reproductive Physiology and Biochemistry have been producing amazing results. There are the two calves, Frosty I and Frosty II, which were produced by artificial insemination from seed frozen at minus 196 deg C. Then there was the successful transplant of ova from top cattle into inferior stock, who then become foster-mothers to their new seed, after a suitable hormone shot.

This is still too expensive an operation to be put into widespread practice, because it's surgical work. But they are spending over £250,000 a year on it and it will soon be justified if they can make the switch from surgical transplanting to a non-surgical technique, along the lines of artificial insemination.

At the Rowett Research Station's 560-acre farm in Aberdeen there are 4,000 animals under study from cattle and sheep and rabbits, to rats and mice. But even so, there's still not enough in the annual budget of £1,200,000 to do everything they'd like, says the director Kenneth (*Spartina Townsendii*) Blaxter. So some of his work, into Highland deer, virtually took on the nature of a hobby.

Then suddenly the research became practical. Venison shot up to 50p per lb last year, and the Highland Development Board put up some money to start experimental breeding in the upland grazing areas which have always been too sparse for other livestock.

Research people themselves are not usually responsible for developing their work. ADAS does this – the Agricultural Development Advisory Service; through the agricultural colleges, trade literature, exhibitions, and so on. But as we showed last week, and the fish research people found out, it is one thing to present your findings, quite another to gain acceptance for them.

Even the promise of raising your lambing by a third, has been slow to catch on among farmers. There is the capital investment in a building, because your sheep must be indoors where you can regulate feed (low in pregnancy, high at lambing time) and also adjust the light. You have to indicate winter by short artificial days, lengthening them hurriedly until they think it's spring-time and lambing-time. It is not just the building; you will need responsible staff to manage it too.

And very much slower has been acceptance to the idea of using leaf proteins. It is over 30 years since N. W. Pirie pioneered it at Rothamstead. He has always hoped the cheap powdered protein could be made in parts of the world where children have a protein deficiency, which causes irreversible brain damage, and he's always been angry that the FAO refuse to support the idea.

But now, with the cost of animal feeds shooting up, first America and then Sweden put their men to work researching grass proteins with animals, not starving children in mind. But we have had it all the time, and only now are we on the verge of getting the simple machinery to a practical level to suit farm systems. It is a very appealing process. Grass, or lucerne (the alfalfa grass of Steinbeck's *Of Mice and Men*) is crushed in rollers. The residue is fed to cattle, for bulk. The protein in the juice, which grown cattle do not need, is processed for pig feed. Growing pigs, like growing humans, need all the protein they can get. And this is a pretty cheap form, considering you've already had the benefit of the residue once. A warming thought: our intensively-reared pigs need never suffer irreversible brain damage.

Snags: they have not got the machinery right even now. Dr Pirie complained that when a Swedish firm wanted to make the equipment, they produced a vision of stainless steel Rolls-Royce-type machinery; he was quite shocked, because he says it can be done with rough and ready equipment not much more expensive than an old banger. The sort of machinery that would make sense in, say Southern India, and the poor places of the world. British farmers are likely to be given something sturdier, but it may need a Churchill to bully it through.

And this is a very real dilemma for the men in research. They are not Churchills and nor would they want to be. At the Food Research Institute in Norwich, Arnold Tomalin, their chief liaison officer, suggested we'd probably need the impetus of a crisis to act on known research and get things moving quickly. 'I remember the introduction of the dehydrated potato, Pom. From the basic idea to the pilot scheme was only a year. Given the stress, the expertise was there. Though I can't say it was aesthetically satisfying.'

But are there not many areas of research which need a push and a shove? Pom eventually grew up to be quite a big boy in the commercial world, all the snags ironed out, a pleasantly untasty dish, which offends few, indeed a Smash hit for Cadbury Schweppes.

'Ah,' said Tomalin. 'Are you postulating a society which says what it wants? Or a Big Brother society where they might say, *rabbit is more efficient*, and switch all our resources to rabbit breeding? There's a danger of going overboard.'

So we're left with Professor Woolhouse up there alone in Leeds wondering if one day he'll be known as the man who put *Spartina Townsendii* on the map. But at the rate we're going, his fame may well be posthumous.

The Cost of Vitamin C

Woodrow Wyatt, the MP and writer, believes along with Dr Linus Pauling, the Nobel Science prize-winner, that massive doses of Vitamin C keeps colds at bay. He buys it for his own staff, by the hundredweight, at £190 for a 50-kilo box.

Wyatt's Vitamin C cost him a third of a penny per gram. That is a penny a day, if you take the massive three grams-a-day dose recommended by Pauling. Or if you merely wish to top yourself up to the minimum required dose recommended by the Department of Health & Social Security, 30 milligrams, it will cost you just a penny a month.

These figures highlight the huge difference in the cost of Vitamin C if you buy it at the chemist in its various advertised forms. Instead of 30p a month for the high Pauling dose, you can pay £11.16 for a month's equivalent supply of Vitamin C if you buy C-Compleat; £10.53 if you take your Vitamin C by way of the product Acerola, and £10.35 if you fancy Sanatogen Vitamin C. If you take it with Vitamin A and D, you can pay £22.50 for a month.

What extra do you get for your money? In most cases, a degree of fancy packaging and the promise built into it by a strong advertising line, usually in health food magazines.

For example, health food people emphasise the natural Vitamin C from sources high in it: rosehips, blackcurrant juice, green peppers. But there is no difference in Vitamin C in plants and the ascorbic acid made synthetically.

Most of the products have special instructions on the labels, and some have leaflets. None of them suggests, and it is isn't in their interests do so, that most of us get more than enough Vitamin C in our daily diet if we stick to the minimum figure laid down by the government.

Those who wish to follow the Pauling theory of doses of three grams a day – and up to ten grams a day to counter a cold – will be wasting their money if they buy Vitamin C in the fancy, promising packs. The two best buys at the prices we paid are Linus and Boots powder. They show only a 400% mark-up on the basic wholesale figure, compared with some which show a 3,000% mark-up.

Good Beef about Bad Beef

No wonder women see red when they buy meat in high street butchers. Red is the colour they look for in meat, so red is what the butchers give them – never mind how tough and immature.

According to the farmers, most butchers are selling the customer short. They say a side of beef should hang for two to three weeks at just above freezing point, in order to break down tissues and develop flavour and tenderness.

But well-hung meat has a brownish colour and most shoppers think there must be something wrong with it. So if butchers aren't selling meat which is tough and raw, or sprinkling nitrate crystals on it to make it red, they put it in display cabinets under brilliant pink lights. For their *son et lumière* techniques, full marks. For butchery, nil.

Who cares? The International Wine and Food Society does, and it has just launched a campaign among its 8,000 members to try to put things right – to educate members to demand that butchers improve their craft.

A pity the shopper can't eavesdrop on one of the society's beef days. She would soon discover why she's not getting the best.

Russell Smith, a Hertfordshire farmer, declares that matters get worse all the time; instead of helping the housewife to learn about meat, the butchers cash in on her ignorance. 'In Ware, only a week or two ago, I saw cattle in the market one day, and on the butcher's slab the next. It's economics, time is money. If the butcher has to hang meat till it's good, he suffers a weight loss of about two pounds a week. Then there's the problem of storage space. The meat is tough and tasteless but the butchers don't care.'

The society's model for good beef is Captain John Stewart's 4450-acre farm near Olney, Bucks. He is an ex-Marine commando and parachutist who runs his farm with the deliberateness of a Salisbury Plain exercise, together with a John Bull brand loyalty to what's best in British beef.

He grows his Hereford/Friesians to a maturity of 21 years before finishing them for market. He has nothing but scorn for the intensively-reared one-year-olds (which taste like tough veal) or the semi-intensively reared 18-month-olds.

He has tried every kind of beef farming, and even now is experimenting with the Continental breed, Simmenthal. 'They don't speak the lingo,' he complains. What's more they are extremely unhandsome, with ugly dewlaps to their jaws. 'Camels without humps,' says the Captain ungraciously.

'I don't want to knock foreign breeds, but the same goes for the French Charolais, the main French breeds. Unless they are intensively reared and you chuck stuff down them all day, they are no good at all. You can't rear them well on grass. And there's no fat on them. Meat without fat has no flavour, whatever the housewife may think. And that's why you can never buy a decent bit of beef in France.'

What's worse, we are getting these Common Market leftovers, thanks to our ignorance about meat. The butcher prizes the 'well-made, expensive, rear end' of the beast rather than the forequarters. The front half, the forequarters, come at nearly 20p per lb less wholesale, averaging about 26p per pound, including bone. The Continentals have been flogging us inferior forequarters from intensively reared animals at 11p a lb, and they are being snapped up by freezer firms who cash in on undiscriminating customers.

The meat may taste better but won't it cost more the Stewart way? 'No,' he says. 'Two year beef is grown on the cheaper system, mostly on grass. The one-year system is capital-intensive.'

Whisker-Licking Good?

Last Tuesday's BBC's Nationwide exposed the myth that different pet foods vary in real value. In nauseating detail, Nationwide showed just how uniform is the basic contents of each tin of cat food. If you are looking at pet food from a nutritional point of view, buy the cheapest. And if you are thinking it might be a cheap human food be very careful.

But what about the taste? Just because some food is good for you, it does not mean you like it. John Craske, a journalist who owns three cats and three kittens has tasted 19 brands. So have his cats.

Their joint tests showed substantial differences in flavour, with a major divide between fish and non-fish. Craske says cat foods, to human taste, are nearly all nasty, but the less he liked them, the more his cats enjoyed them.

The pet food manufacturers Spillers and Pedigree Petfoods (a subsidiary of the giant US Mars Group) say pet foods are quite safe for humans, although they say they cannot risk children eating from animal food bowls and being poisoned.

The Department of Health disagrees: 'Pet food manufacturers do not have to satisfy such rigid standards. There are degrees of safety. We say do not eat them.'

So do we. This is not a guide to cat food for humans, but cat food for cats. Here are John Craske's findings, along with those of kittens Noisy, Gimpy and Num-Num.

We give the name of the cat food, the makers name, John Craske's comments – and the cat rating in bold.

Felix Meaty Chunks (Quaker)
Gritty texture. Gravy tasted meaty. **No miaow.**

Big Value (Spratts)
Fishbone stuck in teeth. **Miaow.**

Kit-E-Kat (Pedigree)
Really horrible. **Four miaows.**

Choosy (Spillers)
Pink, soggy, fishy, slimy. **Three Miaows.**

Katkins (Pedigree)
Looked, smelled and tasted like Choosy. **Two miaows.**

Whiskas Neptune (Pedigree)
Knee-buckling. Must be the jellying agent. **Two miaows.**

Top Cat (Spillers)
Over-powering fishiness. **Two miaows.**

Whiskas Supercat (Pedigree)
Pungent smell, watery taste. **Two miaows.**

Bonus (Spillers)
Nondescript. **No miaow.**

Prime Kattomeat (Spillers)
Five star feed. **Two miaows.**

Nine Lives (Pickering)
Grey meat swimming in dishwater. **Three miaows.**

Bounce (Pedigree)
Too much powdered bone. **Two miaows.**

Go Cat (Carnation)
Tangy hit for wine and cheese party. **Two miaows.**

Munchies (Pedigree)
The crunchiest. **Miaow.**

Purina Liver Dinner (Ralston Purina)
No shortage of roughage. **Miaow.**

Felix Meaty Rabbit (Quaker)
Soggy old cornflakes. **Miaow.**

Felix Tender Morsels (Quaker)
Sheep's droppings. **Miaow.**

Cupboard Love (Pedigree)
As above. **Miaow.**

Purina Delikat (Ralston Purina)
Sickly. **Miaow.**

Whatever Happened to Carnivores?

Now you wouldn't call Ted Ray or Leo Tolstoy cranks, would you? Or Pete Murray and Mahatma Gandhi. Or John Peel and Buddha. Or Barbara Kelly and Leonardo da Vinci?

All vegetarians; and members of a cult which is suddenly becoming very respectable, very ecological.

Everybody's doing it now: Brigid Brophy, Lord Fenner Brockway, Yehudi Menuhin, Malcolm Muggeridge, Lord Soper, Dame Sybil Thorndike, Dr Barnes Wallis, Jomo Kenyatta.

Socrates, Ovid. Milton, Wordsworth, Shelley, Voltaire, George Bernard Shaw lit the torch. Katie Boyle, Dora Bryan, Spike Milligan and Marty Feldman carry it on. They are all doing their bit. It's the decent thing to do in a world which is eating up the resources of the environment.

And yet it's only 14 years since the first of the good vegetarian restaurants chose the tongue-in-cheek name Cranks, because the vegetarian image was so comic when it opened off Carnaby Street.

Dr Alan Long, secretary of The Vegetarian Society, says he's seen a big increase in serious interest from medics, from young people who are excited by the mysticism of eastern religions, and from the ecologists.

'The first reason most people give today is the ecological one,' says Dr Long. 'They believe we're using our world resources wastefully in growing grain to feed cattle.' The same land can produce up to 20 times the protein yield if it's used to grow grain and cereal for direct consumption.

It's not actually a new idea. Another well-known vegetarian was advocating it before the war, Adolf Hitler. The Führer (who was also an intolerant non-smoker and non-drinker) thought the Fatherland should be ploughed up and land used for growing beef should be devoted to the potato.

One of the biggest boosts to the movement has been the growth of 'natural food' shops. They should not be confused with the commercial operations of the health food chains, where you can buy vitamin supplements you don't need at up to 20 times their actual value.

New food firms, like Ceres and Harmony Foods specialise in foods for macrobiotics, with a heavy emphasis on grain, like wild rice, brown rice, buckwheat, and nuts and seeds. They have their own magazine *Seed* which disseminates the spiritual advantages of the wholefood way of life.

Seed was founded four years ago and has a modest circulation of 3,500. 'But readership is high,' says Gregory Sam, the 26-year-old American co-editor. 'In one commune it has a readership of 63 for one copy.' Sam also helped found Ceres, the 'natural food' shopping chain. Seven years ago Ceres had one shop – today it has nearly 30.

Sam says that people come to natural foods because they are vegetarian, or they are concerned about the Third World: ' But the main reason they go on buying them is because they taste better. Brown rice simply wins out on white rice.'

This is a different approach from Dr Long's longer-established Vegetarian Society, which runs a newsletter of a circulation of 50,000; the emphasis is on the shock-horror of cruelty to animals.

They also feature stories on the Pete Murrays and all other personable vegetarians. They even run to a vegetarian crossword, by the Guardian's crossword puzzler who is also vegetarian, eg Ten across 'Cook poultry – but only for the primitive (eight letters).' Try *heathen*.

Vegetarianism has a strikingly non-violent record; from Buddha himself, through to Martin Luther, and then John Wesley who founded Methodism, and General William Booth who started the Salvation Army, and more recently nuclear disarmers like Canon John Collins and Lord Brockway.

Psychiatrists believe that vegetarianism sometimes has its roots in childhood feeding. 'A baby may become fearful about its aggressive devouring of the breast,' a psychiatrist told us. 'If the quality of the mother-child relationship is "not satisfactory", the baby may not be able to cope with its natural fear and anxiety about what it thinks it has done. Later on in life; at times of anxiety, he may be fearful of eating meat with its cannibalistic associations.' So you see what Buddha's mother started, to say nothing of the mothers of Luther, Wesley and Hitler.

GLOSSARY

Vegetarian: don't eat meat, fish, fowl.

Lactarians: no meat, fish, fowl or milk.

Ovo-lactarians: and no eggs either.

Vegans: no animal products of any kind.

Fruitarians: only eat fruit.

Herbivores: only eat plants.

Granivores: only grain.

'Whole' food: organically-grown

'Natural' foods: whole grain, nuts, seeds.

'Health' foods: all this and vitamins too.

It's very kind of you indeed but I'm afraid I wouldn't know how to cook them

Me and my morally sound diet – five vegetarians give the reason why.

Dr Barnes Wallis, inventor, has been vegetarian for nearly 15 years. He's a healthy 88. 'I suffer from migraine headaches and a vegetarian diet helps alleviate this. Also, I feel I cannot take advantage of another man doing something that I couldn't do myself. I could not possibly kill an animal. Mind you, I drink milk, and I'm not sure I could milk a cow.'

Eleanor Bron, actress, eats fish, but no flesh or fowl. 'It's not for moral reasons. I don't like the smell or fibrous texture of meat or the way it's prepared. Fish is cleaner, and I believe it's better for you. It used to be thought faddish, but now more and more people join in, people think I'm less quirky. There are good ecological reasons for doing it.'

John Peel, the BBC DJ, has been vegetarian eight years. He's 36. 'I got into it in the Love/Peace Flower Power era, like a lot of people in the glamorous world of Rock-a-Boogie. Everyone draws the line at what they're willing to kill, mine's a bit further down the evolutionary scale. I say, you don't eat me, and I won't eat you.'

Brigid Brophy, 46, writer and critic. 'It's a question of rights. I have a right not to be killed just because someone wants to eat me. Ecologically speaking, it's cheaper to feed vegetables straight to people, instead of first to the cattle, then feeding the cattle to the people. As a child I thought it unfair to eat animals, but I couldn't believe my nice parents would do anything wrong.'

Carla Lane, who writes the BBC Liver Bird scripts, has been vegetarian for 10 years. 'Maybe I'm a bit unbalanced about it, but I'd like to close down every abattoir in the country. It all started when some friends bashed a bumble bee to death in front of me, and it landed in my bowl of custard. Such a lovely thing killed for nothing. My husband still eats meat.'

Ginseng and Tonic

Are you over 40 but can't stop chattering like a five-year-old? Or are you a pensioner who has been overtaken by the sexual appetites of a teenager?

Then perhaps you've been taking too much Ginseng, the fashionable herb remedy from China which is supposed to confer the magical properties of rejuvenation and virility. If we are to believe the claims.

Who's taking it? Miss Barbara Cartland, for one. It gave her the energy to complete 18 novels and a cookbook last year, bringing her life's total to around 170. And she's 73. She says the Kissingers take it, too, booming their way round and round the world by jet. It counters the strain of jet-lag.

How does one find out about this magic healing balm? Well, you read advertisements in magazines like the *Health Food Trader*,

Here's Health, Prevention and *Seed*. You learn about a strange root which must grow for seven years in shady places beside water. An expensive root. And profitable for the people who advertise it, therefore.

The Advertising Standards Authority which administers the Code of Advertising Practice allows no great claims for ginseng on the grounds that there has been no research into it in this country. (Martindale, the pharmacists' bible, goes as far as saying it has sedative and demulcent – soothing – properties, or may even act as a stimulant on the heart. But nothing about rejuvenation or virility.)

The March issue of *Here's Health* carries several advertisements in clear breach of the CAP rules. It is a special ginseng issue. On the cover is a picture of the creamy coloured root, entwining like medieval mandrake, beside it, a headline announcing the Barbara Cartland article: Spotlight on Ginseng.

Inside the magazine is her three-page article and two other editorial mentions, one for the root and one for a face cream that incorporates it; there is also one advertisement which is passed off as editorial, entitled Claire McIver reporting. Another breach of the CAP rules. What is ASA doing about it? It has now seen the ads and says they are in breach of the code. The magazine replies that it does submit ads to CAP for approval. 'We can't remember if these particular ads were shown to them; the CAP is certainly clamping down very hard on ginseng.'

They don't seem to be very effective clamps. Here is the claim of Healthcrafts who have a three-page advertisement. 'Korean ginseng has been reverently used in the Orient for several thousands of years, and is reputed by the Chinese to be of great value in preserving strength, vigour and vitality. They also call it the rejuvenation herb, and its enthusiasts consider it the panacea of all diseases.' Of all diseases?

Healthcrafts and *Here's Health* are both subsidiaries of the same firm, Booker McConnell, better known in the City as the sugar kings.

Another ad which missed the CAP 'clampdown' is the Liverpool firm of Korean Ginseng products: 'Try ginseng for strengthening vitality and stamina, mental fatigue and dyspepsia, disturbances of circulation and liver function, anaemia, hypertension, diabetics.' (It will cost you £4.50 for 500 ml of the ginseng solution).

Power Health Foods of Pocklington, Yorkshire, also escapes the clampdown. Under the Claire McIver by-line it says: 'Nothing can change the fact that we grow a little older every year, but if you believe it is important to remain young in mind and body, remember that ginseng has been reputed for many thousands of years to improve the function of the brain and memory as well as restoring virility.' (£2.20 for 48 capsules.)

The other ads are not quite so boastful. Emperor ginseng, which costs £1 for 10 grams: 'It doesn't just go to your head, it gets everywhere.' The Aromatic Oil Company is 'for Go-Ahead people'. Ortis makes no claim, but doubles the mystical appeal by mixing it with royal jelly (the liquid which bee babies drink). Panax is alone in making no claims for its ginseng at all.

But back to Miss Cartland for the strongest endorsement of all. She first heard about it, she writes, from an important stockbroker, five years ago in Hong Kong. The important stockbroker pointed to the Chinese in sampans and said: 'Everyone is working and saving so he can buy ginseng . . . they consider it is the most fabulous tonic in the world and believe it will not only prolong their life, but also improve their sexual capabilities.' (Is one to believe the important stockbroker or the quite unimportant Chinese clerk who told me that what they were actually saving to buy was opium?)

Miss Cartland puts it to the test, as she puts all health foods to the test. Each morning at breakfast she has a cup of ginseng tea and two ginseng tablets, and it's doing her a lot of good, she reckons. She also takes 90 separate vitamin pills a day, which are also doing her a lot of good. And a brain pill called Celaton CH3 Tri-plus (the magic 4 of Celaton CH3 plus Heart plus Brain plus Intrinsic Factor Vitamin B 12). It has powdered sheep's brain in it and it is very strong, she says.

Query. How can she tell which of all these magical pills is the one doing her so much good, sustaining her word power? Well, she just knows. 'I am convinced that ginseng is a magical healer, both physically and mentally.'

The Pie that Stares

Frenchmen come to blows about the right way to prepare a bouillabaisse fish soup. Spaniards raise their voices to describe the definitive paella. And every Cornishman swears he knows the only recipe for stargazy pie.

So what's the difference between the Frenchman, the Spaniard and the Cornishman? This. The French and Spanish relish their national dish. The Cornishman never eats his at all. In Penzance, the top hotels had never prepared it; try St Ives, they suggested. 'That's where the pilchards are landed. But you'll be lucky. The pilchard is dying out.'

In St. Ives, not one of the four main hotels had ever served it. There was no demand. In any case, it was a Mousehole dish. (Pronounce it Muzzle.)

In Mousehole they have two famous seafood restaurants. The Lobster Pot and The Coastguards. They remembered it nostalgically. 'It used to be served the day before Christmas Eve,' said a girl assistant. 'In memory of Tom Babcock. They were starving in Mousehole and Tom Babcock went out end caught every kind of fish imaginable. And they all ate stargazy pie. There's a song about it.' No, she couldn't sing it.

In St Austell (pronounce it Nozzle) they said, not here; try farther west. Farther west, at Land's End, they said not here, try farther east.

In Falmouth, they said it's not a pilchard dish, it's made with herring, try Newquay. In Newquay, they agreed it was made with herring, but with mackerel and pilchards, too. But not in Newquay, it wasn't.

In Truro, heart of Cornwall, at Chez Leon, the top restaurant, they said with certainty: 'You'll never find a stargazy pie in Cornwall today.' Why not? 'Well, it's rather robust, isn't it; the heads hang out of the pastry. I don't think anyone could really face it.'

But we did find one. In the little fishing village of St. Mawes, where it is cooked at the Idle Rocks restaurant and eaten with curiosity by visiting Americans.

What must once have been Cornwall's cheapest dish now stars

on the menu, hovering around the £2 mark. But it's not as if they are paying for a cheap local fish. The pilchards for the pie I ate had come from Paddington on the train before mine.

Every cookery book gives an authentic recipe, and no two agree. In *Traditional British Cookery* compiled by Maggie Malpas Pearse for the International Wine and Food Society (David and Charles), she has it with pilchards or herrings, stuffed with chopped onion and herbs, and baked in pastry, the heads protruding.

The Cornish Women's Institutes have other variations. Some have the fish boned, some not, some make it with mullet and it's gamey. Some mix vinegar with the cream for sharpness. Some cook it with diced potatoes; others have a mashed potato covering instead of pastry. Many place the fish on a bed of breadcrumbs.

Chef Dick Belt at the Idle Rocks doesn't do it any of these ways, and he's the one who's right, he insists. 'I got the recipe from my mother, and my mother got it from her mother.' If that wasn't enough, he adds for emphasis: 'My great great-grandfather landed fish here in St Mawes.'

We joined two Americans, lawyer Ken Novak and his wife Debbie, for Dick's stargazy pie. We ate it outdoors on a balcony where seagulls swooped low over the harbour wall. The pie was produced staring with starry, starry eyes. It was very, very good, said the Americans.

Black Pud gets Fishy Face-Lift

Fat trout from Lancashire's Ribble valley, stuffed with puréed black pudding, a garnish of hazelnuts, diced apple and pickled black walnuts: or would you prefer young Manchester pigeons, pot-roast in the French mode, dished up with a couple of faggots and a splodge of pale green mushy peas?

We are talking of Manchester Cuisine, 1975-style, as presented at Sir Charles Forte's Post House. The Manchester Menu was created this year by a group of Manchester's top chefs, and promoted with determination by Marcello Giobbe, 35, the Italian-born Post House manager.

Marcello's imagination has been fired by the new *Cuisine Minceur*, where chefs are producing high-class menus low in calories, short on cholesterol.

Giobbe, who has been, manager in Manchester for three years, had no problem in presenting a low-calorie menu. But the *haute cuisine*? Manchester is the world's first workshop, the birthplace of the industrial revolution, with a cuisine to match. Think of Manchester and you think of wet Sundays, fish and chips, bread and butter and tea, black pudding, tripe and faggots.

With the enthusiastic urging of Giobbe, and the technical advice of ex-chef, catering lecturer Jack Neighbour, the Manchester chefs designed an amazing menu of attractive, high-class dishes, using local ingredients. 'Local ingredients, with a foreign element,' explains Giobbe.

The menu includes the trout and the pigeon; Morecambe Bay shrimps with soured cream; pâté from lambs' sweetbreads; Salford pancake (stuffed with black pudding, Lancashire cheese, mushrooms and chicken); steak, mushroom and cowheel pie; and cream of tripe soup. How does that grab Manchester's expense account eaters?

'It's like everything else,' says Giobbe. 'People come to it slowly. Some people are horrified, of course. One lady rang up to book a table for seven, "on condition you don't serve me any of your regional food".

Response has been generally good, though. 'Food is like fashion and it changes. It's time that regional food changed. There are only seven notes in music, but with seven notes you can create symphonies. There are many more flavours in food. You need to marry them.' The most notable marriage of the year seemed to be the trout stuffed with black pudding, which is traditionally blood sausage with some fatty bits in it. This was the invention of Chef Hodgson of the Piccadilly Hotel, but Giobbe was giving it pride of place at the Post House.

'It's a marriage of the essential earthiness of the flavour of black pudding and the earthy flavour of trout. The stuffing keeps the trout moist in cooking.' My views of marriage being more cynical than his, I commented on the gobs of hard white fat rolling around my tongue with the trout bones. Marcello frowned: 'Hmm. The chef should have sieved it through first.' No marriage is perfect. 'But the taste is good? We make the black pudding into a purée with cream. And as trout has a dry, rather flat taste and very little texture, the garnish of apple and hazelnut and pickled walnut gives it more interest.'

Pot-roast pigeons, faggots and mushy peas was a more obvious combination. There is just a little bit of firm, dark breast on the plate, and the softer, plainer flavour of the faggots marries well. Mushy peas? Well, that's how Lancastrians like them. None of that costly deep-frozen stuff. Good, dry hard peas, soaked all night, cooked until they crumble, and beaten to a pulp.

Test your Nerves on Guga

Now here's a delicate soup you can't get from a can: sheep's head broth. First you singe the head over a peat fire (which gives it that special flavour of burnt cardigan), then rub the brains over the head to moisten it. Simmer for hours, then serve the soup with the whole head, eyes staring, tongue sticking out.

This is one example of the true regional cooking that exists in out-of-the-way places, where it is harsh reality rather than romantic folklore.

You can step into this world, through the kitchen door of the Acre Hotel in Stornoway, on the Island of Lewis in the Outer Hebrides. It's as strange as walking through Alice's Looking Glass.

In the hotel dining-room, to the Sound of Musak, they are flambéeing dishes, as they would in international hotels anywhere. Guests are overseas tourists, or wealthy anglers who've come for the salmon.

On the other side of the kitchen door are the real islanders talking in their lilting Gaelic. People whose idea of food is as strange to us as their language. Fish liver dishes like flakki, mugilden, and hagga-muggi; krus and krampus, krappit and kroppen. Porridge dishes called brose, broomie and burston, fuareg, pram and clapshot. People who eat seabirds and seaweed.

The chef, Celum MacMillan, has prepared some local dishes with his assistant cook, Dolly Graham, a grandmother. Celum spent a week of his summer holidays digging a year's supply of peat for his mother. Dolly, when she's not cooking international cuisine for the guests, prepares simple local dishes for her family, like sheep's head soup and stuffed cod's head.

Hello, Dolly's got a cod's head here right now. She scoops some gunge out, stuffs the head with oatmeal, onion, fish liver, salt and pepper, and sews it up with needle and cotton. She simmers it in water until the eyes turn opaque and the bones go gluey. You eat it with potatoes boiled in their jackets.

Celum stirs a big cauldron. He's cooking the special delicacy, guga, a young gannet. It is a protected bird. These islanders are the only people allowed to take and eat it. Once a year a dozen islanders make a dangerous 40-mile trip into the Atlantic to catch the young birds on a rock; this year they caught a thousand and every single one was sold on the quayside at Ness at £1 a time within hours of returning. Those that aren't eaten by the islanders are sent round the world to exiles, a taste of home.

But what a taste! Guga is built for sturdy palates. When it's caught, the bird's beheaded and gutted, and the rib-cage cut out. So all that's left is the four pieces of meat, the breasts, and the legs adhering to the thick, grey spongy skin. It is first dried, then salted. Celum has been boiling it in the kitchen for three hours and in three changes of water. 'It's very salty, and very tough.'

It smells of fish; which isn't surprising as the bird lives on mackerel. The flesh is brown, like duck. It tastes like salted ham that hasn't been soaked. It's a taste sensation you have to grasp firmly, like a nettle, for there's a wave of nausea hurrying towards you, ready to overwhelm you if you hesitate. The flavour lingers on. And on and on.

Later, to steady my nerves, I went for a walk round Stornoway harbour. The sea was at low ebb. There was a stench of decaying matter in puddles, of seaweed clinging to greasy rocks, and an odour in the salty fishing boats of stale gutted herring and caked engine oil, and then I knew what gannet tasted of. The unmistakable taste of home.

Earlier I'd met Roddy Macleod, 51, one of a family of nine, who remembers when, in his childhood, a plate of brose barley-meal porridge was sometimes all they had to eat in a whole day. Seabirds like puffin and cormorant were eaten as well as gannet. Even though they were thought dirty feeders, they would be put in to feed with the chickens for three weeks. 'We all believe here that we have a right to the birds of the air and the fish of the sea,' he says.

If this is the last remaining, stronghold of true British regional cookery, no one the other side of the kitchen door would know about it. In the dining-room that night, spring-heeled Stornoway waitresses bounced between tables, and a waiter was flambéeing for two Americans. The menu had nothing more horrific than a Steak Lewis. 'It's steak from the mainland, flamed in whisky,' said the English-born manager, Terry Atkinson. 'With asparagus. A bit of a cheat, really.' Not like the gannet.

Even if it's Only Eggs, Scramble them with Style . . .

Have you ever been preparing a recipe step by step, a few hours before the guests arrive – and turned the page of your cookery book to see the next stage which reads : 'Now leave to marinate for seven days ...'?

...Or have you ever been so disorganised in preparing your meal that by ten pm, when it's finally ready, the first of your guests are announcing that they must get back to their baby-sitter in Carshalton?

Or maybe wanted to impress a senior colleague at work and attempted some ambitious dish like chicken Kiev and, when you've served it, instead of spurting out a jet of garlicky butter, it opens to reveal a frozen lump of butter clinging to the uncooked, pink chicken flesh? Well, I have.

There's a message in every meal, and it's one which isn't always flattering to the guests. So when you don't have the skill of a Robert Carrier (who once treated a hundred guests to a gourmet meal conceived entirely in 'gold') and when you don't have £10,000 to spend on a banquet for your friends (like the Lord Mayor of London), how can you make sure the message doesn't misfire?

None of us is in the position of Cleopatra. When she was shacked up with Antony in their Roman pad, they had guests to dinner who rudely remarked that they didn't think the meal could have been very costly. 'Is that so?' said the Egyptian queen taking a large pearl and tossing it into the salad. 'Well, now it is.'

Money is the most eloquent message of all. But most of us have to make the meaning in our food clear in other ways, in selecting the menu, buying choice delicacies, or taking a lot of trouble over the preparation. That's the message most easily understood.

Elizabeth David, one of our most talented food writers, likes the story of a French cook, Hélène, who cooked for Gertrude Stein. Hélène took a dislike to Matisse, the great painter, who would come without warning and expect a meal. 'If he's staying for dinner,' Hélène told Gertrude Stein, 'I will not cook an omelette but fry eggs; it takes the same number of eggs, and the same amount of butter, but it shows less respect and he will understand.'

I've been talking to some of the people whose business is putting a message into food, and asking them to explain their attitudes to this unique means of communication. The first thing that strikes you is how impossible it must be to entertain any of them. Since their standards are so much higher than ours, how can they fail to view us critically?

I put this question to Caroline Conran, a marvellous cook and, ironically, author of *Poor Cook* (Sphere, 60p). She is married to the millionaire head of Habitat, Terence Conran, who also just happens to own the Neal Street Restaurant, and used to be a cook, too.

'People never ask us out to dinner,' says Caroline, 'and when people come to dinner with us, they expect it to be perfect and it never is.' That's the price you pay for being an expert. But, daunting though the Conrans might seem, their principles are cheerfully simple, their message friendly and unselfconscious.

'I believe simple is good,' says Caroline. 'As the French put it, *fait simple*. I'm lucky because I have lots of time for cooking and the average housewife hasn't. But there are a lot of things you can cook which are good, like vegetables from your own garden.

'I admit, I do try extremely hard for guests, though I do have one rule: don't do things that you haven't done for yourself before. I remember one disaster when I was cooking for Robert Carrier and I made *Imam Bayaldi* (the aubergine scooped out of its skin, fried with onion, put back and baked in the oven); I forgot to fry it first and it tasted terribly bitter. It's a mistake to go for special effects which aren't true to you. It's better not to do lots and lots of things, but to be terribly generous, have stacks of roast potatoes, masses of watercress salad, two huge chunks of cheese.'

Mightn't the message in such a meal be *too* simple for some of their grand business contacts? Caroline disagrees. 'If it's someone very important to Terence, I get out my white table-cloth and probably serve English roast lamb or roast beef. People are so happy not to be eating in an hotel or a restaurant and they love it, especially if you serve home-made bread. That's the way to knock them for six.

'Dressing up the table is the worst thing to do. On TV and in women's magazines, there's all that fancy stuff to make people feel grand and posh. But it's not good cooking. Spend time making the food taste good, not making the accessories look good.'

You want to do something special for friends, of course, and Caroline says she'll try to get something like quails' eggs (from a farmer near her home in Berkshire) or puff balls from the fields. Most of all she likes to cook with someone else. 'I have a friend who is particularly fond of Middle Eastern food and we cook together. It's much nicer with two people. Entertaining should be fun, not an obligation.'

For Robert Carrier, cooking is much more than fun; it's life itself. Robert Carrier is a showman – he made a start in life as an actor – and he's still putting on a show, searching for applause. Food is the message. 'I'm not interested in religion. I'm not interested in politics.' He speaks through food? 'That's it.'

Robert Carrier's message is certainly profitable. No one has made so much money out of it, no chef, no other cookery writer, on television or off it, in this country or abroad. There are his cookery books : *The Robert Carrier Cookbook* (Sphere, £1.30) which begat the *Great Dishes of the World* (Sphere, 95p) which begat the *Robert Carrier Cookery Course* (W H Allen, £8). And his distinguished restaurants, one in London's Islington and the other in Suffolk, a stately eating-place called Hintlesham Hall, a Tudor building with an eighteenth-century façade in cream and white. Inside, where the BBC came to film him for the programme *One Pair of Eyes*, is the roomy restaurant where he sits in state, like an English country gentleman. Not really an English country gentleman because he's an American with the name of McMahon, whose mother was German and father an Irish-born lawyer, and who came to England by way of France (editing a magazine for de Gaulle) and Italy.

Food is also a paradox: 'I love *not* to eat anything for a while and, after a week of not eating, I have a desire for a greasy banger, or pasta. The sensation? It's like trying to describe love to someone who doesn't know what it is. It's like being in the sea before the big wave breaks, and you jump into the surging froth. It's a physical experience. I'm not being kinky or masochistic but it can be quite a painful experience : you come out of the sea, and find you are bleeding from head to foot and didn't know it; it's like an orgasm. I believe we reach climaxes in our work and in our pleasures; a great meal is an energy-releasing bounty. You have your Christmas dinners in England where people eat until they almost drop dead.'

This rather alarming message, somewhat modified, is the one which he tries to incorporate in his restaurant cuisine. But might it be too overwhelming for the average home? On the contrary, he would argue. He's very particular about food. He's selectively sensual. He's never liked milk products a great deal, he hates the sickly smell of a butcher's shop, he doesn't like the sweetness of the baker's shop.

He's no puritan, has no concern for the economics of the household as we expect from our native good writers. 'Food is for communicating pleasure,' says Carrier. 'For bringing people together. It welds friendships, softens interviews [it softened ours, most deliciously – over galantine of duck, Moroccan chicken, rice pilaff with toasted pine nuts, fresh raspberries with raspberry sorbet, and raspberry liqueur]. Food is an easing thing, food is love, food is calorific warmth. Food is one of the basics: love, sex, sensuality. We fight for food, we kill for food. It's biblical. If you give someone salt, you won't harm them, if you aren't given salt, you're in danger.' (You're in no danger in a Carrier restaurant, plenty of salt in everything.) 'When you meet someone across a desk, there's a barrier. When you meet round a table, food brings you together, it's a joy.'

Being Robert Carrier, he's rung all the changes in food sensations. 'I've eaten bull's balls, sheep's eyes, parson's nose, coxcombs (the cockerel's comb), jellied eels, and I love tripe. The big duck producers once sent me duck's balls to see if I could create a dish around them – and I couldn't; the fish meal they feed the ducks on seems to get concentrated there.'

How do you become a sensual cook? 'All you need is a drop of cream, some white wine, brandy, Pernod, carrots, olive oil, butter, eggs and herbs – add a bit, just a pinch – and you begin to cook.'

Carrier doesn't like to be bored. And he doesn't like to bore people. When he visited the big restaurants he found the same lack of choice ; the smoked salmon, the avocado, scampi ... 'I do only what I want ... I don't serve a single slice of smoked salmon as such, but smoked salmon *quiche*; don't serve smoked eel, but puréed with cream as smoked eel *brandade*; the avocado as soup – so simple anyone can do it. We created a cold soup here at Hintlesham – so simple – you blend chicken stock and cream, with a little curry powder, add diced tart apple soaked in lemon juice, chopped watercress, served ice cold. It's a knock-out.'

Here's one of Carrier's specials with which he celebrated his fiftieth birthday. Gold is his colour and the sun is his motif, so he treated his hundred guests to a meal conceived totally in gold ... even decorations were done in gold, like an ornate frieze over the fireplace, artichoke heads and plastic grapes sprayed with gold paint.

To start with: a double consommé of fish (that's a concentrated fish stock made with sole bones, cod, a lobster shell with Pernod dribbled over it, clarified with eggshell, flavoured with tomato and fennel, coloured gold with saffron) plus one clam, one oyster, one tiny piece of sole, and one slice of fennel added to each serving.

Then: brioche (yeasty, eggy bread coloured with turmeric for yellow, glazed with egg yolk).

Foie gras, which is pink, but coloured golden with aspic jelly.

Chinese duck, with ginger, glazed with orange syrup.

Courgettes souffléd (cut lengthwise, poached five minutes, the centres scooped out, mashed with egg yolk, Parmesan and Gruyère, blended with beaten white of egg, piped back in shells, and returned to a hot oven till they puff up – about 20-25 minutes).

Corn and potato croquettes (*pommes dauphine* and sweet corn put through the blender).

Salad mimosa (green salad with baby spinach leaves and herb flavourings over which he sieved hard-boiled egg yolk into a sun pattern cut out of cardboard).

Mango ice-cream and golden cake.

Christopher Driver, Editor of *The Good Food Guide*, sometimes described as the man who's had more hot dinners than most people have had hot dinners, wouldn't go along with Carrier's vision of an enlightened public.

Christopher followed the great gourmet and classical scholar Raymond Postgate into the job seven years ago. He thinks the British are hopelessly self-conscious about food. 'Private hospitality is something the English are not good at. Hospitality tends to be an American or French attribute. Entertaining forces us to be something we are not. Our way is nearly always with drink, we do it with drink in the home or outside it. At home, when we are on show, we get inhibitions. We wonder – are we spending enough? We all have something at home we're ashamed about (I know I have) and insecurity is the message which comes across. People always add the extra ingredient, making it *too much*, rather than too little.'

What are his guidelines? 'If I were entertaining a millionaire – and millionaires are intrinsically mean – I'd choose a fairly expensive restaurant, but something less expensive than you'd expect. Hotels are often better than restaurants, especially if they have historically accumulated wine lists like the Connaught or the Ritz. I had a good lunch at the Berkeley, surprisingly good value for the price. I think you'd want to convey to the millionaire that you had good judgement rather than money, you'd want to show him you had a filing system which directed you to such places. How do you show you appreciate someone? By spending time on them, or being knowledgeable.'

If he wanted to put a message over to a girl, I suggested? 'Ah,' he laughed, 'I've just seen the very place. It's a Chinese restaurant called Chicken Bang-bang.'

The most direct message in a meal is the advertising message and none more direct than from J Walter Thompson, the leading food advertising people. They put excitement into Horlicks and Kraft cheese and all the celebrated Heinz products. They have a two-way experience of food: addressing the public and addressing the client, two very different messages.

John Humphrey, the PR and advertising executive for Kraft, is a former ad agency creative head; he sees presenting food as a creative, imaginative exercise. What can you do to entertain Mr X whom you know can afford to hire the Savoy to come and do his party?

'Use your imagination. In India, we had a friend whose wife had died – he'd been nursing her in America. He'd lived in Bali and had Balinese paintings. We moved into his house, and got a painter to enlarge all his paintings to make a mural on white paper which we hung on his walls. Then we took the legs off his table, and arranged a Balinese meal on his Bali dishes, sitting round on cushions, all lit with Indian oil lamps. When he arrived, dressed in his bowler hat, we were all waiting in sarongs and bush jackets, with his Balinese records playing in the background.'

Now that John Humphrey lives in Reigate both servants and Balinese paintings are in short supply, but the principle of entertaining is the same. 'We psychoanalyse our guests. If they have been eating in expensive restaurants the whole time, we wouldn't give them smoked salmon or caviare. I'd just give them the biggest letdown, a starter so simple it just isn't true. If you were a fisherman, it might be a trout you'd caught – build it round yourself. How many people have got the courage to serve a ham they've prepared themselves? If you've overseas visitors, try to sell Britain – a lot of them think British food is awful. So we won't give them roast beef but real veal and ham pie or pheasant or grouse casserole. Some tired businessmen don't want the misery of a sweet, so we just serve something like the fruits of the season, some fresh raspberries or blackberries or mulberries in a wineglass with a little gelatine and colouring poured over them as it's about to set, chilled overnight in the fridge, with a dollop of cream on top.'

All these grand entertainers have the cash to spend, and the time to prepare it. Perhaps you could get away with it if you 'cheated'? Delia Smith, who's the *Evening Standard* cookery columnist, wrote a book called *How to Cheat at Cooking* (Coronet, 35p) and it sold 20,000 copies in the first three months when it went into paperback. So somewhere there are 20,000 women (and some men, too, no doubt) cheating like mad.

But if you cheat your friends, don't they feel cheated? 'I feel I'm away from cheating,' says Delia defensively. 'I'm not a cheating cook, but my book has a lot of cheating recipes. This book was for people who don't like cookery, but do like eating. I say, "why not put your imagination into junk food, and disguise things?"

Delia says there's a difference between entertaining guests and creating magnificent works of art out of food. 'Do you want to be pretentious, creating in the kitchen like crazy, or do you just want to entertain, and not get yourself into a fluster, not have to be doing things all through the meal?

'Cheating isn't presenting rubbish,' she explains. 'Learn about the good bakers, the best delicatessens, find out about specialist fruits, unusual cheeses, the best coffee, things which aren't any trouble. Cheating is using easy non-stick pans, oven-to-table ware.'

She doesn't see why you shouldn't use canned soup, considering all the trouble the manufacturer has put into making it. Add a spot of red wine to minestrone, sherry to oxtail, brandy to crab or lobster, soured cream to consommé or tomato soup. Decorate with garnishes like parsley and mint, and *croûtons*, squares of fried bread, flavoured with garlic if you like.

Instant potato? Yes, the trick is to disguise the texture rather than the taste. Buy Smash and beat in cream and butter and chives, or finely chopped onion.

To Harold Wilshaw, *The Guardian*'s distinguished cookery expert, there's no heresy more wicked than cheating. The food is more important than the guests : 'I choose the food first, then the guests. When I plan a dinner, I plan for weeks in advance. I bought a jar of white truffles in Italy, and I'm planning to make poulet marengo. It will be a labour of love and I'll ask people to whom I owe a special dinner. Every now and then I give a dinner I can't afford.

'Of course, the people are important, too. The mistake is to have the wrong people meet the wrong people. I go along with Elsa Maxwell who said: 'If you owe a bore a dinner, send it to him.' Harold Wilshaw puts down his interest in food to a tolerant mother who encouraged his kitchen experiments.

We've talked to those who see food as sex, food as fun, and food as prestige, but Harold Wilshaw was the first who'd seen food as punishment. He was investigating British institutional cooking, schools, hospitals, old people's services, prisons. He visited Oxford prison which is so medieval there's only room for twenty-five people to sit down to a meal; the others have to take food to eat alone in their cells. 'The food is frightful in Oxford prison. Food is part of the environment, and it is humiliating. The porridge is made with water instead of milk. Except on Christmas Day.' That's what they mean by 'doing porridge'.

The judges who send these men to prison are accustomed to rather better fare. They are the recipients of some of the grandest public and private dinners served in this country, like that given by the Lord Mayor-elect for the Lord Chancellor and senior judges, about twenty in all. It's a fine old feudal custom. So grand is it that John Coombe, head of the City's old and distinguished banqueting firm, Ring and Brymer, won't discuss it. He feels the economic crisis is so grave people might question expenditure of this sort.

Then the Lord Mayor goes on to entertain 700 or so guests in the Guildhall – sharing the cost with his two sheriffs. Today the message in this prestigious meal is a humbler one than it's ever been – course after course has been lopped away, year by year. Even the tradition of turtle soup has gone because of protests by Peter Scott, the nature conservationist. Turtle soup is actually one of Britain's sole contributions to the international gourmet scene, and a bizarre one it is. It amounts to about the same thing as serving lark's tongues at a Roman feast, or the Chinese practice of bird's nest soup (it's perilous collecting them) or shark's fin soup (the process takes weeks).

To feed all the Guildhall guests the caterers used to import up to a dozen turtles, live, and set each one down in a corner of the kitchen until the reluctant beast put its head out. At this point, they were lassooed, hung up from the ceiling and – plonk! Breaking and entering the shell is rather like dismembering a tank, and the cuts of meat are so tough they have to be stewed for seven hours to extract the flavour. The merit of this soup is doubtful – and I have actually tasted it at a Lord Mayor's banquet. I thought I discerned a flavour of tea, but I now put that down to the tannin in the sherry which is added. In any case the meat juices are blended with beef consommé, and the flavour is further improved with herbs like thyme and marjoram and coriander. What makes it decidedly different from any other soup is the two pieces of something floating in the bowl in front of you. One is brown, and it is meat. The other is green, and is turtle fat.

If you can't impress your guests with turtle soup, how can you do it? The City isn't noted for imagination, and John Coombe says the main call is for caviar, oysters, *foie gras*, partridge, grouse. 'People like out-of-season asparagus and wild strawberries flown in, and that sort of thing. But to make a banquet distinctive, you must have the great wines of France.' A third of the cost of most banquets is the wine.

That may be what City gents would like to eat, but precious few can afford it. The cost of status-seeking is rising all the time, and there's no one in the City today who'd be prepared to pay up for a banquet like this one, taken from Ring and Brymer's files of fifty years ago : 'No one has the time or the capacity either,' points out Coombe. 'The banquet began at six-thirty p.m. and they ate through till ten p.m.'

The guests started with the traditional turtle soup, followed by casserole of *sole Veronique*, mousse of *foie gras* and tongue, then cuts from a baron of beef, some roast partridge accompanied by salad mariette (cooked carrots, quartered in sauce vinaigrette), finishing with orange jelly, maids of honour, kirsch-iced soufflé, fruit and coffee. They washed this lot down with refreshing glassfuls of punch, sherry, hock, champagne, port and brandy or Benedictine.

When he's not doing banquets for the Lord Mayor, insolvency practitioners, and the crowned heads of Europe, John Coombe is entertaining at home, and by now he should know a thing or two.

Does he have any rules? 'The food should be good, to stimulate the conversation.' So he literally starts with a Talking Point. 'The first course is not exactly experimental, not exactly a throwaway, but it's possibly a gimmick, like a variation of some lobster or salmon dish. It helps if it can be prepared in advance.'

The main course might be a *filet de boeuf Wellington* (fillet of beef in a pastry case) and he'd go straight on to cheese, missing out a dessert. 'So that you can go on drinking the claret or burgundy right through the meal, continuing with it as long as possible.' That's a pretty straightforward message. 'And I never have to worry about impressing people,' he added, 'because I never ask anyone home except my best friends.'

Perhaps we can't expect to organise a meal with the expertise of John Coombe, the flair of an advertising man like John Humphrey, and certainly not the flamboyance of Carrier. But at least we can take a cue from the *bonhomie* of Wilshaw or the spirit of generosity of Conran. And friends are forgiving, even of the worst disasters – as long as you mean well. Caroline Conran describes how her sister entertained a dozen friends for dinner one night: 'When we'd finished the meal and got up from our coffee, we all felt terribly hungry. "What a simple little meal," we said to each other. "A bit too simple, perhaps." Then my sister went onto the kitchen and found three chickens in the oven . . .'

Baby Big and the Magic Milkmen

Food scientists are striving to achieve the perfect milk for Britain's babies. But need they bother?

After 80 years experimenting with dried milk formulae, British medicine has finally arrived at the perfect mix.

It's a formula for baby milk which has exactly the correct ratio of vitamins and trace minerals; the right balance of carbohydrates, fat, protein – down to the last of the eight amino acids essential for growth. What's more, you can dispense with tedious preparation time in the kitchen, boiling water and sterilising bottles, because it's presented at stable body temperature.

The new milk is available to all prospective mothers and it comes in a superbly attractive twin-pack, with washable teats. It's called the mother's breast.

Yet seven mothers out of 10 in Britain believe that they are doing the best thing for their babies by starting them on powdered cow's milk from birth. Only one mother in 20 is determined enough to go on breast feeding her baby from the breast for more than three months.

Why should this be? Inertia, possibly. Mothers are quite likely to go on doing what their mothers and grandmothers did before them, despite a Government report last year which stated unequivocally that breast milk is better for a baby's growth and development. The report, Present Day Practice in Infant Feeding, pointed out that there are hazards in artificial feeding; the high level of phosphates in cow's milk which can weaken the baby's resistence to disease in the first fortnight, for example.

There are other hazards in cow's milk feeding: mothers may not be clear about the dangers of incorrectly preparing the mix – they don't realise what happens, for example, if they 'add one for the pot' and give the baby too many feeds in the day.

Powdered milk has three times more sodium than breast milk, and excessive feeds can raise the level of sodium to the point where the baby dehydrates. This is now believed to be responsible in part for the large number of unexplained 'cot deaths'.

What is the Government doing about the recommendations of the report? 'We can't order people to do things,' says the Department of Health. 'Although one would expect note to be taken of the report.'

Some doctors, however, believe that British mothers have been badly misled – and that the Government should act. Dr Michael Church, a London lecturer in nutrition, who has studied infant feeding, feels very strongly about it.

'People have been led to believe that modified milk may be better than breast milk,' he says. 'There's the mystique of the manufacturing process: and then there's a picture of a smiling baby on the packet. People talk about the convenience of bottle feeding but there's nothing more inconvenient. You have to get up in the middle of the night, sterilise the bottle, measure out the formula, add the boiling water, wait for it to cool. It's incredibly inconvenient.

'After all that, the balance of the milk is wrong. Cow's milk was designed for baby cows, not baby humans. All mammals' milk is designed to fit its own kind perfectly, not other mammals.'

Cows' milk, for example, has less carbohydrate than human milk, but more protein, and too much saturated fat. This may explain the contents-list on a packet of baby-milk, which goes:

Ingredients: Skimmed milk, lactose, unhydrogenated palm oil, unhydrogenated palm kernel oil, unhydrogenated corn oil, unhydrogenated soya bean oil...

Nor does cow's milk have the same vitamin or mineral balance. Therefore the list goes on (and on)...ascorbic acid (Vitamin C), ferrous sulphate, DL-alpha-tocopherol acetate, zinc sulphate, nicotinic acid, calcium pantothenate, copper sulphate, riboflavine, thiamine hydrochloride, pyridoxine hydrochloride, Vitamin A, folic acid, biotin, Vitamin D, cyanocobalamin.

There is nothing sinister about this list. It's just that these precious vitamins happen to occur in breast milk in exactly the right proportions. In cow's milk they have to be added.

The two big baby's milk firms are Glaxo and Cow and Gate and they share a huge £15 million retail market. Neither of them actually claims that their milk is better than breast milk or even its equal. In fact they both say they're deeply concerned over the fear that dehydration from hypernatraemia may possibly occur when the instructions are not carefully followed.

Glaxo, makers of Ostermilk, say they've been in business 80 years and hypernatraemia has only just come to light. 'It's a terrible thing,' says a Glaxo lady, 'but the average British mother listens to the average British grandmother, and the average British grandmother listens to her average British grandmother.

'Instead of giving babies some boiled water between feeds when they cry they make another feed. And they put in extra spoonfuls, thinking they are giving extra nutrition, saying to themselves, *there can't be much goodness in water.*'

That's how babies get on the road to excess sodium. And, naturally, baby milk manufacturers do not put scary warnings on their packets saying: *This milk may be dangerous to your child's health.* (Sodium-rich Marmite, for example, is still advertised on TV with the slogan 'babies love its delicious savoury taste.')

Glaxo, who have the world's most modern drying plant in Kendal in the Lake District, feel virtuous about their role in feeding babies, but not half as virtuous as Cow and Gate, which has just created at a cost of £250,000 the equivalent of a mechanical breast.

Cow and Gate have built a huge plant in Wexford, Eire, which can process the whey from the milk, and reduce the level of trace minerals by electrodialysis to almost the exact level of the minerals in the breast. In fact they take so much out they have to put some back in artificial form.

They believe the investment was necessary in the light of modern medical findings. To put it plainly, it's an admission that cow's milk hasn't really been the right food for babies for all these years, in spite of the rosy picture of the bonny, bouncing ones on Cow and Gate packets.

[In fact fat babies are distinctly out of fashion. Recent surveys have established that by the time they are a year old half of Britain's babies are overweight, because they are crammed full with milk and cream and cereals. 'Cereal foods end up as pacifiers,' says Dr Church. 'Give your child cereals and they stop crying. But there's a satiety factor. They get overloaded with calories, and by the time they are a year old they are overweight, and this may set a pattern of obesity for later years.']

Cow and Gate's new product is called Premium Baby Milk, which the firm claims is the one modified milk in the world nearest in composition to breast milk.

Three cheers for breast milk, they cry. Peter Hawke, the Cow and Gate spokesman, says: 'A mother should feed from the breast for the first 10 weeks. That's essential. From four to six months is good. If she does it longer, she's doing the best for her child.' And if they did that, they wouldn't need Premium? 'That's right,' says Hawke.

It has taken seven years to develop Premium milk. Ron Hendey, Cow and Gate's chief scientist, explains: 'You take the protein down from 3.4 per cent to 1.8 per cent; raise lactose, the milk sugar from 4.8 per cent to the level of breast milk, 7 per cent. In fact you alter the protein, the sugar, the mixture of fats and oils, the whole amino acid structure.'

It's a bit late in the day to introduce the idea now, but Hendey admits that almost any mammal milk would be easier to modify than cow's milk. Pig's milk is actually the nearest to human milk. Camel and mare's milk have a better balance for humans. Sheep's milk is OK and so is goat's. Reindeer milk would be a bit fat, dog's milk a bit-thin. Now, otter's could be just right. Perhaps we should look into it.

A Taste of the Times

The pattern of eating out in Britain has changed more in the past 25 years than in the past 25 centuries: but it's not something you can put down to the Queen.

The biggest change in British eating habits has been the end of our traditional suspicion of foreigners, says Christopher Driver, editor of *The Good Food Guide*, which was started by Raymond Postgate 25 years ago last March. Driver says we have completely surrendered to the influence of foreign food; from taking wine with our meals, to eating Indian, Chinese, Italian, Greek, even Indonesian and Japanese food as a matter of pride. 'People forget that 25 years ago it was considered quite extraordinary to ask for wine with a meal. You had great difficulty in getting a waiter to understand. It was considered pretty eccentric to drink anything but beer or ginger beer when you ate out. British food as such has almost disappeared, in this time, only to reappear again in the past few years as a rather *recherché* thing as The Taste of England. Even the good old British institution, the fish and chip, is dying, almost as fast as fishmongers' shops. But the amazing thing must be our easy acceptance of foreign foods.'

The greatest change in British eating was the arrival of the hamburger, claim Lyons, who introduced Wimpy Bars in 1955. Now they've just sold the Wimpy concession along with all their catering interests. Raymond Marquis, a Lyons executive, has seen the change from Lyons teashops (with pre-war waitresses in frilly aprons, called Nippies) to the Jolyon restaurants (the last one closed in 1976). 'One of our directors went to the States in 1955 and saw them in operation,' says Marquis, 'and we bought the European rights. This has been the big change of our time. The move away from restaurants to *fast-food outlets.*' (e.g. 'We had dinner last night at a lovely little fast-food outlet.').

The biggest change is social, says Egon Ronay. He opened a restaurant, the Marquee, in 1952, before he'd conceived the idea of a restaurant guide. His diners-out were literally all ex-public school-boys who had no idea of what food could be. 'I did a survey of public school eating. It was rubbish. Horrendous. Really horrific. Public schoolboys never had a chance to find out what food was all about, and as long as it wasn't blancmange, they thought it was wonderful. The food at grammar schools was infinitely better. I'd put the date of the change at 1960; a new generation starting to make money who didn't come from the public schools. They hadn't been conditioned to think it was bad manners to discuss food, or complain in restaurants. And they bloody well did open their mouths. It opened the door to the trattorias; the revolutionary change in eating-out has been the people who eat.'

The biggest change has been the disappearance of snobbery, says Humphrey Lyttelton. 'Humph', jazz trumpeter, Old Etonian, was for many years a witty restaurant critic (he once decided to eat in an unsavoury Northern cafe, because 'ten thousand flies can't be wrong'). In his younger days Britons had an inferiority complex about eating out. 'You were absolutely scared stiff. You had a wine waiter who looked like Eric von Stroheim, and he gazed at you as if he had a deep respect for you and the wine you chose. It's probably gone too far in the other direction now: I was eating in the Café Royal, which has one of the best wine-cellars in London, thoroughly enjoying a slow examination of the wine list, when I saw the waiter getting edgy. Finally he prompted me: "What about a nice red, sir?" The British really want to be liked, and if you look at *The Good Food Guide*, you'll always see little remarks like "food nice and service *friendly*". In France they don't go to be loved. And in Germany they go to restaurants to shout at waiters and be shouted at back.

'We are almost petrified at the idea of complaining. Eating out has completely changed since the old tyrants in restaurants have died out. Out went the French style of waiter, and in came the Italian style, who are so friendly they practically fall into your soup. I'd put the date of the change as late Fifties, with Mario and Franco's restaurants, waiters all ebullient and leaping about. They were fun to go to.'

The biggest influence on restaurants in 25 years could be gay power, suggests Michael Smith, a little mischievously. Smith, a former restaurateur and food historian says food has only really improved in restaurants since more women and gay folk started to run them. 'Gay people are really good at entertaining, with a painstaking attention to detail, to the *mise-en-scene*, silver, china, tablecloths, decor. Possibly 15 out of the top 20 restaurants in the country have a gay hand guiding them. I'd put the date at around 1967. Back in 1952 people hardly had any restaurants to go to, they ate in hotels. Coffee bars came in the Fifties and we thought they were the bees bloody knees. Trendy, with-it and chic. Then people who'd been abroad came back and began to demand something better, and all the best places have been started by amateurs. The British think catering is an abysmal profession, socially. They think a chap should never go into catering, unless it's the management side. Which is how your brilliant amateurs emerged; no competition.'

The biggest change is yet to come, says Graham Kemp. Kemp is an ex-Birds Eye food man, now a publisher and communications adviser responsible for the National Catering Inquiry. 'It's started already – a big switch to food and snacks. Pubs have this huge potential for the quick food business. Industrial canteens have moved into fast food from the freezer. More young people are eating out than ever before. They want to eat where there's no formality, no waiters. The home freezer produced a big change in eating about five years ago, but the effect on restaurant catering has been halting. Most restaurateurs respond to the Egon Ronay snobbishness that vegetables should be fresh. So they don't equip themselves with proper storage freezers and micro-wave ovens. Now they themselves are on the wrong foot. Cheaper restaurants have never had this hang-up about frozen food. In 10 years' time the revolution will be total.'

1951 Raymond Postgate's *Good Food Guide* launched: London, a bleak desert of restaurants.

1953 Milk bars give way to coffee bars; Tommy Steele will be discovered in one of them.

1955 Lyons introduce Wimpy Bars: Egon Ronay launches his restaurant guide.

1958 Cod War with Iceland starts: and the beginning of the end for cheap fish and chips.

1959 Mario and Franco start first of the Italians trendy tratts and set a new eating style.

1960 Chinese pouring in from Hong Kong at increased rate and opening restaurants.

1965 First Kentucky Fried chicken counter: now you don't even have to sit down to eat.

1970 Indian restaurants outgrow Chinese; Greek-Cypriot kebab houses multiplying.

1977 Revolution complete with curry houses, kebab houses, Chinese take-aways, American McDonald hamburger bars; fast food everywhere.

The Good Prison Food Guide

What do the 42,000 prisoners in Britain's jails eat? The Home Office allowed us to visit six jails to find out.

Prison catering is rather like cooking with wartime rations, but instead of a ration book there is the Dietary Scale, in which the Home Office lays down the strict limits within which each prisoner is fed. Just £3.80 per head is allowed for the raw materials – per week.

The rules require the food to be 'wholesome, nutritious, well-prepared and served, and reasonably varied and sufficient in quantity'. We visited six prisons and tasted the main meal on the day we were there. Although these jails may not be representative of all 125 establishments, we found that the requirements were generally met. But the quality, preparation and presentation, depended very much on the skills and ingenuity of the catering staff.

Only recently has a choice of menu been offered, but the amount of choice varies and, at Pentonville, there is none at all. Like most institutional food, too much was sweet and starchy, sometimes vegetables were overcooked, and there was not enough fresh fruit or brown bread. In some prisons, pepper is regarded as a highly dangerous substance and forbidden, and the luxury of a soft- boiled egg and toast is unknown. 'Food is always a focus for dissatisfaction because it plays an important part in a prisoner's otherwise dull existence,' says Martin Wright, director of the Howard League for Penal Reform. Offenders used to be put on numbered diets as a punishment – No. 1 diet which was one pound of bread, and water, for three days at a time, was abolished as recently as 1974. Special diets are allowed on vegetarian, religious or medical grounds.

Most of our local prisons were built before the turn of the century and no communal dining rooms were provided. Now, it is general policy for prisoners to eat 'in association', but most still have to eat 'banged up' in their cells while the prison officers are off duty. The food may be lukewarm by the time the prisoner has returned with his tray to the cell, and it takes a steady hand to avoid the soup flowing into the custard. Overcrowding means about 16,000 inmates live two or three to a cell originally designed for one man, and they have to eat in cramped and sometimes insanitary conditions.

Those prisoners who are on their own have to eat alone, even on Christmas Day.

The prison day usually starts around 7am, and most prisoners have porridge with their breakfast. (Sometimes there is cereal if the milk allowance of half a pint a day is stretched.) 'Doing porridge' has become synonymous with serving time – a prisoner has breakfast before his release and the term arose from saying: 'I've got six days and a porridge left to do.' One prisoner told us that the porridge made excellent glue for sticking up pin-ups, and he had once made a papier-mâché sculpture with porridge and newspaper.

The main meal starts between 11.30 and 12.30; tea is usually a cooked meal, and supper is just a fillip. The Governor has a statutory duty to taste the food, although the prison officers do not eat the same meals as inmates. If prisoners have facilities for 'brewing up' in their wings they are able to buy tea and biscuits, and Mars bars (together with tobacco) are often used as currency. Mars bars sales had rocketed at one prison because of prisoners gambling on the World Cup.

To provide some variety the Home Office allows 18p a week for extras for men, but 19p-22p for women: the Home Office thinks that women are more food conscious. Each prison also levies a small tax from the average earnings of £1.50 a week which go to pay for additional entertainments and Christmas. 'The dietary scale allowance is usually used up week by week and there is not much room for saving,' says Peter Stephenson, catering manager for prisons in England and Wales. 'Prison caterers usually buy items like turkeys in bulk before the prices go up and they are kept in store until wanted. Few prisons have deep freezers.'

Much of the food including all salad crops, bacon and pork is produced on prison farms, from which it is bought at market prices. There is even a prison jam, made from mixed fruit, at Hollesey Bay, Suffolk. And most prisons bake their own bread. Except for fish fingers, convenience foods are virtually unknown, in fact, many prisoners probably get more 'home cooking' than they did when on the outside.

Lincoln

Local prison for all types of offenders. Mid-Victorian fortress built for 350 but with 560 inmates, sometimes two or three to a cell. Prisoners line up to be served from insulated trolleys, helping themselves to soup and gravy. Meals eaten in cell.

Daily menu. Breakfast: unlimited porridge, tea, bread and margarine, choice of three or four cooked items. Dinner: four or six choices of main dish and up to six choices of pudding. Tea: Usually five cooked dishes with cold meal on Sunday.

Supper. Half a pint of tea and cake or bun.

Main meal. Vegetable soup, roll. Fried whiting with cabbage and sauté potatoes. Blackberry trifle. Tea.

Kitchens. Principal officer caterer Edward Shillabeer runs kitchens with two officer caterers, a relief officer caterer, and 25 inmates. He believes good presentation of food is psychologically important to prisoners. Kitchen refurbished four years ago, spotless with gleaming metal. They prepare vegetables, bake bread and do their own butchery.

Verdict. Good presentation. Although carrots were most popular vegetables there was good, firm cabbage. Delicious trifle made from juice left over from tinned blackberries and sponge which had been a teatime cake.

Wandsworth

Local prison built in 1847 and overcrowded with 1542 inmates. Includes top security prisoners with no privileges – no TV, table tennis or association. Governor says: 'It's stern discipline but they know where they are here.' Takes 17 minutes to serve 1500 meals from the 'serveries' on the wings. Food eaten in cells.

Daily menu. Breakfast: pint of tea, three slices of bread and margarine, half pint porridge and often choice of something cooked. Dinner: soup and always a choice of three main meats and three courses, Always mint sauce, apple sauce or mustard with appropriate meat. Choice of puddings. Tea: pint of tea and up to five slices of bread and margarine. Cheese or boiled ham and usually fruit. Supper: half pint of tea and a scone or biscuit.

Main meal. Oxtail soup, bread roll. Faggots made with chopped meat, liver, bacon, minced onions and herbs. Swedes and creamed potatoes. Mince tart and custard. Tea.

Kitchens. Chief officer caterer Gordon Reed has a staff of principal officer, four officers and 45 inmates. Victorian kitchen with a high glass roof which makes it a hothouse in summer and freezing in winter. Most food prepared in the kitchen except fish fingers and ice cream.

Verdict. Very good soup and tasty faggots. Mince tart full of mincemeat. In general, prisoners seem appreciative.

Pentonville

Local prison built in 1842 for men serving mainly short sentences. Overcrowded – 1200 inmates, about 900 doubled up. Meals go on to the wings in insulated containers and are served on warm trays. As in most prisons, the cutlery is plastic. But pepper is allowed. Meals are eaten in cells. Smell of urine, disinfectant and old cabbage.

Daily menu. Breakfast: porridge, scrambled egg, bread and margarine. Tea. Coffee an extra every couple of months. Dinner: no choice for main meal, three vegetables, pudding and tea. Tea: usually cooked meal, sausages in gravy with peas and creamed potatoes. Bread and margarine. Supper: tea and a bun.

Main meal. Vegetable soup and as much bread as you want. Chicken pie, boiled potatoes, vichy carrots, peas. Strawberry blancmange with Farmatt cream topping. (This is bought by 'tradingback' flour left over from the prisoners' ample allowances.) Fruit and tea.

Kitchens. Chief officer caterer George Forsyth is assisted by one principal officer caterer, four officer caterers and 30 inmates. Kitchen holds seven days rations in advance. They bake up to 400 loaves a day. Usual steamers, fryers and rotary ovens.

Verdict. Large portions of unimaginative, institutional food. Overcooked potatoes. Prisoners seem to appreciate pint mugs of tea but as one told us: 'The food doesn't compare with home.' The prison we were most glad to leave.

Kirkham

Open prison an old RAF camp in Lancashire. 400 men serving four years or less. Kitchens also provide about 240 meals on wheels a week for four local villages. Three dining halls, one called The Silver Grill for the over 45s. Won a gold and a bronze medal for pork pies in the prison catering competition this year. Prison wages at about £2.30 a week are higher than average, so more is bought from canteen.

Daily menu. Breakfast: porridge alternated with cereal, always something cooked. Dinner: usually soup and choice of three main dishes in the week, two at weekends. Always tea and bread and marge. Tea: choice of three cooked meals (like ham and egg pie) with a vegetable plus tea and bread. Supper: tea and a bun, but prisoners usually brew up for themselves and buy biscuits.

Main meal. Individual steak-and-kidney pie, gravy, carrots, creamed potatoes. Raspberry tapioca. Tea.

Kitchens. Principal officer caterer Peter Givan has a staff of two officer caterers and 16 inmates. Kitchens equipped with large steamers, fryer, etc. Vegetables prepared in old aircraft hangar.

Verdict. Presentation poor but baking good. Steak-and-kidney pie had less meat than one would expect at home. Vegetables unattractive black bits in the diced carrot. Puddings rather dull, but the raspberry tapioca was better than we remembered from schooldays.

Dartmoor

Training prison built in 1806; 538 medium to long-term prisoners. Single cell accommodation, no sharing. Fresh food from own dairy, salad crops from market gardens, and they rear their own pigs. Bake a total of 2000 loaves a week. Canteen service on each wing, meals taken back to cell. Some meals eaten in 'association'.

Daily menu. Breakfast: porridge five or six times a week plus cooked items like boiled eggs. Dinner: usually a choice of three to five main dishes. Always two vegetables besides potatoes (or rice). Tea: cooked meal, sometimes a choice. Supper: tea, bun or crisps.

Main meal. Vegetable soup with unlimited bread rolls. Gammon with pineapple with cabbage, carrots end sauté potatoes. Sponge pudding with custard. Mug of tea.

Kitchens. Run by the popular principal officer caterer Terry 'The Bear' Davies. Has to be prepared for siege conditions in winter; last winter supplied local villages. Gets bargain deals with local traders on one-offs like mis-labelled tomato sauce. Runs City and Guilds catering courses for prisoners – eight passed last year. Thirty inmates help in the kitchens.

Verdict. Excellent – the miracle of firm cabbage. Brown bread and fresh fruit two or three times a week. If you had to go to jail at least this one would offer good food and plenty of fresh air.

Askham Grange

Open women's prison, a converted mansion near York for women serving short sentences or finishing longer ones. 113 inmates and 12 babies. Extra milk or eggs for those pregnant. Canteen-style service from hot plates, food then carried to dining rooms. Sandwiches provided for those working outside, with a cooked tea when they come in. Some vegetables grown in market gardens – strawberries, blackberries and raspberries in summer.

Daily menu. Breakfast: cereals with porridge, toast and jam. Coffee at Christmas and on bank holidays. Dinner: choice of two, sometimes three, main meals and usually three vegetables. There is always a roast on Sundays. Tea: often fry-ups with chips. Supper: tea and a snack.

Main meal. Savoury pancake, carrots, cabbage and creamed potatoes. Prunes with as much custard as you like. Tea.

Kitchens. Peter Fawcett, officer caterer, has nine women prisoners working in the kitchen and two cleaning the dining rooms. Catering can be unpredictable – the kitchen can cook 120 meals, only for 20 women to decide they want to go on a diet that day.

Verdict. Simple, wholesome food, lots of fruit and salads. One prisoner said she had put on a stone after 12 weeks here, getting back to her normal weight. Greater use could be made of women's cooking skills to make more imaginative dishes. But one woman told us, 'It's the best of the three prisons I've been in.'

Big Bang Beans, Aloo Baji and Æbleskiver

Civet de Lapin, Aloo Baji and Æbleskiver are among the delicacies tried and tested by children from the John Evelyn Infants School in South London. If they can't always pronounce the names, they certainly know what it takes to make them. (Civet de Lapin is stewed rabbit from Mauritius, Aloo Baji is a vegetable side dish from Bangladesh and Æbleskiver are Danish pancake balls.)

There are children from nearly a dozen different countries in the school. 'The cookery lessons started as a community thing to encourage the children to try recipes from all round the world,' said June Harold, the deputy headmistress. It was an immediate success. The food has been so tasty and the lessons aroused so much interest that they decided to put the recipes together. The result is *The Deptford Cook Book.* The first edition, carefully typed by teachers, with a cover designed by the children, is already decorating the classrooms and new recipes are being prepared for addition to the loose-leaf booklet. The inner London Education Authority is very interested in the idea, which it feels helps the children learn about and accept their different cultural backgrounds. LEA is therefore considering publishing the book.

Mothers come to the school when they have a spare afternoon, bringing ingredients and recipes for food from their home countries which they then cook with a group of four or five children. For each lesson the children wear brightly-coloured aprons, help with the stirring, mixing and weighing, lay the table and eat the results.

Nicole Jordan, five, is English but she's getting quite knowledgeable about foreign food. 'I've had Turkish bread – it's flat with little bits on top – and salad and Turkish cheese. The bread is better than English, but I don't like Turkish cheese. It's too salty.'

Leyla Gungor, who's six, enjoys her native Turkish food, but declares: 'I like fish and chips and big bang beans (baked beans).'

Gourmet with a Conscience

On the one hand, Christopher Driver is eating like a king as editor of The Good Food Guide. *On the other, he is concerned with the plight of the hungry as a member of Christian Aid. How does he reconcile the two roles?*

Do you remember the thousands of nomads starving in the Sahara drought last year? It was enough to make the *boeuf stroganoff* turn sour in your mouth. Especially if you happened to be editor of *The Good Food Guide* like Christopher Driver, who is also a member of the Christian Aid board which was mounting the rescue operation.

This year sees the 25th anniversary of *The Good Food Guide,* with the new edition to be published next week. It finds Driver, 43, trying to reconcile his two roles. It's not easy. On the one hand, he's deeply committed to radical Christianity: anxious to do what he can for the world's starving. On the other hand, he's a deeply committed and fussy eater, dedicated to guzzling excellent and often expensive food in rather pleasant surroundings.

His wife doesn't think it's right. Nor does his mother, who has been a missionary and teacher in India. 'I do sometimes feel guilty about him,' she says.

Driver's wife, Margaret, is a social worker who looks after handicapped children. 'I feel Christopher shouldn't be doing this,' she says. 'I get this terrible hang-up, because I have to tell families how to screw out an extra pound. And we are eating meals which cost £10 a head. I do feel guilty spending in restaurants.'

Driver says he thinks about it a lot. But he comes to the conclusion it's a fruitful contradiction. 'It's a fruitful tension. Having this undercurrent of Christian radicalism means I'm less likely to go along with the chi-chi, expense account, big-spending type of restaurant.

'It's obvious there are a vast number of people in the world who haven't got enough to eat, and there's also a tiny number who are, rightly, incensed about what they have got.'

Driver took over as *Guide* editor from Raymond Postgate seven years ago. Postgate, scholar and wine-bibber, founded it in 1951 when the British restaurant scene was particularly bleak. When Postgate invited readers to send in their own comments, he upset a hornet's nest of pent-up fury about British restaurant food and service.

Driver continues this tradition and claims they are even more strict today. 'Under Postgate the *Guide* mellowed. We flung a lot of places out. We know a lot more about what restaurant food should be like today.' Only two London restaurants have survived the 25 years of the *Guide*: L'Etoile and Au Savarin.

Now that the *Guide* is under the wing of the Consumers' Association it has a sound financial basis. It has 40 paid inspectors, but still relies heavily on the response from readers. Often they are helpful, but occasionally their voices become shrill, which prompts Driver's many critics to accuse the *Guide* of snobbery, pretentious-ness and elitism.

Driver is used to this criticism. He lets each lash fall patiently, then says: '1 hope we are not snobbish. Snobbishness excludes peo-ple. Elitists are always looking for now recruits.'

He's really proud to get the response he does. 'People are extremely shy of complaining. They are not used to eating out, and they accept what they get.' He hopes the *Guide* is a corrective to this attitude.

It doesn't read like a campaigning pamphlet; more often it echoes the pained voice of Pooter in the Victorian classic, *Diary of a Nobody*. Like Pooter, the *Guide*'s readers are always being snubbed. They are always being refused meals or put in seats near the serving hatch. The waiters bring them stale cheese and burnt omelettes. Sometimes the enraged proprietor bundles them unceremoniously out of the restaurant, because they've come into the dining-room without a tie.

Driver looks an unlikely person to be champion of middle-class eating. He actually looks as if he's in disguise, perhaps to confuse restaurateurs when he's inspecting. His thick-rimmed glasses add an owlish, academic look which could be deliberate. He's proud that the reason why Postgate took to him at first was because they both read Greats and could exchange pleasantries in Latin and Greek. Postgate used to write restaurant notes in Greek on the menu so that peeping proprietors couldn't read his remarks. Driver makes jokes in Latin. You must be wondering how a fastidious Puritan with a peculiar line in Ancient Latin jokes became Britain's arbiter of good taste?

It wasn't anything he got at home. When his parents came back from India, he was 14 months old. They settled down to a typical doctor's family in Leominster in Herefordshire. His mother remem-bers he would go and play with the cooks in the kitchen. But that was all.

School didn't inspire him. At Rugby the food was terrible. He wrote to the school magazine complaining about the wartime prac-tice of making the butter go further by mixing the marge in with it.

His mother used to send him food parcels. 'He used to beseech us. I would go hungry, I used to use up my points from the ration book, sending things to him, like baked beans, things he wouldn't look at now.'

He was still at school when Postgate published the first edition of *The Good Food Guide*. When he went up to Oxford he would carry it everywhere. His parents were hugely amused. 'We used to tease him about it,' said his mother. 'We said it was his bible.'

The student Driver drank wines beyond his imagining at High Table. He made tentative steps as a food critic. He still cherishes an entry he sent to the *Guide* written in the spiky little writing which Greats scholars assume. It was about the Garrick Hotel in Charing Cross Road: 'The sole caprice showed some signs of having been kept for some time. There are not many places where you can get such a fine Hermitage at such a price. The soup was good. You may print my name.'

He missed National Service. He registered as a pacifist, feeling rather violent about the Government's policy on the H-bomb. He had to join the Friends Ambulance Brigade instead.

His mother said: 'I thought it would be a waste of time. But within a few months he wrote to say he was cooking for the whole of the headquarters.' Driver was thrilled: 'I cooked through the Penguin Bee Nelson.' He also got on very well with the Japanese wife of the brigade secretary. She taught him Japanese and Chinese cooking.

Then into newspapers. *The Liverpool Post*, then the *Guardian*, where he wrote a food column which he signed Archestratus.

He took a salary drop to edit *The Good Food Guide*, and ekes out a living by doing odd jobs for *The Listener* and *New Society*.

His wife feels strongly about this: 'This is the irony. We have those expensive meals. But it isn't as if we have vast amounts of wealth.'

They live in Highgate. There's a rude blue plaque on the doorpost: 'This is a No Smoking house. Put it out.' His three children, Catherine l6, Penny 14, Beatrice 11, and his wife Margaret, however, are charming hosts. Four moody half-Burmese cats stalk around. Driver hates dogs: 'They are so insanitary.'

Apart from food, the family's real interest is music. Christopher plays violin and viola. Margaret sings and plays piano and viola. Catherine's on oboe, Penny's a grade eight cellist, Beatrice plays the horn. Margaret confides: 'I think it's terrible to spend money on food, but I think it's all right to spend £60 on a viola string.'

Nobody much asks the Drivers out for a meal. 'It's a great deprivation,' sighs Mrs Driver. Christopher adds: 'Actually, we're extremely easy to please. But there's this curious hesitancy about asking us out. But people at home cook much better than people in restaurants.'

It must be embarrassing to go out with the Drivers for a meal? No, because of his position; he daren't complain, he says.

'Though once I was in Glasgow and I sent the waiter back with the pears in red wine. *I suggest you did this by opening a tin of pears and pouring over some raw red wine*, I said. The waiter came back, sidled up to me and said: *Are you in the catering business?*'

Campaign for Real Bread

In 1980, Michael launched the ground-breaking Campaign for Real Bread in the Lifespan section of The Sunday Times. *The weekly debates and events eventually brought about a change to the bread produced and sold in shops and supermarkets up and down the country.*

We believe the consumer has a right to bread which is tastier, healthier, and better value. Today Lifespan launches *The Sunday Times* Campaign for Real Bread.

But isn't all bread 'real'? Of course. But like ale, some breads are more real than others. More real than the technological bread of the Sixties and Seventies.

Throughout these bad times, *The Sunday Times* has always championed the cause of better bread. Now, at long last, we detect a swing in the right direction. Today very many more housewives confidently bake their own bread. Small bakers, who had been disappearing are returning as high quality bread shops.

We are campaigning for health, quality and value.

Health. Most health authorities recommend wholemeal bread as the staple. Wholemeal bread is made from flour which contains the wheatgerm and its essential oils, and the bran, which is vital roughage. Yet wholemeal bread is difficult to obtain and shop assistants often don't know wholemeal from wheatmeal and brown.

Quality. What is lacking from the majority of loaves today is flavour. Most loaves cooked the technological way are underbaked, so they have no appreciable crust. If they had, they could no longer be squeezed to see if they are 'fresh'. Taste and flavour also come from the flour: the more wholemeal flour in the dough, the more wholesome the flavour.

Value. Healthy, good quality bread costs more. But it is good value. Mass-produced bread is cheaper because it is easier to make, and because it contains more water in proportion to flour.

These are our aims:

1. To improve the variety of breads sold in shops.
2. To encourage bakers to tell customers exactly what they are buying.
3. To make wholemeal bread available everywhere.
4. To collect and publish news of good bakers.
5. To find, test, and publish the best bread recipes.

In our Campaign for Real Bread we are criticising plant-baked bread, which is bought by 70 per cent of us. This week we have a reply from the people who invented it, the Flour Milling and Baking Research Association, Professor Brian Spencer:

'I think you should tell all your readers that all bread is good, but it comes into two categories. If you want a Rolls-Royce, and all the comforts, you have to pay for it. If you are not satisfied with plant bread, the answer is to go to the bread shop for hand-crafted bread. You pays your money and you takes your choice. There isn't a problem.

'And there is no way, unless you can rapidly train 25,000

craftsmen and set them up in small shops, that you can change things. But things aren't going to change, the number of small bakers we have in this country is about what the country can sustain. The plant bread strikes helped them, but not all of their new customers stayed with them.

'It is wrong of you to say some bread isn't good. A lot of people aren't desperately well-educated, and if they are told white bread isn't good for them, and they don't like brown bread, they may cut down on bread and eat less nutritious foods.

'All bread is good, but it comes in two kinds, the better-tasting loaf which I prefer, and the plant-baked bread.

'Incidentally, plant-baked bread makes vast savings; it costs the country £80 million a year in subsidies to the EEC to import the hard North American wheats used in the traditional loaf. The Chorley Wood Bread Process uses more soft European wheats, and saves the government millions. You accuse us of making plant bread with more water. But you have to use enough water to make a handleable dough. Plant loaves need slightly more water because of the soft wheat used, but it's less than is used in brown, and much less than in wholemeal.

'I think what you printed was your opinion given as stated fact.'

An ABC of French Wine

A is for *Appellation d'Origine Contrôlée*, the French wine law designed to protect the customer. B is for Burgundy and Bordeaux, the most fashionable wines of France which sell at premium prices. And C is for cheating. Cheating undoubtedly goes on, so it's worth knowing your ABC of French wine. The biggest scandals are usually outside France. Some years ago in Italy, for example, Gianfranco Ferrari made news with his no-grape wine. Sludge from the bottom of banana boats was one of many ingredients he used to make his chemical brew.

Wine of sorts can be made of any fruit, berry or vegetable, by fermenting the natural sugars to create carbon dioxide and alcohol. It only needs a chemist to balance it and create an illusion of wine by adding flavour and colour. This the chemists cheerfully do.

In court it was explained that Ferrari made a thousand gallons of un-wine every eight hours, despatching it as Chianti, Valpolicella, Barbera and other famous Italian products. French wine, of course, has a better name abroad than Italian, and this is what appeals to cheats. A poor wine can always be improved by a better label.

For many years the *Appellation d'Origine Contrôlée* (AOC) has ensured that dozens of regional wines fulfil the requirements of a 'controlled name'. Some, like *Appellation Bordeaux Contrôlée*, cover large areas, others like *Appellation Brouilly Contrôlée* (in Burgundy), small villages. The law is strictly administered and every AOC wine travels with a green document of identification. Yet the cheats don't need to switch the wine. They switch the dockets instead. The world looks to Bordeaux for its great vintages. The English were first to 'mother' the wines of this region and they affectionately call them clarets (the French pronunciation of 'clear red'). They have traded from these parts for centuries (since Henry II accepted the area as a marriage dowry) and they are suckers for wines labelled with the names of its chateaux. But there are chateaux and *cheateaux* and even among the bona fide one needs to be careful. Some producers use the label Chateau La Tour – sounds innocent enough, a castle with a tower. It just happens to sound like Chateau Latour which is one of the world's grandest wines.

The most noble of all French wine comes from four great chateaux in the Médoc whose limits were defined in 1855, and a fifth, from Graves, which was 'assimilated' later. These houses produce what are called *premier crus*: they are Latour, Margaux, Mouton-Rothschild, Lafite-Rothschild and the added Haut-Brion. Innocents with a little learning see a Laffite, with two Fs, and think they have the real thing (although they may have something good); likewise with a Mouton-Cadet, which is not at all the same as a Mouton-Rothschild.

But innocents they will remain. For they have wandered into the aristocracy of wines where they have no place. A single bottle of one of these great wines, bottled around 1805, broke a world record in Texas a few years ago, selling at $15,000; recently the London auctioneers, Sotheby's, sold a dozen Lafite 1961 for £1,350. An auction is probably the right place to find such wines. Like antiques and rare books they accrue in value with age. In the year of its bottling, this wine was selling at only £20 a case. (A tip: buy into the 1982 Bordeaux clarets, a great vintage and an investment for 20 years on.) Those who buy these wines – and many rich Americans collect them as they would stamps – need well-paid advisers. The advisers prefer not to know that their clients sometimes can't tell a Chianti from a Chablis. I once overheard a group of Americans heatedly discussing the merits of wines on a restaurant list, arguing about which would suit their meal best. The wine waiter finally approached them for their order, asking politely: 'Would you gentlemen like a little wine?' The host replied, rather too quickly: 'Hell no. We want a lot.'

The good name of French wine invites cheating. Seventeen years ago, a wine company in Ipswich, 100 miles from London, made news when it was caught out making up blends in its bottling line, and putting on Burgundy and Bordeaux labels. The ensuing exposé entitled The Art of Cooking Bogus Burgundy, opened a Pandora's box of similar tales. Such as a party visiting a wine company in Portugal which reported that they saw local red wine being put into bottles labelled Produce of France. When they pointed this out to the manager, he replied engagingly: 'Yes. But this is all right: it's for Canada.' Others told of journeys on boats plying a passage between Barcelona and Marseilles carrying wine from Spain labelled Bordeaux Red.

In these instances, France has been more sinned against than sinned itself. And this was the general picture until the so-called Winegate scandals in 1974. It was Bordeaux again. The role of scapegoat was adopted by a wine merchant. He was found guilty of bringing in wines from Provence (where yields of wine per acre are much heavier) and relabelling them Bordeaux; of handling large stocks of wine designated unfit for consumption, and chemically treating them to alter colour, taste and smell.

He complained on his conviction that he was only carrying out the usual practice: 'I am guilty, but so are thousands of others. In 30 years in the trade, I have seen fraud practised everywhere among owners, dealers and professional associations. Baptising – as we call it in the trade – is common practice.'

Wine-growers will tell you that there are four kinds of wine: great wines, especially those from 1976 and 1978, which are plainly and simply authentic; authentic wines from goodish years, like 1975 and 1977, which have been given a leg up by *chaptalisation* – a little sugar is added in the fermenting to increase alcohol strength, and therefore price; authentic poor wines; and finally illegal, beefed up wines.

Illegal vintages can be falsified in four ways. By blending (a process which can also improve wines) or adding sugar after fermentation, to disguise nasty acid products. By changing labels, which is plain dishonest. By introducing other fruits from whatever excess crop there is (potatoes, turnips, apricots, apples, pears) and adding citric acid to give fruit flavour. But worst of all, by the chemical treatment of crops which have gone mouldy and bad.

Chemical trickery is harder to spot than you might expect. The French government offers a £20,000 reward to the chemists who can produce a way of detecting chaptalisation, for example. The Germans have used carbon dating apparatus to try to detect frauds. On one occasion they were examining a bottle of port said to be a 1963 vintage. Port is a rich red wine, fortified by the addition of a spirit which must be grape brandy by law. The German scientists found to their puzzlement that the spirit in their sample was much older than 1963. Then they discovered the reason. It wasn't grape brandy at all, but imported potato spirit from Russia – which just so happened to be older.

On the other hand, some wine-growers will defend the chemist's role. The grower who has invested everything he's got, his money, time, energy, resources, in a crop which is then spoilt by rainstorms, hailstorms, frost, blight or disease, is not going to chuck it all away; he'll be determined to get something back from it. In the poor wine-growing areas of Gascony and Charente, the thin, acid grapes are not fit for wine, so they go to make the spirits of the area, Cognac and Armagnac. No one complains of the ways they direct their skills. To save bad harvests, French oenologists (the wine scientists who have replaced the craftsmen of old) can kill off unwanted bacteria and in some wines you can spot the preservative and anti-oxidant sulphur dioxide, a bad egg smell. They can also adjust poor vintages by judicious blending of wines of other years or from outside the region. French wine law carefully allows for this, and it is quite legal to add up to one fifth of imported wines, usually from Spain, Italy and *Algérie Française*, the hot, full-bodied wine giving strength to the thinner ones of France in certain years.

It's not only a question of taste, but economics. The soil and climate of Bordeaux, and in particular Burgundy, which produce such fine wines, do not give high yields of grapes per acre. They would expect 15,000 litres of wine per acre; but the neighbouring area of the Midi, with its hot Mediterranean climate, produces 4,000 litres of wine per acre. And Sicily in the sunny south yields 10,000 litres per acre, along with southern Spain and North Africa. (When France lost Algeria, the quality of certain French wines dropped immediately.) Experts say that in the lowest class of wines, the *vin de table*, it is quite right to beef up the product. A thin local wine and a robust imported wine benefit by association with each other. But when the customer thinks he's getting something rather special and he's not, the question of cheating arises. This doesn't happen with the wines of the South-West and the Midi which are rough and ready, and even the wines of the Rhône and Provence which are fairly basic, and not in great demand. But price comes into it as you go further north and out of the heavy Mediterranean sun; to the Upper Rhône valley and Burgundy, a small area which houses the even smaller area of Beaujolais, and the even smaller villages of Beaujolais like Morgon, Moulin-à-Vent, Chiroubles, Juliénas, Brouilly and Fleurie. Recently there was a case of Pouilly Fuissé, the great white Burgundy, being exported to the States and sold at up to $20 a bottle. It was found to be a quite ordinary *vin blanc* from the South.

In good years these wines have the wine writers rolling around in paroxysms of delight; and so mystique has grown up around them. This is good news to the merchants, who price their wines accordingly, and many are the times it has been said that more Beaujolais is drunk in Paris alone each year than is produced in Beaujolais.

With premium prices, you can see that the temptation to cheat is enormous, but here the French don't need to. Because the name of Burgundy sails so high, the less scrupulous wine-growers replant poor ground, where poor vines have been grubbed up, in order to have grapes growing within the defined legal limits. Then they supplement the inevitable thin years with heavy wines from the South.

People who swear by the name Burgundy have been innocently drinking wines far different from those praised by the experts. True, the wines are from the area, but as wine expert Anthony Hanson has recently pointed out in an important book on Burgundy, the real wine of the area is made from the quite light and delicate Pinot Noir grapes. He created a stir last year when he challenged the wine merchants with over-pricing these wines. He said: 'Most red Burgundy today is mediocre, without quality, and poor value for money. Briefly a rip-off. The Burgundians are coasting along on their reputation.'

Until recently Burgundy was thought to be a quite heavy full-bodied wine. Burgundy, a long way north from Mediterranean climes, only produces a really great vintage once every four or five years. The growers therefore build up the thin-bodied wine by doses of full-bodied and rich imported stuff. Fashions change. Not only is the true Burgundy made with Pinot Noir back in fashion (at anything from £8 a bottle in restaurants) but Beaujolais Nouveau from the same area is enjoying an astonishing vogue.

Beaujolais Nouveau is served only six weeks after the grapes are harvested, and it's the thing to drink it the day it arrives (the race to get it to Paris and London is particularly bizarre and a wonderful public relations exercise for the growers). In good years, this wine, properly called a *primeur* (the first wine) is a pleasant, lightly alcoholic fruit juice; in other years, fairly awful. Serious wine critics allow the young thing its day; it doesn't keep. Last year's *primeur* is like yesterday's newspaper, but probably someone somewhere will still manage to sell it to you.

The Hidden Side of Majorca

The African black vulture considers there's only one place in Europe safe to settle for the summer. It's Majorca. Strange, considering that in Majorca he'll be in the company of three million Britons. Yet, Britain's favourite Mediterranean island supports 50 miles of wild coastline, and some rare wildlife.

Most Britons travel in July and August and arrive at Europe's busiest airport, Palma, in frying pan heat. They are bussed to the hotelscapes of Palma Nova and El Arenal, and set about building up a burn, later taking to the discos to drink their weight in Pina Coladas.

But if you travel in May and June or September and October, when it's hot but not baking, you can experience a totally different world in the northern-most of the island's two mountain ranges only an hour's drive from the airport.

It won't suit the holiday maker intent on a package, because there are almost no sandy beaches, and your main pleasure comes from climbing up and down steep tracks in the valleys and rocks. But the scenery is spectacular. There is wildlife that deserves study, and there is good walking. climbing and swimming.

The only way is to stop the car, get out, and start walking. And at once the charm of this beautiful island can begin to work its spell, and soon you understand why it's called *La Isla de la Calma* – the Island of Calm.

Among the extraordinary sights are the 1,000-year-old olive trees, with trunks twisted by the winds over the centuries. Olive-growing was started by the Moors, who built tiers of dry stone walls rising to 2,000 ft, an engineering feat comparable with the drystone walling of Cuzco, the Inca city of Peru.

The north coastline starts at Valdemosa, a monastery town made famous by the short visit one winter of the pianist Chopin and his girlfriend, George Sands.

The road runs east through small villages and towns, down to Puerto Soller, then up to the grand chasm of the Torrentes de Pareis (unpassable in winter, but a great five-hour walk in summer when it's dry); then Pollensa, and finally the promontory of Formentor and its hotel (favoured by Prince Rainier and the Duke and Duchess of Kent).

Only one small town has a ready appeal for the tourist, Puerto Soller, a Spanish naval base with a shallow sandy bay and a pretty promenade, lined with boutiques. There is a charming old railway with open wooded carriages linking it with the inland town of Soller.

Walks along the mountain range are spectacular (but go with a guide and a party, taking heavy boots and thick trousers against the prickly shrubs); the walks down to the coves are superb, through olive groves where sheep with bells scamper.

The most sought-after area is Deyá, known as the Poet's Coast, because the great English poet, Robert Graves, now in his 80s, retired to live here.

The valley of Deyá, a hilltop town tucked into a protective arm-chair of mountains, is one of the joys of the island. A stream tumbles down, swelling to a thunderous river in winter, In the humid micro-climate fragrant tropical foliage flourishes alongside Mediterranean cypresses, oleander, bougainvillea.

Life on a holiday like this is very slow. Breakfast in the hotel or pension is coffee and *ensaimada*, a fluffy, yeasty sweet bun. Then a slow climb down to the cove, 30 minutes or so; swimming and sitting out on the rocks (no sand), picnicking in the pine woods, or lunching off grilled fish caught in the morning; by late afternoon, the slow haul back, this time a 40- or 50-minute climb, then a doze before supper.

On the Island of Calm this routine becomes hypnotically compelling. You listen with curiosity to other hasty guests who've made a breakneck, hairy tour of the island. They've seen *everything*. And yet they've seen nothing.

Gastronomic Grand Tour

Your friends won't be at all surprised to know you enjoyed a week eating out in Belgium. But they may be surprised to see that you haven't put on ten kilos doing it, particularly if you've been tempted into that paradise for game, the Ardennes.

Nouvelle cuisine, the lighter style of cooking which has become almost universal in France, was ignored by the Belgians until fairly recently. They simply preferred to gourmandise in the traditional way, enjoying rich game and fish with creamy, buttery sauces.

Just look at *Waterzooi*, the national Belgian dish celebrated around the world. It is usually a fish soup (there is also a chicken version) with carp, perch, pike and eel, poached in white wine and running with butter.

And the tradition of eating rich and sweet food doesn't stop in restaurants, cafés and bars. Stop in any small town square and gaze in wonder at the rich sweet tarts and cakes, with rich and buttery pastry, and thick sweet fruits in sugar syrup and dredged, or drenched, in icing sugar. Tarts of *myrtilles* (blueberries), gooseberry, cherries, finely shredded rhubarb, strawberries, apricot jam, apple turnovers in brioche, rice and egg custard tarts, *galettes*, waffles, éclairs, frothy flan cases, nougat with almonds, and pancakes stuffed with *crème patissier*.

But it seems that Belgians too are becoming conscious of the warnings the doctors have been urging these last ten years. It's interesting to sit at a pavement café in Liège to see some of the fattest and some of the thinnest people in Europe walking by.

The fat people have been gorging themselves on the treats in the local restaurants; here they serve grills, traditional dishes of *grenouilles* (frogs) and *escargots* (snails); *pommes frites*, mussels with mayonnaise, rich and sweet pancakes, and even Chinese and North African specialities. The thin people have obviously renounced the Belgian cooking traditions completely.

Happily there is now a compromise, and you only need to go to the *Michelin Guide to Belgium*, with its strict standards, to discover a long list of new style restaurants which respect your waist.

I chose the Ardennes for what you might term my cook's tour for the simple reason that even I realize there's more to a holiday than eating. This southerly region of hills is covered with beautiful forests, traversed by a web of rivers and studded with historical towns and villages. They have a chequered history which embraces not only the neighbouring French, Dutch and German cultures but

Austrian and Spanish too.

For me the Ardennes is also a marvellous area in which to walk up a healthy appetite. The real pleasure of the deep mysterious forests is only apparent when you park the car beside a path and go for a stroll. Here you will walk on a carpet of pine needles, with pines and firs closing to a roof above your head 40 or 50 feet high. There is dappled sunlight. Birdsong. Tranquillity. The air is still and warm. You begin to see velvety green mosses, ferns, pine nuts, wild mushrooms, cones, old tree stumps to sit on. Peace is yours as you step away from the other world which races by.

Besides walking, the Ardennes offers the obvious sporting amenities of cycling, riding, canoeing and camping. First class roads knit the area together and you need never fear to follow your map when you see a weak or wavy line. These roads are good roads. The biggest danger will be avoiding helmeted racing cyclists swooping downhill like bullets, wobbling as they climb their way slowly up the next hill, thighs slowly pumping.

To make the most of the region you really do need to study the guide books; and certainly if you mean to make the most of Belgium's great cuisine. It wouldn't be a complete waste of time to take pot luck, because even the cheapest food is good: yet with so many gastronomic treasures to exploit, it's like going to Rheims to see the railway station instead of the cathedral.

So when it comes to gourmandising how do you find the best? We set ourselves to solve this problem in the little town of Rochefort, on our first day. It bustled with plenty of cafés around the main crossroads. It is a popular tourist centre with a safari park a few miles away, many multi-coloured underground grottoes and stately chateaux sited elegantly along the River Semois.

The guide books recommend Auberge Falizes. We found it quickly and liked its elegance, its promising gourmet menu, and the charm of its pretty setting under the trees. But at the beginning of a holiday we wanted to share the experience of the locals, so we asked at the local tourist office which restaurant? All are good, they smiled diplomatically.

We picked the Limbourg, full of plump, local businessmen and Belgian families. It was a marvellous meal, wonderful clean setting, good service, delicious food. Fresh green celery soup; terrine of game, juicy and chunky; crudités, grated carrot with mustardy dressing, red pickled cabbage, tomato, finely grated raw onion, slices of cucumber in vinegar dressing: wild boar for one of us; rare steak smothered in mushrooms and a creamy sauce for the other: for sweet, a tasty custard caramel and a raspberry sorbet.

It can be boring to read a plate by plate account of meals; like making love, it is immensely enjoyable for those taking part, but the sensual pleasure of eating is largely subjective.

But I did find it interesting to have experienced two quite opposite sensations eating in the Ardennes. On one occasion, we were almost bludgeoned into oblivion by a restaurant's gourmandly attitude to providing a meal and then on another, we were so subtly seduced by temptations we did not think ourselves greedy when we had consumed the lot, nor did we begrudge the size of the bill.

For the gourmand, rather than the gourmet, perhaps we should describe Le Sanglier des Ardennes in Durbuy, half an hour south of Liège. Le Sanglier figures in most of the articles written by the world's travel writers, so it sets out to create a memorable experience. And it does, but like the Eiffel tower (and the North Face of the Eiger) you may not choose to go that way again.

The stone building, beside the bridge, looks centuries old but a plaque set in its baroque walls proclaims it is only from 1904. We wanted to stay there in the hotel, but the rooms have no bathroom or shower so we chose to stay in the smart annexe across the road. On this hot summer night it was a good decision, especially returning from our meal at midnight, when we reached greedily for the cold cans of crisp Spa water in the bedroom fridge.

Back at the restaurant, as this was to be our introduction to Belgian grande cuisine, we asked for the Menu Gastronomique; perhaps it should be called La Grande Bouffe.

As we sat down at a window table overlooking the calm river trickling in the evening light, we sensed an ordeal to come. First the glasses. In front of us, snaking in an S-shape, were six slim glasses. Three each were for the three white wines which would accompany our first three courses.

The meal unfolds, served by an anxious team of young boys and girls carrying plates covered in silver cloches. To begin, an aspic of poached trout and salmon trout and a glass of Vecchio, a dry Italian white. Then a piece of grilled trout, off the bone, criss-crossed with a hot skewer to make an attractive trellis pattern, served with a pink tomato sauce speckled with shreds of red sweet pepper; this came with Chenin Blanc, a full-flavoured white wine from South Africa.

Pleasant dishes, but frankly not surprising. Then an original dish: tender, slow-simmered snails, with a purée of watercress, the nutty flavour of the snails perfectly complemented by the hot tang of the green sauce. With it Greno, another Italian wine with a dryness which perfectly matches the dish.

Now comes an interval and the white wine glasses are removed to be replaced with six red wine glasses. We're invited to choose pear William sorbet or jellied consommé to refresh our palates. Then back to the serious meal.

Now comes saddle of rabbit with a salad of curly endive and lamb's lettuce; we tuck this away and immediately the next dish arrives, nuggets of wild boar, served with a savoury game sauce. With the rabbit comes a simple claret, a Bergeron from the Haut Médoc; with the boar, a meatier claret altogether, Château Mayney St Estèphe 1977.

Give up? No. On to the cheese. We can't manage the rich brie offered and ask for a local cheese, and are served with thimble-sized goat's cheeses; they do well in the company of a rich burgundy, Château Charles I Mercury 1978.

The final act is the dessert, a colourful plate of red fruits, strawberries, redcurrants, myrtleberries, with a raspberry coulis (strained, crushed fresh raspberries). A seventh wine glass appears: we are drinking a pink champagne with it.

We've been in the restaurant over three hours: darkness has fallen: the river sparkles still. We're finished. We stagger to our feet and feel the relief of moving our bodies again. Enough of the Grande Bouffe.

So Belgium is still a country which honours the spirit, the notion of a great repast. But it has also responded to new attitudes to cooking, and it was notable that the meals we ate in Michelin-starred restaurants showed great restraint in the richness of the food.

The most recommended restaurant in the Ardennes is probably Moulin Hideux, at Noirefontaine with two rosettes. As it was fully booked, we drove on to a one-star establishment in Robertville, almost as far to the east as you can go within the Belgian Ardennes. We arrived there after exploring the Hautes Fagnes, high forest land, and having visited the highest spot, the Point Culminant de Belgique, some 700 metres above sea level.

The meal was exquisite and light; we had Ogen melon with Ardennes ham, smoky slices cut as thin as tissue paper – Ardennes ham, a speciality of the region, is smokier, saltier and moister, than most – a gourmet experience in itself; a salad of thinly sliced ceps with morsels of foie gras, pine nuts, lettuce and walnut oil dressing; langoustine pungently flavoured with chervil and the tiniest portion of minute green noodles, garnished with tomato. And an extraordinary *tour de force*, a feathery light, frothy, warm slice of lobster terrine, swimming in butter and fresh herbs, served in a cradle of shredded carrots and beans, spinach purée, tomato concassé, pieces of salty samphire – a rare, tender plant which grows in salt marshes.

In a dreamy daze of gastronomic satisfaction we swooned into the pleasure of marvellous plates of scented fresh red fruit and frothy ice cream soufflés; and for me a plate of warm strawberries. Then dark chocolate petit fours and good strong coffee, outside on the garden patio.

On to Alle in the farthest south-west of the Ardennes. We'd intended staying in the medieval town of Bouillon but it was so noisy due to a fête that we looked up the guide books, rang the Auberge Alle, and booked a meal and a room there. The road which winds from Bouillon to Alle is one of the loveliest in the Ardennes, climbing and falling to valleys where until recently the main crop was tobacco; you still see the wooden sheds used for drying the pungent leaf. You pass many enchanting villages before you find Alle, and the Auberge is set, with some dignity, back from the main village.

M. George, as he likes to be known, took over the Auberge 16 years ago and runs it, with his wife and daughter, like a country inn; although it's full of oak beams and panels, with a painted ceiling which might belong to the 16th century, it was, amazingly, built in 1949.

There is nothing novel or strange or exotic about the menu. The cooking is simply perfect from a vegetable terrine (which was really a pleasant new way with Russian salad, and a country pâté of pork and rabbit, jellied with aspic; *truite au bleu*, from the fish tank, looking like a grey flying angel on the plate; nuggets of saddle of lamb with a tiny piece of fat adhering to give flavour, crisp outside, tender and pink inside; a sauce of the meat juices with a suggestion of cream and Dijon mustard; a plate of fresh red fruits you'd swear were hand-picked minutes before, served with a tart and almost too cheesy crème fraîche. Lastly, coffee, sweet, bitter, black and smooth. You'd love to go back again and again.

The World's Top Chef

The world's greatest restaurants are usually found in cities like London, Brussels, New York and Paris, or else in lovely rural settings among hills and parks, lakes and rivers.

Frédy Girardet's restaurant is in Crissier, a village of 4,000 inhabitants on the outskirts of Lausanne in Switzerland. To reach it you may have to drive along a curving dual carriageway through a cheerless industrial estate. The restaurant is on a busy crossroads, a building of unremarkable bourgeois dignity which looks like a town hall. That's exactly what it was, the municipal town hall.

But one step inside, and you encounter a magical world of comfort and delight.

Frédy Girardet is a proud, shy Swiss, an almost entirely self-taught chef who has spent the last 17 years transforming himself from a modest bistro cook to the man now fêted as best chef in the world. Some say the greatest chef since Escoffier 90 years ago.

The British restaurant critic Egon Ronay describes Girardet as 'the best cook in the world'. Richard Binns, author of *French Leave III*, claims he is head and shoulders above the French chefs. Even Paul Bocuse, who invented *nouvelle cuisine* 20 years ago, pays this homage: 'Girardet is a genius in the kitchen. He is the only chef who ever surprises me.'

Frédy Girardet is a grey-haired man of 48 with the worried look of a bulldog. He is nothing like the smiling fat chefs of popular image who've eaten too well and too often. He has the lean tough frame of the athlete hardened by constant exercise – racing his bicycle over the Alps. He goes cross-country skiing in Sweden. He plays football with his staff, or goes jogging. He is also plainly scornful of other people's greedy attitudes to eating.

Girardet is one of the new breed of Europe's chef-patrons who reign supreme in their own restaurants. They've taken over from the chefs who used to work for the great hotels and restaurants. They are the stars of gastronomy and are treated as celebrities on television. Some travel the world demonstrating their skills in New York, Tokyo, on ocean liners. But Girardet never leaves his restaurant. 'My work is my obsession,' he explains.

When you eat at his restaurant you may well find that your fellow diners are the rich and famous. Prince Philip, Bjorn Borg, David Bowie, Richard Burton, the Chaplin family and Peter Ustinov have eaten here and a host of other world personalities. Richard Nixon turned up unexpectedly once. After midnight.

Girardet is flattered by this attention and realises that it is good for business. But he is more proud that half his customers are Swiss and come from nearby. In order to maintain his superlative standards, Girardet presents himself as a hard, almost impossible man to deal with. But he is harder with himself than others and he does create a smiling atmosphere of happiness and hospitality in the restaurant.

The family presence is evident: his mother Georgette greets guests; his wife Muriel and daughter Rachel help him; a friendly Airedale, Santos, wags his tail; and a highly polished and friendly team of waiters (14 staff serve the 60 diners) are utterly attentive; in the kitchen the 18 keen young chefs are smiling and welcoming, happy to show you what they're doing.

The restaurant is clean and unpretentious. There are bare brown tiles, simple high rush-seated chairs, brown tablecloths; on the walls, paintings by Girardet's favourite Swiss artists. The real showpiece is the kitchen – 'a laboratory where base products are turned into gold' is how one critic described it. It is large, light and well-ventilated, and there's almost no smoke, no splashed fat and no cooking smells. Twice a day it is cleaned so spotlessly that when mother Georgette sometimes takes guests on a tour before they leave they remark with bewilderment that there is no food to be seen at all.

A meal, any meal, in Girardet's restaurant is unforgettable. You're welcomed in his upstairs bar with a glass of local Swiss wine, grown specially for him.

The first taste of a Girardet dish is an appetiser – an '*amuse-gueule*' to tickle the palate. It is a tiny sliver of savoury egg and onion tart, sweet, frothy.

Girardet sets out to present dishes you would never eat anywhere else. So the first course is just that: you have never had anything like it. A square of puff pastry with tender girolle mushrooms and garlic-scented tiny white balls; but what are they? The meat is from frogs' legs, skinned and removed from the bone!

The next course is fish. The plate is as decorative as a bright, abstract painting. Here is a fillet of John Dory with anchovy butter, served with a tiny mousse of sweet red peppers and sautéed vegetables.

Another fish dish follows. It's called a *cassolette* of shellfish. It consists of a large Dublin Bay prawn, rosy and orange in hue, and a tender lobster tail with scarlet and ruby patches. The large prawn has been tossed in a frying pan for moments only; the lobster is put into boiling water, but before it can harden, is removed, shelled, and baked in a low oven for 20 minutes.

The dish is vividly decorated with thin carrot discs, cut into rose shapes, floating in a pool of natural juices to make up the sauce. There is a hint of fresh herbs: chives, celery, lovage.

You're thinking this all very clever, all very pretty, when in comes a succulent roast duck. Its skin is crisped to a caramelised sweetness. Then the leg is taken away and returned to the oven to cook 15 minutes longer. It will be ready by the time you've finished eating the breast. It is served with slices of bitter-sweet baby turnips, overlapping like 10p pieces, grilled quickly with a dribble of cream.

A 'salad' is served. But put out of your mind visions of drowning lettuce. This artist-chef shaves fine ribbons of rusty-green radic-chio and arranges it beautifully with crunchy purple leaves of batavia, twists of curly endive and shreds of baby carrot dressed with wine vinegar and a hint of hazelnut oil.

Now they wheel in a cheese trolley under glass, like a terrarium. If Girardet's main produce comes from abroad each day, these cheeses are wholly Swiss – a selection of 30 from mountain farmers he has urged to develop their own style. Some style! Juicy, tasty, creamy and sharp. The local Swiss red wine rolls round them in your mouth.

Now comes the sweet. Rather, the sweets. The waiters will encourage you to try them all. Some are very sweet, like Vaudois Tart and Oriental Oranges. Others are sharp with fresh fruit, like Passion Fruit Soufflé, but some are immensely rich like Black Forest Gâteau, but offset by a hard back-taste of plum brandy.

Just for an awful moment you wonder if this fabulous meal might founder on a sweet and sickly note. But no; he hauls you back with a powerful shot of strong black coffee. (Why can't everyone make real coffee like this?) The petit-four, a winningly seductive bit-ter-sweet chocolate truffle, vanishes in your mouth, like so many of his creations. There is no after-effect, no sense of over-indulgence.

It is now time to leave. Customers will have paid from £60 to £100 a head, but it seems well worth it: 'He honours your desires,' said one contented lady diner all the way from Chicago, 'but he makes your desires honourable.'

Girardet's life story is extraordinary. His ambition was to become a professional footballer, but he seemed destined to follow his father in the kitchen, when, at 18, his parents took over a mod-est bistro in Crissier.

Very suddenly, when Girardet was 19, his father died, and his mother asked him to take over.

It was a traumatic experience. He wasn't ready for the responsi-bility, and he didn't want to cook. He still wanted to be a footballer. It was some years before he discovered that cooking might be a wor-thy career.

When it came, the conversion was as sudden as St Paul's. A reg-ular customer, a lorry driver, invited Girardet on a trip to Burgundy.

There he introduced him to a friendly wine-grower, Jacques Parent, who took an immediate liking to him. He took him to lunch at the Troisgros Restaurant in Roanne, run by two brothers, Pierre and Jean, who were fast becoming two of the most famous chefs in France. Jean died last year, sadly.

'I realised I had slept through life until now,' says Girardet. He had never even been to a great restaurant before, let alone trained in one. 'I suddenly understood that there was an art called gastronomy and that I had a talent for it.'

Nouvelle cuisine, the style to which he was introduced, which was developed 20 years earlier in France, exploits natural flavours, rejecting conventional creamy, rich dishes which are the essence of traditional restaurant cooking. Girardet was inspired by the idea of the chef as an artist, making the food look beautiful on the plate. Until this New Wave, it was unimportant, something waiters did at the table in front of the customer.

For three years Girardet devoted himself solely to experimenting and composing dishes.

He did not become an overnight success, any more than a boy inspired by a football comic steps out to play in an international. 'The price was a lot of long, lonely and painstaking research,' says his friend Catherine Michel, who helped him prepare his recipe book, *La Cuisine Spontanée*, recently published in France (Robert Laffont, 160F).

When he was 33 he went to the bank for a loan, and without giving up the family bistro was able to buy the ground floor dining-room in the local town hall. It took him five years of very hard work before he came to the notice of Paris food critics. But his success from that point was assured and today they rave about him.

How did Girardet achieve this excellence? By indulging an obsession for perfection and taking fresh produce from all over the world each morning, and only using it on the day of arrival. He will not keep even a live lobster a second day. 'After that,' he says, 'the texture of the flesh begins to suffer, I'm sure. Fish can never be kept overnight. The taste disappears. It loses firmness.' So, every day fresh lobsters arrive at Geneva, flown in from Shannon; oysters and shellfish from Brittany; crayfish and shrimps from Greece; lorries bring in the individually cared-for chickens from Bresse, a few hours away. Local winemakers make wines specially for him, and local suppliers send cheeses as well. A baker in the village makes rolls and breads to his specification.

Freshness and quality are essential, but Girardet's real genius is his instinctive knowledge of the essence of each ingredient. He searches out extremes of taste and flavour to appeal to all the senses: juicy, savoury and salt, spicy and smooth, bitter and sour, smoky and burnt, tart and acid, scented and rich. Like a composer or a painter he seems to push a note too far, then magically resolves it. Gourmets speak of Girardet's 'fabulous creativity' and his spontaneity: in the more traditional kitchens the chef creates a dish and then his staff reproduce this exactly week after week, often year after year. But Girardet changes his creations every day. He is never satisfied. His work seems more a passion than a pleasure. In his quest for perfection he can't take life easily. He worries as the pressure mounts each day in the kitchen. His face goes glum as he confronts a fault, and sometimes his face blackens to a thundercloud, and the chefs stay out of his way till the moment passes. Is the day's produce fresh enough? Do the chefs understand his new dishes? Have all the customers arrived? Because he has not learnt from other chefs, he tends to make original discoveries. No one cooks a lobster the way he does. The same with a soufflé. To prevent it from drying out, he controls the initial temperature by nursing it in a bain-marie on top of the stove to start it; he finishes it in the oven. It comes out creamy, gentle and light. His Passion Fruit Soufflé has this quality, but is sharpened by the juice of this uniquely tart fruit.

He uses cream, but you barely notice it in sauces. He prefers small quantities of the natural juices. He 'deglazes' a pan in which he has sautéed goose liver with a little wine vinegar, stirring hazelnut oil. That's all. He disarms the crude garlic bulb by simmering the cloves in water till soft to make a scented purée. He takes humble parsley, fries it with shallots and cream and serves it as a vegetable.

A dish of rice, his special risotto, becomes an Aladdin's cave of treasures, with morsels of foie gras, frogs' legs, truffles. We may not have the same superb ingredients to experiment with, but Girardet's message is clear. All of us can succeed if we're prepared to trust our senses, learn from our failures and try and try again. The rewards, he assures us, are vast beyond imagining.

The Emergent Cookery of Australia

Australia must be the last great country in the world to discover cookery. But now the art of cuisine has hit them like an ocean wave, and they are tackling it with the sort of demonic commitment and invention they put into everything from their rugby and their sailing to their wine-making and their films. The results are prodigious.

In the immortal words of Paul Hogan, star of Crocodile Dundee, 'You can live on it, but it tastes like ****'

He was talking about some grubs he'd dug up in a crocodile swamp. But he might have been describing Australian cooking.

In 200 years Australia hasn't won any prizes for its gastronomy. 'This cuisine is elementary, not to say abominable,' was the comment of an early French gourmet.

In the Fifties, when Poms were emigrating on £12 assisted passages Professor Denis Brogan, the BBC Brain's Trust personality, claimed that cooking a potato was 'beyond the culinary resources of an Australian hotel'.

Australians find their fellow countryfolk's food pretensions very funny. They laugh with glee at Dame Edna Everage's portraits of Melbourne's middle-class mums swapping recipes like Pavlova cake, while they pick at the Vegemite sandwiches and Lamingtons (Australian chocolate-covered cakes rolled in coconut flakes).

We also assume from Paul Hogan's lager ads, that most Australians dine off eating charred steaks from the barbie, swilling it down with crates of chilled tinnies.

So how would we know that 12,000 miles away they no longer call you a Pinko or a Pooftah if you ask for a glass of wine in a bar? And that in the last 20 years, the Australian wine industry has risen like a phoenix to become the envy of the New World.

And far from cooling down on the lager, smart young Australians take a wine-box of Australian Rhine Riesling to the beach; and what they don't finish they take to one of the thousands of pleasant, casual, easy-going BYO restaurants – Bring Your Own.

A restaurant revolution has followed the wine revolution. But it's so new that the Australian Tourist Commission has only just dared British wine and food writers to see for themselves. They weren't disappointed.

Of course, news of changes have been filtering through. David Frost, surely the most widely travelled diner in the world, raves about the great seafood restaurants of Sydney; crayfish as large as lobsters, huge, sweet-tasting mud crabs, tender little mussels, nutty rock oysters from Sydney harbour. And strange little natives like yabbies, a freshwater crayfish, and Moreton Bay Bugs, a small flat nose lobster.

And Carol Thatcher the PM's daughter, no gourmet, came back from a job in radio thrilling at their healthy diet; an abundance of seafood, vegetables and fresh tropical fruit; everything from avocado and bananas to mango and paw paw grow in Queensland's tropical sun.

The explosion in eating out is very recent. The new *Sydney Good Food Guide* is testimony to this. Like the New Wave it is in its infancy, only two years old. But what it records is the mushrooming of ethnic restaurants, the immense success of cheaper styles of eating, Vietnamese, Thai, Malaysian, Mexican, as well as the firmly rooted Greek, Italian, Japanese and Chinese.

Some of the Japanese and Chinese restaurants are better than any you can get in London, says David Wolfe, a British expert on Asian cooking. The chefs are nearer 'home', working with familiar Pacific ingredients at peak of perfection.

Some of the Japanese restaurants are very classy, like Sydney's Suntory. And you're not welcome in casual clothes, a reminder that Japan is Australia's number one trading partner. But others are cheap and cheerful, especially those around the Kings Cross area of Sydney, a delightfully sleazy area which reminds you of Fifties' Soho.

Many Chinese restaurants are terrific. Sydney and Melbourne both have large Chinatowns – the Chinese came to Australia in the 1850s to work the gold mines. You can tell from the large number of

Chinese eating in them that they are authentic. And in Sydney, the Imperial Peking Waterside is one of the great Chinese restaurants in the world, equal to many in Hong Kong.

The swank hotels have stepped up their acts, too. The major hotels in the big cities have to have classy restaurants to net the wealthy international travellers. French classical cooking is the model, but there are increasingly confident overtones of native Australia.

Melbourne's newly built Park Royal Hotel boasts a fabulous range of Pacific fish, from Barramundi and ocean perch to St George's Bat Whiting, Black-eyed trevally, blue-eyed grenadier, gemfish, oilfish, jewfish, swordfish, blue swimmer crabs. And the new Intercontinental in Sydney, with its incomparable views of Sydney Harbour Bridge, the full-sailed Opera House, and Botanical Gardens, supplements its wine list with Australian classics. Like the 20-year-old Grange Hermitage they poured for us – pretty good but at £200 a bottle, it ought to be.

The grandest hotel in Australia is probably Burnham Beeches, set in the splendour of the Dandenong Hills, north of Melbourne. It is one of the prestigious French Relais and Chateau chain, and has French, Japanese – and Australian –chefs. The youngest Australian recruit to the staff was bubbling with enthusiasm; for the first time in Australia, he said, to work as a cook was a step up the social ladder and not a step down.

But somewhere between the grand hotels and the ethnics, a new chic style is emerging. Stephanie's in Melbourne, run by Stephanie Alexander in an Italianate Palace, offers not only the city's best food, but it is the best place to be seen. In Sydney, Chez Oz is the new in-place, with designer food and designer décor, and a smart young crowd dressed in studied and expensive casual wear. The food is good and the prices high. The owners of this kind of place have usually had no professional training in the kitchens. Many are women, and highly-educated too.

The superb example is Berowra Waters Inn which was started by Gay Bilson, a Melbourne University Arts student, and her boyfriend Tony. She now runs it with her Greek-born chef, Janni Kyritsis, a former electrician. Between them, they have established world-wide recognition, and many consider the restaurant Australia's best.

They break all the rules. The setting of the restaurant itself is a fierce expression of commitment. It is far from potential customers at the heart of Sydney, 30 miles away, an hour's drive to a maze of deep rivers jungled with steep cliffs of eucalyptus.

You can drive north out of the city, taking in Botany Bay where Captain Cook landed with his botanists, Greville and Banks. From then on you'll pass through the wondrous Bush, populated by scarlet and orange wattle and bottlebrush. Into the wooded creeks, dotted with vermilion poinsettia trees and purple flowers of the jacarandas. Then to the wide emerald tributary of the Hawkesbury River, where you must take a boat for the last half mile to the restaurant, to dismount on a landing stage on the fern-lined bank. (Some customers fly in by aeroplane.)

In front of you is this functional modern building designed by the architect, Glenn Murcutt. It's in what they call Australian vernacular, which is to say it looks like a sheep-shearing shed with a long flat corrugated roof. But once inside, you turn to embrace a spectacular view through the louvred 12ft high glass windows, the sight of steep cliffs crowded with eucalyptus and white boned angophora trees. It's as if you're viewing from a verandah.

The décor is minimalist; light beige, mushroom, pale olive. There are no flowers on the tables. 'They detract from the view,' says Gay, straight-haired blond young owner.

'I don't have flowers. And I loathe pretty plates. I don't like mixed-up flavours either. I like everything to be very clean. Like champagne is clean.'

With her chef, Janni, she says she has set out to create experiences which are more than a meal. 'It's not the food that you eat, it's the memory that you'd like to linger. I think of meals I've had in France and Italy.'

Like many Australians of her generation, she has travelled the world, and what she does in Berowra is a synthesis of what she's brought back, and what she finds in Australia. 'I love French food, but I want to get away from that model. Their sauces are marvellous, but I avoid strong reductions. I love Italian food, it's so gutsy. I love olive oil. But I also love the tastes of the Orient. Japanese raw fish, seaweed, hot radish. And Chinese fresh ginger, and star anise, and other spices. I love our fish. And our tropical fruit. I think of the passion fruit as Australian – it's easily my favourite.'

The meal she created that day was indeed a meal to linger in the memory. As the sun powered down on the deep waters where families cut swathes with their leisure boats, we enjoyed a succession of delights.

Baby goat cheeses, dressed in virgin olive oil; saffron yellow shellfish soup with lobster wantons; a salad of squid with pancetta (crispy Italian cured ham) and black noodles which are coloured by the ink of the squid.

Steamed ocean perch, sautéed skate, roast rock ling. A caul of pigs' trotters with minced ox tongue (she may have re-invented haggis). For sweets, baked quinces with coeur de la crème, a roulade of pancakes as thin as tissue paper, filled with orange butter and pralines, a chequerboard of anise-flavoured ice-creams.

True Confessions on a Plate

After 30 years of publishing sponsored restaurant guides, Egon Ronay has produced his first unsponsored book. It is a record of his life in the food business and is called *The Unforgettable Dishes of My Life* (Victor Gollancz, £17.95).

It is a life which brought him from pre-war Hungary, where he and his father, and his grandfather before him, ran fashionable restaurants, to the gastronomic desert of post-war Britain – a land of long-boiled cabbage and dried-up, curling sandwiches, where he was to raise the standards of mass catering almost single-handedly.

On one level, he has policed popular catering for 30 years, campaigning for better food in motorway cafés, airport restaurants, airline catering, and over-seeing the efforts of institutions such as schools, hospitals and canteens.

Inevitably, Ronay's criticisms have made him enemies, none more powerful than Lord Forte, of Trusthouse Forte plc hotel and catering fame. Forte is suing him for an article about London airport restaurants in the newsletter of the British Gastronomic Academy, which Ronay founded two years ago. 'I was asked to apologise but I refused. I have no fear of speaking my mind, and if it upsets people, it can't be helped. I wouldn't back down if it came to selling my house.'

On another level, Ronay has raised the standing of British chefs. In 1977, in one of his boldest entrepreneurial initiatives, he took five British chefs to Maxim's in Paris to cook for 200 international food critics, altering at a stroke the French disregard for British restaurant cooking.

And year after year, he has singled out the best of British chefs. Many chefs, first discovered by him in their early days, are now considered as good as their counterparts anywhere in the world. He was first to single out Pierre Koffmann, now chef-patron of La Tante Claire, when he was chef for Michel Roux at the Waterside Inn, and to praise Raymond Blanc when he opened his first restaurant 10 years ago in an Oxford suburb.

Egon Ronay is a quietly spoken, intensely courteous man. But his eyes are keen and watchful, and with his spiky crest of short hair he resembles a small but pugnacious species of Amazonian bird. Three decades of eating in restaurants have done nothing to swell his figure. Now in his seventies and looking more than 10 years younger, the 'Public Stomach' is as trim as he is slim. He has sold the Egon Ronay guides to the Automobile Association, remaining as consultant only, and spends less time in his London home. This is close to Bibendum, where a former guide inspector, Simon Hopkinson, is chef and partner ('What a down-to-earth, anti-snob approach to food,' says Ronay). He now spends more of his time at his home in the Berkshire Downs, a short drive from Blanc's Manoir aux Quat'Saisons. He has built a cellar in his 300-year-old timbered home, where he stocks wines which will not mature for a long time. 'When buying wine, you have to make the assumption you will live for ever,' he says.

Egon Ronay's family were from Transylvania before it was submerged into Hungary. 'It was one of the great cuisines of the world,' he says.

His first visit to England, as a teenager, was a rude shock. 'It wasn't so much that the food was inedible: it simply had no interest in it. Nobody was interested in food.' Ronay cites the humble cucumber, ignored here as a limp garnish, but celebrated in Hungary as a dish in its own right, with paprika, salt and sour cream.

When Egon Ronay returned to Britain in 1945, to escape the Russians who were sending white-collar workers to Siberia, he arrived without a penny, and a wife and two young daughters to provide for. After two jobs as a restaurant manager, he boldly opened his own restaurant, The Marquee, in Piccadilly. It proved a unique vantage point from which to observe the beginning of a revolution in social attitudes to eating out. 'When I first came you could eat well in top-class restaurants and hotels, where there were French chefs, but there was nothing in the medium range, apart from Lyons Corner Houses, where you could get a good breakfast, kippers, bacon and eggs. Some of the food was unbelievable, those strange tennis-ball things, Scotch eggs, very badly done.

'The people who influenced food at this time had been to public school, where the food had been not just without interest, but horrifying. So you didn't discuss food.

'The big social change came in the Sixties, when people who had been to grammar schools, and eaten good food at home, started coming to restaurants. They were used to speaking their mind.'

The Daily Telegraph asked him to write a dining-out column, and a new career opened up. He sold the restaurant, and eventually put together his first restaurant guide book, based on 170 London restaurant reviews, which he published himself in 1957, thanks to getting the Ford Motor Company to take adverts in it. It set the precedent for sponsorship for his guides (from the British Motor Corporation, British Gas, Lucas) and gave him the commercial footing to build up a commercial inspectorate, distancing him from his main rival, the essentially amateur *Good Food Guide*. In those days the latter was an immensely readable but not always reliable compendium of comments sent in by readers.

But in 1958 he had an inspectorate of one: with a colleague, he made a painful journey around the whole country, eating two lunches each a day, and two dinners. 'It was a gruelling experience,' he remembers. 'The food was almost always dreadful.'

There must have been some funny stories? 'No. It made me very angry to see how things were. To see how little needed to be done to turn things round. Why not good coffee? You have the coffee, you have the water, and the heat. It puzzles me. Why shouldn't the simplest things be marvellous?'

He determined that his inspectors should be people with eloquent feelings about basic standards – not gourmets assessing the correctness of a lobster bisque. Although he is no longer at the helm, he writes the introductions to the growing family of guides – the Egon Ronay PG Tips *Just a Bite*; the *Coca-Cola Guide* (food in pubs); the *Access Guide* (European restaurants). Next month he is godfather to a new baby: Egon Ronay's H J Heinz Guide *And Baby Comes Too*, places which cater for small children.

In *Unforgettable Dishes*, Ronay celebrates home cooking (especially his wife's), but the palm is awarded for those he considers the true artists, worthy of the respect offered to painters and musicians. In Britain he singles out Pierre Koffmann of La Tante Claire. 'I think he is the best chef in Britain, such finesse, but with a rough, peasant rustic side.' And the outstanding chef in the world has to be Frédy Girardet of Lausanne in Switzerland. 'I have had four or five of the best meals of my life at Girardet's. Every dish is remarkable and each meal is like a symphony. I have never had such dishes of unlikely ingredients. You can copy him, as you might play a melody by Mozart, but no-one can compose like him.'

He has no thought of retiring. He continues to write (attacking irradiation of food on aesthetic as well as safety grounds) and will publish more books. They will not have food pictures, which he believes act against the appreciation of cookery. 'Photographers make dishes look perfect and unrealistic. You get a complex. You feel you'll never be able to achieve them. Homely dishes are unphotogenic.'

He reflects that there has never been a successful food magazine here as there are in other countries. 'I think it's because we go for presentation, the visual effect, the snob appeal. It's food for voyeurs, but it's not sincere. It doesn't come from the heart. Cooking is a matter of love.'

1. HOW WILL YOU START, SIR?

2. SOUSED NORWEGIAN HERRING?

3. THEN, HOT INDIAN CURRY...

4. OR SPANISH PAELLA?

5 THEN MY OWN TURKISH DELIGHT..

6. OR OUR SPECIALITY "ANGELS ON HORSEBACK"

Smokescreen

Hardly a month goes by without some new smoked delicacy surfacing on the supermarket shelves. And not just traditional hams and fish, but chicken, turkey, pigeon, quail, cheese.

Safeway's, who introduced smoked Scottish venison this year, are so pleased with the results, they've become smoke-crazed. 'Smoked food is suddenly considered exotic,' explains the Safeway's buyer. 'It adds a little excitement.' But what are we to make of their weirdest novelty, smoked garlic? How do you eat it? 'Cut it into slivers and stuff them into incisions in your Sunday roast,' he suggests.

This revived taste for smoke is certainly an upmarket thing. Harrods Food Hall has doubled its sales of smoked foods this year, especially imported smoked meat from Germany, Switzerland, Italy, France and Poland.

Fashionable restaurants don't feel they're ahead of the game unless they have some new smoked item on the menu, like smoked meats in a salad. Anthony Worrall Thompson, the entrepreneurial London restaurateur, read an article on a chef making sauces with smoked butter, and decided he had to have some.

He asked a smokery if they could make it. Smoke is hot, so how do you stop the butter melting? It was damn tricky but they obliged. You refrigerate the smoke.

British smokeries are on the crest of a wave and the best of them are weathering the storm unleashed by the EEC, whose new hygiene regulations threatened to see off Britain's antiquated smokehouses. A few have gone to the wall, but the rest report ever-increasing sales.

The more traditional smokers are regarding the expanding market with astonishment. John Brown of Inverawe Smokery, who uses a traditional brick smokehouse to produce exquisite smoked rainbow trout, smoked cod's roe, and eel, looks on at the changing trend with suspicion.

'There's a movement afoot; if it moves, smoke it.'

That might well be the motto of one of his neighbours, Macdonald's smokery, where they smoke alligator and ostrich, barracuda and flying fish, not to mention mussels, scallops, quail and, this year, frogs' legs. It was he who smoked Mr Worrall Thompson's butter.

People with long memories will be amazed at the trend. Throughout history, the object of salting and smoking food was preservation rather than delectation. Smoked salmon in the mid-19th century was a crude affair, heavily salted and smoked. Although, Kettner's *Book of the Table*, published in 1877, says a slice grilled is 'a dainty breakfast dish, if you can get one fresh which has undergone the kippering process for not more than two or three days.'

Achieving good flavour was usually of secondary consideration, and although the smoking of hams was often taken to a high degree of excellence, in the old days many smoked foods were barely edible. The introduction of preservation by freezing in the 1930's mercifully ended the need to preserve food by heavy salting and smoking (salting draws out water in which bacteria would otherwise multiply; and smoke provides a resistant varnish seal), although in some parts of the country, they still produce the old heavily-smoked, tarry bloaters and red herrings that our grandparents knew – arguably Britain's most pungent foods.

But evidently it is custom, not the palate, which determines what is a delicacy, for red herring and bloater pale to insignificance compared with some of the world's traditionally-preserved specialities. The repellent ammoniac smell and choking taste of salted shark which has been buried for an Arctic winter under the shingle of the sea shore is considered delicious only in Iceland. Even more repulsive, with the taste of a seagull dredged from an oil slick, is the salted guga, a baby gannet the size of a supermarket chicken which the islanders of Lewis in the Hebrides lovingly post to exiles around the world at Christmas as a pungent reminder of home.

The smoker's art has traditionally elevated the herring, at its most magnificent as Loch Fyne and Manx kippers; it has ennobled the common haddock to produce Finnan haddie (the split fish cold-smoked) and deliciously moist, delicate Arbroath smokies (small, whole fish, brined, and hot-smoked for 30 minutes).

The traditional wisdom is that slightly oily fish smoke best, mackerel, herring, eel, trout and salmon, and it was the emergence of lightly-smoked salmon which altered our perception of smoking.

Conserving the salmon in chill cabinets did away with the role of salt and smoke as preservatives, and a much lighter-tasting product took off.

Fatty meats, like ham, bacon, pancetta (the Italian roll of back fat) were also thought well suited, so it's surprising that a dry meat like venison should be one of the new success stories.

'I can't explain its success, but I suppose it's because people are looking for something new,' says Leo Barclay who runs the Rannock Smokery near Pitlochry in Scotland which pioneered smoked venison seven years ago. 'I used to think venison was unsuitable for smoking. I must admit I don't really like all those new gimmicks.'

Leo Barclay says he was looking for a way of adding value to the red deer he was farming, and was doubtful that smoking would work. But using the unsmoked Italian cured beef bresaola as a model, he was able to produce something very similar. He slices it thinly and sells it in windowed vacuum packs for around £4 for 100g.

So at £20 a pound he's certainly achieved added value. This he justifies by the slow process in which about a third of the weight is lost. He injects the fillets from the haunches with a brine of sugar, salt and saltpetre to soak for three days, drains them for 24 hours, then smokes them for three days.

His smoked venison is well-received in Spain, Italy and Greece, and in Britain has sold well in delicatessens and restaurants; they tend to serve it like an Italian carpaccio, drizzled with olive oil or with an oily mustardy dressing like a gravadlax sauce. Now that Safeway have taken it up, it's enjoying wider currency.

One of the first of the new smokers to exploit the potential of various flavours was Anne Petch who runs Heal Farm in Devon. 'Traditional smoking used to mean a heavy, tarry result which repels both flies and customers,' she says.

While most smokeries use oak chippings or sawdust solely, she varies the woods; apple cuttings for pork, for example, and rosemary branches for lamb.

Eighty per cent of her sales are mail order but the range of fresh and smoked beef, lamb, mutton and pork she sells has put her in the EC firing line. The new EC requirements mean she would have to install no fewer than 14 different preparation rooms and nine different cold stores. Now she's hoping to persuade our Food Minister, the Hon. Nicholas Soames, to put a case for small producers under a scheme called Artisanal Producers with a Non-industrial Base. Hopefully, Anne Petch may bring some common sense to the debate. She may just succeed, being a determined lady – whose ancestors include Sir Robert Peel, famed for repealing the Corn Laws.

Real Chickens Don't Eat Sheep

This is the Year of the Horse in China; in Britain it could be the Year of the Chicken.

In the sixteenth century, King Henry IV of France promised his people a *poule au pot* every Sunday, but this grand design was not achieved until our own times. Post-war biologists and chemists have managed to put a broiler chicken in our pot, or at least microwave, every day of the week. Mass production has brought the cost down; the price we have paid is a loss of flavour and texture. The modern broiler, the intensively reared, deep-litter fowl, has no definable taste, and the texture of wet wallpaper. But now what happened to keg beer and white, sliced, factory bread is happening to broiler chickens. There is a rising demand for chickens which taste better.

While the deterioration in taste has been gradual, a sudden desire for change has been prompted by the revelations of last year – the discovery that our broiler flocks are gripped by *salmonella enteritidis* and the conclusion that this is caused by feeding chickens on waste offal from pigs and sheep. Consumers are now asking for 'real' chickens.

Colin Spencer, a food campaigner and chairman of the Guild of Food Writers, is sure the time has come for a change. 'Nothing is so barbaric as the way we treat our poultry. The muck and chemicals given to boost them is unimaginable. The birds are killed at 40 days but they need at least three months to reach adult size. I think it is vile, and you end up with a very inferior product. Eight out of 10 chickens have *salmonella enteritidis*. It is carried in the cavity and in the edible offal, and the onus is on the consumer to kill it – by making sure the chicken is fully cooked.'

In this new climate of opinion the demand for free-range birds doubled last year; and the demand for organically reared birds exceeds supply. The Minister of Agriculture, John Gummer, blinks at the idea of making all our birds free-range: 'You'd have to turn an area the size of the South-East into a bloody great chicken coop.' But labelling to disclose the birds' origins and history, be they the euphemistic 'farm fresh' or free-range, is growing more complex.

The French were the first to produce customised chickens, the famous blue-legged *Poulets de Bresse* from Burgundy, with their own *appellation contrôlée*, each one numbered and labelled, reared outdoors and fed a gourmet diet. 'They are very happy birds,' says Marc Beaujeu, who sells them at La Boucherie Lamartine (229 Ebury Street, London SW1 at premium prices, £4.20 per lb). The Boucherie also sells French *fermier* Red Label chickens – 12-week-old free-range birds – at £2.60 per lb. *Fermier* is the French equivalent of our free-range. 'They are lovely birds with a lot of flavour and texture,' says Mr Beaujeu. 'They are more mature and they use their muscles to run about. You have to be careful of the word free-range; the British definition is different.' *Fermier* Red Label birds are guaranteed to have had unlimited space to roam, 75 per cent cereal feed and to be at least 80 days old, twice the age of the English broiler.

Tesco is now selling *fermier* Red Label chickens from south-west France, having acquired exclusive rights to a million-hectare forest in Les Landes. The chickens, a variety called *Cou Nu* (which means bare-necked) grow satisfyingly burly on an 80 per cent grain diet, provided by a co-operative of 600 farmers who harvest maize as their main crop. The chickens make up the rest by foraging through the pines, chewing needles and pine kernels. The *Cou Nu* costs a premium £1.60 a pound for a bird of 3lb or more, compared with £1.30 per lb for the normal free-range, 96p per lb for standard broilers and 70p for frozen birds.

But even more elite than the *Cou Nu* are the organic chickens. Organic is a strictly defined word, and means that 80 per cent of the diet of the birds must have been produced without chemicals, insecticides and so on. Demand outstrips supply, says Francis Blake, secretary of the organic producers' watchdog, the Soil Association. 'Farmers cannot get enough grain to feed their birds, because most of it is wanted for human consumption. The public is hungry for organic food of every kind, and can't get it.' Mr Blake believes this is a cue for the Government to step in, especially since John Gummer is an organic crusader himself and founder of the UK Register of Organic Foods. (The Soil Association can send you a list of their organic farmers: 86 Colston Street, Bristol BS1 5BB.)

French organic chickens (not to be confused with *fermier* Red Label), killed at 14 weeks, are becoming available in small supply by mail order. They have been certified by a distinguished-sounding body called *La Fédération de Défense de la Culture Biologique*. (Mail order from Greenway Organic Farms, Freepost, Edinburgh EN1 0AQ)

Harrods sells free-range *fermier* chickens (at £1.85 per pound) and a semi-organic 'traditional' chicken. Semi-organic? The feed is organic but the store cannot put their hand on their heart and claim that the grazing meets organic standards.

The biggest-selling free-range chickens in Britain are the Moy Park brand from Northern Ireland, which, it is claimed, are virtually salmonella-free. They are sold by Waitrose, Safeway, Asda and Gateway. Purists do not accept that they are truly free-range, as they pack in 4,000 birds to the acre (the EC recommends 350 birds to the acre), but it is indisputably a better-textured, better-tasting bird than the standard factory-reared broiler. Their sales doubled last year. Moy Park is launching a Farmhouse chicken in mid-February – a bird kept indoors at all times, with open-sided walls, to let in air and light. Asda already sells them.

If this is really going to be the Year of the Chicken, we could be moving towards individually labelled birds: 'This 15-week-old White Cornish chicken was bred by Farmer Giles, whose family has been raising poultry outdoors for five generations. It has been fed on pesticide-free wheat, maize, soya oil cake and vegetables only, and is certified by the Soil Association. It is best eaten at oven temperature with a good Côtes du Rhône or Australian Shiraz.'

If you have managed to buy a superior chicken, simply roast it in a shallow pan in hot oven at 450F for 20 minutes to the pound plus 20 minutes, turning and basting, until it is golden. It should be rubbed with salt and softened butter, and to enhance flavour and gravy, put a peeled onion, half a lemon and herbs to taste in the cavity. (Michel Guérard spreads a blend of chopped parsley, garlic and two ounces of butter between breast and skin, which should be loosened with fingers.) The bird is done when its juices run clear when it is pricked with a skewer.

1 June 92   At 8am the cock crows.

Snob Appeal on a Plate

In Britain, we now buy 85 per cent of our food in supermarkets.

Do you get the feeling that you cannot go to a dinner party where they aren't serving Marks & Spencer's dishes?

There has not been a bigger influence on middle-class dining since Elizabeth David published *French Provincial Cooking* 30 years ago, when you moved from home to home sampling hopeful stabs at *boeuf à la bourguignonne*. The state of the art is to buy M & S meals, then disguise them: maybe a lemon tart with ginger biscuit, which you elaborate with puréed fruit (from M & S) and whipped yoghurt (M & S). 'Oh Celia, you shouldn't have gone to so much trouble!'

We are talking about ready-cooked meals which you reheat in the oven or zap in the microwave, M & S calls them recipe dishes and they are boom business: half the £300m-worth we bought last year were made by M & S. The Government calls them cook-chill meals and identifies them as an area of serious risk of food poisoning when not handled, stored and cooked properly. But have no fear, M & S has been the nation's pathfinder in food safety.

The company's expansion from clothing to food has been stealthy: going from slabs of cake (before the Second World War) to air-chilled chicken in the Sixties, it has now moved to a 5 per cent slice of the food market. With 260 stores already selling food, some exclusively, and another 60 food stores planned in the next five years, it is set to lead public taste into the next century.

M & S is the envy of other high street stores, if only because it sometimes gets away with outrageous mark-ups. In blind tastings it runs up many more firsts than its rivals, especially for the recipe dishes.

Foodies consider M & S to be the store for unfoodies. But that does not stop them shopping there for butter, cheese, chocolate, chicken, salmon and sandwiches, gateaux and wine, even the recipe dishes, although they will complain afterwards that these are too bland and ordinary.

One cookery writer put it like this: 'M & S responds to a new generation who want restaurant-standard food but don't know how to go about it. It's food for the unconfident. It's food for people who are squeamish and don't like handling real meat, fish and vegetables. It's shopping which takes away the pleasure of foraging. And it's snob-appeal food.'

M & S food is not cheap (which only increases its snob appeal). You can pay £9.50 for a few slices of lobster (tasteless because they are the warm-water variety) in its shell, sitting on potato salad; or 69p for spring onions washed and trimmed, in a dainty windowed package, or 89p for a tray of four baking potatoes. On roadside stalls in the heart of the Lincolnshire potato country, a 56lb sack costs £2.60. In fairness, M & S's loose potatoes at 21p a pound are only 1p more than Tesco's and 2p more than Waitrose's. But step out of any M & S food store into the nearest street market and you will easily halve your greengrocery bill.

M & S will tell you proudly that its stores are customer-led. That attentiveness may explain some of the less wonderful aspects: spongy, light bread, sickly-sweet yoghurt and walls of jumbo crisps. It also means that alarm bells ring when a customer complains. The company received a letter recently enclosing a 'fingernail' said to have been found in an apple pie. It turned out to be the casing of an apple seed. Perhaps M & S has so featherbedded its customers that some have never cored an apple.

Quality and value is the M & S motto, and it is not a vain boast. A team of 400 food scientists, technicians, buyers and 'selectors' have explored the food world to bring back Black Tiger prawns from the new aquafarms of Ecuador and year-round fruit from California's orchards, promoted horticulture at home to grow iceberg lettuce in the fens and filled Scottish lochs with salmon.

Critics observe that in the company's search for consistency, it is falling into the American trap of achieving appearance at the expense of taste.

Control is indeed the key to the M & S operation. Its specifications to suppliers are awesome. They run to 20 pages for each recipe dish, listing each inspected supplier for 40 ingredients, temperature controls and microbiological checks for bugs. High-risk areas in the factories are defined (M & S call them high-care) where staff wear red-peaked hats and may wash their hands 30 or more times a day.

What M & S gives its customers is 'added value', which is what the food industry is all about. If time is money, M & S really does give added value; it saves time shopping, preparing and cooking, and by consistency removes fear of failure. The success of M & S is to have identified the British shopper as a food victim: someone who likes eating but has little time to cook.

Beyond Paella: Spanish Food Gets Serious

An astonishing armada of tapas bars is threatening to overwhelm England. They have names like El Quixote, Bodega, Bodegón, and Bar Escoba (Trust House Forte opened this one in South Kensington in a converted pub). Or they have geographic titles: Marbella, Andalucia and Las Canarias. Or the names of their owners: Benito's, Roberto's, Mesón Don Felipe and Mesón Doña Ma.

The emergence of the tapas bar is a phenomenon which completely mystifies the commercial staff of the Spanish Embassy who are entrusted with promoting food and wine from Spain. British package tourists have been going to Spain for 30 years without ever eating authentic Spanish food, according to Maria José Sevilla of the Spanish Promotions Centre in London. 'The cheap packages affected the quality of cooking in all the Costas. In gastronomic terms, mass tourism was an atrocious disaster.'

Britons who chose Spain for their holidays came with blinkers on, she says. 'They came for the sun, the sea and the sand, to get burned as furiously as they could and to drink as much as they could.' They mostly ate steak and chips, fish and chips, pizzas, spaghetti – not the food of Spain. They may just have had a paella on the beach, a Spanish omelette with potatoes, and some olives at the bar. If asked for an opinion, they would say they didn't like Spanish food because it was greasy (the bitter fumes of cheap frying oil are indeed pretty nauseating).

In hotels, tourists still get Anglo-Spanish cooking. The meat is from Argentina. In the smart restaurants they encounter little which is authentically Spanish because real Spanish food is so honest and unassuming you can't justifiably charge outrageous prices for it. The food in posh restaurants has been French in style but now a Spanish version of nouvelle cuisine is emerging.

The real cooking of Spain is done in the home, based on regional produce, inexpensive, prepared and cooked slowly with care. Spain has been unfortunate in never having had the Elizabeth David treatment. Nearly a quarter of a century ago she told me how much she admired the food of inland Spain, the simplicity, the honest, good ingredients, but she never chose to live in Spain. She said: 'I've been a Greek bore and Provençal bore. I'm not going to be a Spanish bore.' So we have had to wait a very long time to find the quality of writing about Spain which derives from people who have lived there long enough to put its cooking in context.

But now it is happening. A handful of authentic books on Spanish food have recently surfaced. Books by Maria José Sevilla: *Life and Food in the Basque Country* ; Marimar Torres (of the Catalonian wine family) on the new wave restaurant cooking, *The Spanish Table*; Colman Andrews's *Catalan Cuisine*; and those of Elizabeth Luard. Her latest book, the *La Ina Book of Tapas*, with its gross of recipes, is most timely.

Dent and Reuss, marketing people for sherry producers La Ina, explain that the book is no coincidence; they saw a way of changing the dusty image of sherry, which is associated with the older clergy. 'We saw a degree of campaignability if we could link sherry and tapas. It is becoming the food of young people.'

In Spain tapas bars are not restaurants, but bars where you drink before you go on to lunch or dinner. *Tapa* means cover, and derives from the practice of serving a savoury little morsel, a couple of olives, a bite of cheese or sausage, on a saucer placed over the glass. Wandering from bar to bar sampling the tapas is an extremely sociable activity, but the food, though well done, hardly merits serious attention, so it is surprising it should become this year's fad in Britain and in America, too.

Derek Brown, publisher of the *Michelin Red Guide*, says the tapas bar is an idea whose time has come. It is incidental that the food is Spanish. 'The style of eating is appealing. The dishes cost £3 or £4 each, and two, three or four people can order a mixture and share them out. It's fast eating even if it's not fast food.'

It's not fast at all to prepare. Raw anchovies are marinated for hours in wine vinegar (*boquerónes*), meat sauces are simmered for hours for the small dishes (*caracoles*), finest quality meat is minced at least three times for the delicate little meat balls (*albondigas*).

Some critics say it is not fast food but fast bucks. One Spanish resident watches with dismay: 'What's being done here bears no relation to the real thing. Tapas bars have been taken completely out of context.'

The last word is from Maria José Sevilla. 'The Spanish do not find service to be demeaning, so Spanish immigrants don't mind being waiters or chambermaids, they are very good at it. But cooks are different; proper cooks never want to leave home.' She says there is one very serious chef in England – a Basque, at Guernica, in Foley Street, London W1. But this is a restaurant, not a tapas bar.

TWO TAPAS RECIPES

You can also use these as first courses or starters. Frying is rather out of fashion, but good frying is central to Spanish cooking. Food is cooked in olive oil, which is among the healthiest of oils to fry in, and the temperature of the oil is very high, with the result that the outside of the food seals quickly, and little fat is absorbed.

PATATAS BRAVAS – Hot potatoes

Tapas for 8, starter for 4
2lbs large potatoes, peeled
Olive oil to cover pan to $\frac{1}{2}$in depth
Home-made sauce (see below) or 1 tspn each of paprika and
    chilli powder or tabasco or hot sauce
Salt

Cut potatoes into small pieces, about 1in by $\frac{1}{2}$in. Lightly salt and wrap in clean tea towel to draw moisture for $\frac{1}{2}$hour. Wipe dry. In a pan large enough to accommodate all the potatoes in one layer, heat

½ in olive oil till faintly smoking.

Deep-fry potatoes for 10 minutes or till crisp outside, but still soft inside. Drain on absorbent paper. Cover with home-made sauce, or sprinkle with paprika, a teaspoon of chilli pepper (to taste) or hot sauce, slightly thinned with water. Sprinkle with more salt.

Home-made sauce

Fry two tablespoons chopped onion, and chopped garlic clove in olive oil till wilted (about 10 mins); add half a can of tomatoes, strained through sieve, 1 tblsp parsley, splash of white wine, ½ a dry red chilli, deseeded and chopped, a few drops tabasco, pinch of salt. Cook gently, stirring for 20 minutes, adding very little water to thin if necessary.

SPANISH OMELETTE WITH BACALAO – Omelette with salt cod

Tapas for 8, starter for 4
4 eggs
8oz salt cod from a thin cut (soaked in several changes cold
    water for 12 hours)
2 medium onions
Chopped parsley (2 tbsp)
Olive oil, for frying

In a heavy iron pan, sweat the chopped onion on lowest heat till soft and brown – at least 30 to 60 minutes cooking. Remove from heat, transfer onions and oil to a frying pan about 8ins across (you make a thickish omelette). Heat on a medium flame with the flaked cod (or green pepper) and parsley, stirring to prevent sticking. Beat the eggs, and add to the pan. After a few minutes, when the bottom has set, turn the omelette. Place a plate on top, invert the pan, and slide the omelette back the other side up. Cook a few more minutes. (Until the salmonella scare, cooks would say leave the centre a little runny.) Serve hot. If you don't have salt cod, substitute two chopped deseeded green peppers, to make a classic Basque omelette.

Paella

There are many dozens of rice dishes in the province of Valencia, the rice-growing region of Spain, but the one which is famous the world over is paella, so named because it is cooked in a wide, flat, two-handled frying pan called a *paella*. The Spanish are very strict about its exact composition, and the precise cooking method, though they accept that smart chefs in tourist spots break the rules in order to offer, and charge for, a premium product, which explains the delightful garnishes of crayfish, prawns and mussels. This is the original and authentic recipe, and how you break the rules is up to you. You are unlikely to want to include snails, and pork is a fair substitute for rabbit.

Crayfish, prawns, mussels, seafood have their place too, but the name of that dish is not paella, but *arroz marinera*. This is *paella valenciana*. If you do not have a paella pan, use a very wide frying pan, as it's essential that the rice is cooked in a shallow layer.

Serves 4 to 6
12 oz short grain rice (bomba or arborio)
3 pints water
1lb corn-fed chicken, cut into pieces
1lb rabbit cut into pieces
16 cleaned snails (or sprig rosemary)
2 tablespoons olive oil
4 oz green beans, cut into 1 inch pieces
4 oz lima beans, soaked overnight, drained and rinsed
1 large tomato, deseeded and finely chopped
10 saffron strands
1 tablespoon paprika
salt

Cook the soaked, dried lima beans in a pint of water for 45 minutes or until nearly soft.

Trim the chicken and rabbit, leaving the bones in.

Heat the oil in a 16 inch paella pan with a pinch of salt. When hot, fry the chicken and rabbit in it over a medium heat until golden brown on all sides.

Add the green beans and fry for 5 minutes, then add the tomato and cook another 3 minutes.

In another pan, boil the snails for 5 minutes and drain.

Steep and crush the saffron in a little boiling water.

Sprinkle the paprika in the pan, add the water and the rest of the beans and bring it to the boil.

Now add the snails (or rosemary), the saffron, and another pinch of salt.

Simmer, covered with a sheet of foil, for 30-45 minutes until the meat is tender. (If the level of the liquid has gone down, top it up with boiling water.)

Sprinkle the rice into the boiling liquid and cook over a high heat for 10 minutes.

Turn down the heat, and leave to cook without disturbing for 10 minutes until the liquid has evaporated.

If it doesn't seem completely cooked at the end, don't just add more hot water, but take it off the heat and cover it with a dampened, folded tea-cloth, or even a newspaper, for 10 minutes. Left to stand the rice will continue to cook to perfection.

A Famine in the Classroom

Good cooking starts at home but schools should do their bit to encourage it.

Cookery in France is considered an art form, a part of the national culture. If standards are threatened, the Minister of Culture rushes to their defence. And when the minister, Jack Lang, was told that modern French children didn't appreciate the republic's gastronomic heritage, he assembled a commando of nearly 500 chefs and sent them into the primary schools of Paris.

We can smile, but what are British children learning by way of skills to manage and care for their families in the future? Certainly the study of food is low on the list of priorities in the new National Curriculum. Formerly it was taught under the banner of home economics, but now food-related subjects are split up: nutrition is taught in the science course, health and food safety in health education classes, and food preparation is only one of five subjects under design and technology.

Yet cookery has always seemed to me to be a natural subject to teach young children, exercising useful physical skills while embracing so many other subjects, not only farming and horticulture but science and maths, history and geography, and especially the study of other cultures.

That's not how it's seen by the politicians and civil servants who devised the National Curriculum; they emphasised intellectual rather than practical learning. 'The curriculum will drastically affect children when they reach GCSE level,' says home economist Anne Curtis, who teaches at Small Heath Comprehensive, Birmingham. 'Children are losing basic practical skills. We don't teach them how to boil an egg or make toast any more. We have to rely on what they already know, and in the case of some children that's very little indeed.'

But in a straw poll of schools, we found a glimmer of hope. Whereas home economics wasn't taught as a subject until children were 11 (and then only optionally), food under the new order is in the syllabus from the age of five, even if its part is minuscule. Some schools, such as Bournemouth School for Girls, with an ambitious programme in this field, were confident they could develop a good system.

Home economists have traditionally taught skills needed in the family circle (food, clothing, finance, housing, resource management). Many children – and not just poorer ones – do not acquire these skills from the family, and I'm sure home economics deserves its place in the curriculum. When it comes to food, however, I believe it is only in the home that understanding develops. Nearly all the good cooks I have ever met come from homes where the parents have been good cooks.

Home economist and writer Jenny Ridgewell found that the most interested pupils in her South London classes were West Indians, and came from homes where their mothers had been cooking first-rate food. 'They looked at the ingredients I had brought for the first lesson and asked what I was doing with stock cubes? They weren't any good. And why hadn't I brought garlic? The following week I chucked out the stock cubes, brought in the garlic.'

But Derek Cooper, presenter of the BBC's *Food Programme*, feels there is little prospect that schools in this country will ever take food seriously. 'The social, historical and cultural aspects of food have never been taught in our schools. I remember, when my daughter was nine, she came home and said they were going to teach her to make custard, so could she have a packet of Bird's Custard? We removed her to the pottery class.'

The task of making schoolchildren excited about cookery is left to inspired individuals, such as Anna Best. She has been organising a national children's cookery competition for the last 10 years. And who can say British children aren't interested in cookery, when 30,000 of them enter each year, making it easily the biggest cookery competition in the world?

Anna, daughter of a Glasgow domestic science teacher, dreamed up the competition for Thorn EMI who made Tricity cookers, and they ran it until they were taken over by Electrolux, who dropped it. Sainsbury's were only too delighted to step in, and their backing ensures efficient organisation and tempting prizes. The competition is becoming prestigious; one of the previous finalists, Andrew Nutter, now works as a trainee cook at the Savoy Hotel.

If your son or daughter wants to enter, and is aged between 9 and 15, there's still time.

Safe and Sound, but Still not Stylish

Half Britain's shoppers use the Co-op every week, but it may still be left on the shelf.

The Co-op is pure, wholesome and cheap: what a pity it doesn't have style. Yet it was a middle-class movement when it was founded 140 years ago. It only acquired its cloth-cap image in the Thirties, when it was a lifeline to the working class thrown out of work in the Depression. In countries such as Sweden and Japan the Co-operative movement leads the way in quality and excellence, as well as safety and technology. More Marks & Spencer than Mace and Spar.

Now this ancient giant is waking to find itself in the Nineties. 'We realise that we have missed a whole generation,' admits the chief executive, Sir Dennis Landau. 'We were the country's first consumer movement. We believe we should give a lead on environmental issues and food safety.'

The Co-op has made a start. It co-opted enviromentalist David Bellamy to spearhead Green issues, but just when all the other stores had turned a brighter shade of green.

The Co-op also points to its integrity. No additives except those essential to the product. No polyphosphates, which some companies use unscrupulously to increase water content in ham, bacon and chicken. No monosodium glutamate, the insidious 'flavour enhancer'.

The store was also first to reject artificial hormone injections for animals, and it refuses to stock product containing 'mechanically-recovered' meat. Good initiatives. But its rivals in the high street are so wickedly seductive and glamorous. Instead of engaging Bellamy, wouldn't it have been more relevant to bring in someone like Sir Terence Conran to rethink the whole organisation?

Co-op products are notoriously uneven, and at comparative tastings produce both best and worst buys. So why not a panel of food experts to give the products a lift? M & S consults Michelin-starred chefs, Safeway retains Pru Leith, Tesco asks Robert Carrier and Sainsbury's lines up Josceline Dimbleby.

'We have our own panels and experts,' says Sir Dennis. 'Don't forget we are catering to a mass market. We certainly don't always aim to be the cheapest, though it's something we're under pressure to do. But we have started upgrading products.'

Because it is not quoted on the Stock Exchange the Co-op escapes publicity, so many people are unconscious of its scale. Half the shoppers in the country shop in the Co-op every week. It has more customers than Sainsbury's, Tesco, Asda, Safeway, and the Argyll group put together, and more food stores – over 4,000. 'Our great problem,' said the deputy chief executive, David Skinner, then correcting himself, 'our greatest joy is trying to get the co-operatives to co-operate.'

Your impression of the Co-op will be coloured by where you live. If you live in London, you'll find they don't stock such luxuries as good bread, let alone exotica such as wine vinegar. 'London has been our great weakness, if not our graveyard,' concedes Mr Skinner. 'But we're starting to revitalise it.'

But if you live outside London, your regional Co-operative Society may treat you to one of its 68 Superstores. In the Anglia Region they have been rechristened Rainbow stores and will have greengrocery to challenge any in the area, better delicatessen choices, good butchery, fresh fish. They will even have a decent wine selection. 'Good wine at the Co-op? You must be mad, it's dreadful.' Not any more. Two years ago it hired a young Master of Wine as buyer, so now even the plonk is passable. In Scotland the Co-op is the voice of social conscience. It has extended services and put on 20,000 shoppers in two years. If you live on the island of Barra or in other places abandoned by the big supermarkets, you will have good reason to be grateful to the Co-op.

The Co-operative Society was founded by the Rochdale Pioneers in 1844. Food adulteration in Britain had become a national scandal: alum in bread to make it whiter; lead in cider and wine to improve colour; plaster of Paris in flour, and flour to whiten milk.

The society bought the 'purest provisions procurable' for its members, and returned the surplus to the members as a dividend: the 'divi' which survives in occasional branches, such as Ipswich.

By the end of the century there were 1,400 societies. In the Thirties the movement allied itself to the Labour Party, and even today it returns nine Labour Co-operative MPs to Westminster.

The Co-op is a microcosm of society with its members, bank, insurance, shops, factories, farms. It is the country's biggest farmer with 38,000 acres, and also the biggest undertaker, burying one in every four Britons.

It would also claim that its food research laboratories have been the most advanced in the country. 'We have led the way for a very long time,' said Sir Dennis (although M & S is probably catching up). 'We've been in the van on every major food safety issues.'

Sweden's Co-op, Kooperativa Förbundet, arguably operated the world's finest food stores in the Sixties and early Seventies, but political wrangling now finds them stagnated. The Förbundet accepts that it needs to depoliticise in order to carry out essential modernisation. It is a painful situation which the guardians of the British movement understand only too well. Glory beckons. The alternative is too awful to contemplate.

Heartening Times for a Fish called Wonder

The mackerel is the ultimate designer fish, sleek as a torpedo. On the fishmonger's slab its zebra stripes glow green and blue like the hologram on your bank card.

But it is not just a pretty fish. It has suddenly become fervently approved of by nutritionists who have discovered that it contains more fatty acids in its oil, per gramme, than any other fish. The fatty acids containt triglycerides, which thin the blood and keep off heart attacks.

In fatty acids, the mackerel leads the herring, sardine and pilchard by a short head, and it is nearly twice as beneficial as the salmon. Cod, haddock and plaice (Britain's most popular fish) trail way behind.

In other times and climes the mackerel was a fashionable fish, enjoyed with gooseberry or sorrel sauce, or eaten plainly grilled in the spring, when the young fish are at their least oily. But it is only a gourmet treat if it is fresh. Jane Grigson, the much-loved cookery writer who died last month, wrote in her scholarly classic, *Fish Cookery*, that it is not worth cooking a mackerel if it is dull and tired. It has to be so fresh, she said, quoting the expert on tradition-al English food, Dorothy Hartley, 'that the light shines from it like a rainbow'.

As the mackerel is at the bottom of the Ichthyic League, it is the fish we pay less for than any other. When the European Community fleets play at 'quota-hopping', mackerel is considered almost worth-less. Dover sole is king; the Irish will cheerfully trade us 100 tonnes of their cod for 10 precious tonnes of our sole. And we can barter

1,000 tonnes of our herring quota with the Germans, Danes, Dutch and Norwegians in return for 100 tonnes of their cod. But no one trades with mackerel, So we flog most of the 20,000 tonnes we catch to the Russians, who hang around Liverpool with their big processing ships, canning it for grateful Leningrad housewives, or we send it even further, to appreciative Nigerians and Egyptians.

Cod liver oil has long been known as a prevention against winter colds. But the discovery that fish oil is the largest source of essential Omega-3 fatty acids EPA and DHA (Eicosapentoic and docosahexahaeonic acids), is comparatively recent.

Hugh Sinclair, a famously unconventional Oxford nutritionist, set out to discover why Eskimos who eat a diet high in seal fat and oily fish had no record of heart disease, nor indeed many other modern ailments. Dr Sinclair was nearly 70 in 1979 when, in the spirit of scientific curiosity, he embarked on an oily fish diet, eating nothing else for 100 days. He refused the assistance of fellow volunteers for fear there might be dangerous side-effects. He lost two stone, and his experiment established that fish oil has the effect of thinning the blood; the time it took for his blood to clot increased from four to 50 minutes.

Now two British research doctors, Reg Saynor and Frank Ryan have written a book which spells it out: *The Eskimo Diet, How to Avoid a Heart Attack* (Ebury Press). It is climbing the charts, and so are herring and mackerel sales. Eskimos do not eat the Eskimo Diet any more, Dr Saynor admits: 'They eat a Western diet. Every other igloo has a McDonald's sign outside. They are developing the same heart problems as the Western world.'

The doctors would have been justified in calling their book the 'Victorian Britain Diet'. 'There is no record of heart disease in the last century,' says Dr Saynor, 'and records show they ate a lot of herring and mackerel.'

Heart disease, intensified by the consumption of hard fats, butter, cheese, beef, pork and lamb fat, did not make its appearance until the Twenties, and it has only reached epidemic proportions in the last two decades. 'It also coincides with the fall of consumption of fatty fish.'

No one in the nutritional establishment disagrees with the findings, and they would all recommend oily fish as part of a varied diet. Dr Saynor goes further; he adds a fish oil pill to breakfast and lunches off sardine salad or a sardine sandwich. 'I realise that oily fish isn't palatable to everyone.'

Some people would rather die prematurely than live on tinned sardines. So try soused, salted and pickled mackerel and herring, the way they do in Scandinavia. Or marinate mackerel spicily with tamarind, chilli and ginger and fry it, as they do in India and south-east Asia.

Anna Hegarty, the Swedish owner of Anna's Place in north London, minimises the smell of cooking mackerel by wrapping the gutted fish in foil before baking it for half an hour in a medium oven. 'Sprinkle with plenty of salt, stuff the cavity with a wedge of lemon and plenty of parsley.' Cooking it wrapped in clingfilm in a microwave is also effective.

GRAVAD MACKRILL
Serves four as a starter
2 fillets mackerel
3 tablespoons white sugar
1½ teaspoons salt
1½ teaspoons white pepper
Stems of dill

Gravad Makrill is arguably more interesting than Gravad Lax (marinated salmon). Ask your fishmonger to prepare the fillets. The difficult bit is getting out the pin bones; forceps are easier than tweezers.

Lay the fillets skin side down in a flat dish, cover with the condiments and dill, and put a board on top, weighted with a pound or two at the most. It is simple to saw a small piece of wood to shape, and the recipe is so good you will use it again. Wrap a plastic bag round the wood before use.

Leave for 24 hours in the fridge. With a sharp knife, cut at an angle to make rose coloured oblongs. Serve with horseradish sauce. If no dill, a pinch of Chinese five-spice powder adds a touch of aniseed.

When Yellow is a Sauce of Courage

Making hollandaise sauce is one of those kitchen skills that separates the confident from the timorous. It doesn't lend itself to casual, carefree effort, but 5-10 minutes of intense concentration.

But this classic of French cooking adds such a luxurious touch to the special occasion, especially in the summer, that it's worth persevering. Serve it on asparagus, on young vegetables, on salmon which has been grilled, steamed, or poached.

It is also the key to a whole family of warm sauces: the incomparable Béarnaise, which lifts a grilled fillet steak into another dimension; or the pink variation Choron, which beautifully matches salmon too.

Many people try these sauces, and when they curdle or separate decide perhaps that it's not for amateurs. It certainly helps if the cook can understand the principle of making emulsions, rather than follow parrot-fashion the instructions of recipe books. Some of these still give the classic recipes, as laid down by those great teachers Auguste Escoffier (in 1907) and Henri Paul Pellaprat (in 1935).

Escoffier gives a recipe for a quart of hollandaise, using a dozen egg yolks and 1½lb of butter. He adds that good results depend on 'experience alone, the fruit of long practice'.

Today, fortunately, we can resort to the electric liquidiser (I give a fail-safe version from the American cook, Julia Child, at the end). For those who'd like to know about the real thing, come with me to Nico Ladenis's hugely respected, much-praised, classically French restaurant in Great Portland Street, London W1.

Nico is one of the great characters of the kitchen. Bearded like a ferocious Picasso minotaur, he used to be known for being rude back to customers. His book, *My Gastronomy* (Ebury Press, £16.95) – the most entertaining of all the books produced by chefs – includes a chapter entitled 'The customer is not always right'.

But when I visited he was sweetness and light and introduced Tim Johnson, the 23-year-old chef who makes the sauces. He was making a Choron, which is a variation of Béarnaise, which in turn is the same as a hollandaise, except that it's flavoured with a reduction of shallots, wine and wine vinegar instead of lemon juice.

A hollandaise is really a warm mayonnaise. Instead of gradually beating cold olive oil into egg yolks, you gradually beat hot liquid butter into warmed egg yolks. Tim was using 10 egg yolks to 1lb of butter. He suggested the minimum sensible amount to make was five egg yolks to a ¹/₂lb of butter, a generous quantity for six.

Planning ahead is essential. You need a pan to heat the butter; a bowl to beat the egg yolks in; a large saucepan of simmering water to beat them over (or a bain-marie); an egg whisk; and a bowl with your acidic flavouring in it. We're going to use lemon juice for hollandaise, but you would use white wine vinegar and shallots for Béarnaise, and the same plus tomato sauce and tarragon for the Choron.

It's exciting to try to make it by hand, and Tim says you should expect to be passable if not perfect after a few tries. 'The secret of beating by hand is a balance of temperatures between the eggs and the butter. They should be the same, as far as possible.' It's not art, it's chemistry,' says Tim. 'But don't let Mr Ladenis hear you say that.'

Before he started, Tim explained what could go wrong. Get the eggs or the butter too hot, and the mixture will turn into scrambled egg. (Disaster, but don't throw it away. Mix in some chopped anchovies and serve it on slices of toast.)

If you fail to beat the mixture vigorously enough, or try to put too much butter into the egg yolks, the mixture will separate. Not the end of the world. You do as you would with mayonnaise – start again. We'll come to that.

HOLLANDAISE SAUCE
Serves 6
1 teaspoon white wine vinegar
1 teaspoon freshly milled pepper
3 tablespoons water
5 egg yolks
8 oz unsalted butter (melted in a pan, leaving a clear gold liquid and a milky deposit)
juice of ¹/₂ lemon
salt, cayenne pepper

First Tim boiled up the first three ingredients and strained them into a bain-marie. This small amount of liquid, about the quantity of an egg yolk, stops the mixture thickening too quickly, he said. Then he put in the yolks and beat like fury for just a minute or two, till it was a hot smooth cream as thick as mayonnaise.

He picked up the pan of hot melted butter and at first poured it in drop by drop, as he whisked away, gradually getting quicker and quicker. 'If you aren't patient now, you ruin it.' He let the tiniest amount of the melted butter's milky deposit slip in for flavour, but too much would spoil the sauce. It was all done in no time at all.

He whipped in a squeeze of lemon juice, sprinkled salt and a dash of cayenne pepper, then tried it. It tasted superb. It was done. Tim covered it and put it in a warm place, announcing that it would keep all day but would be used within the hour. It will also keep in a deep freeze.

'If the sauce gets too hot, it splits,' said Tim. 'Boil a spoonful of water in the bain-marie, add drop by drop the more solid parts of the sauce, and whisk until it emulsifies. If that fails, start with two more egg yolks, and beat the mixture in.'

To make a Béarnaise, start with 1 tbsp of liquid, made by reducing 2 tbsp white wine, and 1 tbsp white wine vinegar, a finely chopped shallot, white pepper, strained.

For Choron sauce, add 2 tsp of a firm home-made tomato sauce and some chopped tarragon to the final mixture, which is then sieved.

And now the quick version for four. Put 3 yolks in a liquidiser with 1 tbsp of lemon juice. Give it a two-second swish. Pour on 4 oz hot melted butter slowly. Whizz till blended. Tip it out, season it.

It's too easy, isn't it? Experts say the texture doesn't compare with the hand-made stuff. Also you get less volume, although you can obtain more by transferring the sauce to a bowl and quickly whisking in another 2 oz hot butter by hand.

Sixty Ways to Woo your Shopper

Tesco is to Sainsbury's what Avis is to Hertz: it tries harder. As the second largest supermarket chain, treading on Sainsbury's heels, it offers a classless alternative to the middle-class ethos of its rival.

Your own view of Tesco will depend on where you live. You may still be unlucky in being served by one of the outmoded shops which have not been converted; if the Brent Cross superstore is a flagship in London, Goodge Street in the West End was a rowing boat with a hole in it (it is about to reopen with a revamp). Other stores, like the one in Portobello Road, west London, are limping ships in the quickening hustle of the convoy.

The transformation took place in 1985. Sir Ian MacLaurin, chairman of the chain, waved his wand and the television commercials revealed Robert Carrier, the noted American restaurateur and food writer, praising Tesco joints. Some thought it would be the ruin of both Carrier and Tesco.

Carrier, who had once nursed an ambition to act, asked us to believe that Tesco's meat was the best money could buy; but people assumed that Carrier was the best Tesco's money could buy, and did not know who to believe. It never occurred to anyone that the world-famous gourmet might be serious. 'I went through the whole butchery business with Tesco,' he maintains, 'and was convinced it was best. Otherwise I wouldn't have done it.'

Five years later, Tesco identifies with Dudley Moore. Dud's small-screen adventures in the pine forests of south-western France, in pursuit of a very free-range Tesco chicken, have won him more praise than some of his Hollywood efforts.

But it is not merely Tesco's image. In five years, the company has turned itself inside-out, abandoning its working-class origins. The tacky little stores are disappearing, and in their place come an army of superstores, invading suburban fields, shocking with their size and vulgarity; modern country barns on a scale no barn was ever intended to be, which date as fast as they are built.

If they must occupy such vast tracts, why not invite challenging modern architects like Norman Foster and others to create new, exciting landmarks? Jonathan Glancey, architectural correspondent of *The Independent*, suggests Tesco's object may be to get planning permission as fast as possible; more ambitious designs are likely to run into problems with local authorities.

'So you end up with bland compromises. They work in the vernacular to get the approval of local councils, but the vernacular should never be that big, with its gables, slate roofs, and red-brick. It's country kitsch. It's like a pantomime dame, a building in drag.'

If Tesco was once a pygmy, it now stands astride the marketplace like a Colossus, and with about as much subtlety. Never mind the quality, feel the width. The company sells a staggering 14,000 food items, a blunderbuss approach. But is there a packet of biscuits, among the 295 brands it stocks, worth making a detour for? Do we really need to choose from 75 kinds of bottled water? Wouldn't Tesco be doing us a better service if it picked the one or two that were best value and poured the rest back down the spring?

Tesco was founded in 1932 by Jack Cohen, an East End stallholder. His cheerful motto was 'pile it high, sell it cheap', and he had opened about 100 small shops, mostly in the London area, before the Second World War. The TES was not short for his wife's name, as many assume, although he provided the CO from Cohen. The initials were those of T E Stockwell, the merchant who provided the firm's first own-label tea.

Tesco took off after the war, pioneering self-service in 1948 and Britain's first superstore (in Crawley, Sussex) in 1968. Today, Tesco is a mega-company with 140 superstores and 379 shops in total – second only to Sainsbury's in its market share.

For the public, the price of having these great food fairs is the loss of High Street specialists. Fishmongers were the first to go, then grocers (remember grocers?). Soon butchers, bakers and greengrocers were being thinned out, and now the traditional family delicatessens are tumbling.

So the question is not simply whether shopping at Tesco and other chains is cheaper and more convenient, which it obviously is. What really matters is whether these food funfairs recognise they have a duty – to fill the vacuum they have created, and provide real value, quality and choice.

In-house bakeries produce bread which smells good, but no self-respecting French, German or Italian shopper would look at it, let alone buy it. (In Tesco's most upmarket stores, however, there's a black rye loaf that's exceptional.) The delicatessen lacks the sophistication and subtlety, the sensual foreign-ness that makes this kind of food so appealing at its best. The fish is fresh and good, and up to Sainsbury's standards. The good news is the meat counter and the poultry, and the best news is the wine. Who'd have thought old Tesco would win 126 awards at *Wine* magazine's 1990 International Wine Challenge?

Tesco is pretty sure it has the measure of its customers, and works hard to create a club atmosphere with a Tesco life style. It runs consumer advice bureaus in six of its biggest stores, monitoring customers, arranging product testing, giving cookery demonstrations and offering health and nutrition information. The chain was the first to introduce 'healthy eating', and a range of some 50 dishes is so labelled.

This is the initiative of Richard Pugh, director of technical services and Tesco's most public figure. He practises what he preaches, cutting out animal fat, sugar and salt and cycling 150 miles a week. But while Dr Pugh knocks off the calories, Tesco is piling them back on with lines such as 'traditional' steak and kidney pies, leaden with lovely lardy pastry.

Tesco may not be your cup of own-label, but if you're a member of the club it will do its damndest for you. Demand the food you want, and most stores will respond to local needs. Consider north London's Colney Hatch superstore for kosher food, and exotic Neasden, in north-west London, for Eastern herbs and spices.

Red and Yellow and Tartrazine

If tartrazine food dye was a safety risk, the Minister of Agriculture, Fisheries and Food would ban it. But it's not. It only affects a minority of people – like John Gummer's own son.

The Minister is famous for placing his trust in scientific advisers, like those who say there is no danger to humans from mad cow disease (bovine spongiform encephalitis). Mr Gummer has shown faith in them by feeding a beefburger to his daughter at a press conference.

But what about Ministry food scientists who say coal tar and azo dyes are safe food colourings? Mr Gummer has a son who is sensitive to these additives, and becomes hyperactive when exposed to tartrazine (E102) in particular. Coal tar dyes are now banned from his diet.

Tartrazine is one of the most widely used food colours and is common in children's foods such as carbonated drinks, virulently coloured jellies and desserts, liquorice allsorts and boiled sweets; it provides the appealing primrose colour in the batter of fish fingers, gives mustard its screaming yellow radiance, and supplies the iridescent sheen to lumpfish roe, along with caramel.

In *The Safe Food Handbook* (Ebury Press, £6.95) published last month, Geoffrey Cannon says tartrazine, and other coal tar and azo dyes derived from petrochemicals, can cause hyperactivity in children, loss of concentration, migraines, asthma and nettle rash. Tartrazine and Sunset Yellow (E110) in particular have been linked with birth defects, cancers and acute illness.

This is something that informed consumers, like Mr Gummer and Mrs Gummer, formerly Edward Heath's secretary, can find out. The task of isolating safe products is relatively easy, armed with a list of the 16 or so E-numbers and chemical names. But the consequences of a careless mistake are as distressing for the unwitting parent as for the child.

Mr Gummer's Ministry line is that tartrazine and coal tar dyes do not cause illness, although some may 'trigger idiosyncratic reactions in a few intolerant people'. Like his son. This provokes outrage among his critics. 'I'm staggered,' says Erik Millstone, author of *Food Additives* (Penguin, £2.95). 'The official view was that coal tar colouring caused no problems, but now they agree it does, but it's rare.' In the United States, one study suggested that as many as 20 per cent of children under 16 could be affected, but much hangs on the definition of hyperactive.

Concern about additives exploded in 1986, when Britain introduced E-numbers on foodstuffs, E standing for Europe. About 300 additives are regulated in this way, but so great was public anxiety that Maurice Hanssen's *E for Additives* – a dictionary of chemicals – became a bestseller. 'Initially I think my book changed things for the better, but things are starting to back slide. It's not enough to say people can decide from the label, which is the Government view, as additives don't have to be declared in beer, chocolate and takeaway foods.'

Tartrazine was one of the first colours to get a bad name, and many supermarkets have got rid of it. *The Food Magazine* (published by the Food Commission, 88 Old Street, London EC1) details a case of a corner-shop product called Lifestyle Banana Flavour Milk Drink, No Tartrazine, Low Fat. Co-editor Sue Dibb points out that a concerned parent would buy it with a sense of relief, unaware that tartrazine has been replaced with the equally suspicious Sunset Yellow. 'It's a double cheat, because the banana flavour isn't natural either.'

It's made by Lancashire Dairies, which supplies Landmark cash-and-carry stores. Their spokesman said: 'I don't claim to be an expert, but we can't have red banana milk shake.' (In the Gummer spirit, I tested a similar banana milk shake with coal tar dyes on my children, but they didn't go crazy as it was too horrible to finish.)

All the big supermarkets are anxious to point out their own pious initiatives, withdrawing inessential additives. But this seldom includes coal tar and azo dyes, as it's considered necessary to sell glacé cherries the colour of guardsmen's tunics; phosphorescent-green peas; drinks, jellies and sweets a luminous orange and yellow. 'How can children get to know real food if they are always presented with a cacophony of colour?' asks Maurice Hanssen.

For good measure, Geoffrey Cannon also raises the alarm about caramel colouring, which represents by weight 98 per cent of all colours in food. We consume an average of 1lb each per year, in sauces, beers, colas, meat products, soups and chocolate. Caramel isn't the old-fashioned burnt sugar, he says, but a technological chemical, associated in animal tests with swollen guts, swollen kidneys, and diarrhoea.

The Food and Drink Federation, which represents the food industry, argues that testing of additives is so thorough that more is known about *their* effects than about most natural foods. Additives make food safer, preserving it from bacteria and oxidisation and making it taste and look better. But it does accept that people have intolerance to some additives, as they do to foods like shellfish, chocolate and gluten. Indeed, with the Royal College of Physicians and the British Dietetic Association, it has established a databank of food products which are free of additives and other foodstuffs which cause intolerance. (Write to the Food and Drink Federation, 6 Catherine Street, London WC2.)

The Ministry of Agriculture puts the figure of intolerance to coal tar dyes as low as 0.01 per cent of the population, which works out at about 50,000 in Britain – probably children. Dr Melanie Miller, responsible for the Consumer Association's *Understanding Additives*, says that Scandinavia regards any risk as too high, and has banned most of them. Germany and France are more concerned with the fraudulent aspect of colouring, and ban colours from bread (we use caramel to make brown bread look realistic) and meat products.

Geoffrey Cannon accepts that colours, compared with other hazards of modern life like smoking and nuclear emissions, may pose small risks. 'But over time they impose a toxic load, especially on the fragile immune systems of children.' Significantly, coal tar cannot be used in baby foods.

Cannon scoffs at the idea that we need additives. 'Don't think of them as poison as much as legalised fraud,' he says. 'Dyes, colours, flavours and other cosmetic additives are used to disguise inferior ingredients as good food. And not only colours. Polyphosphates are used to hold additional water in chickens, hams and bacon (that's why rashers squirt water when you try to fry them). Starches, celluloses, gums, gels and bulking aids might be quite harmless in themselves, but they are employed to swell food with water, air or other valueless volume. In the nineteenth century, traders who adulterated and contaminated food were prosecuted. Now they are protected by the law.'

His advice, if you're concerned about additives in your food, is to choose whole fresh produce. This is apparently what the Gummers do.

No Need to Beef about Meat

The day may be coming when a cut of prime beef will be sold with its family tree, when only a certificate of a beast's genealogy will dismiss anxiety from the minds of the most suggestible.

In May, the concerns about bovine spongiform encephalopathy (BSE) were compounded by the death of the Bristol cat, Max, from a spongiform disease assumed to be caused by the consumption of 'mad cow' meat. Sales of standard beef are still depressed, but organically-reared beef is enjoying a boom. Purchases are up 20 per cent or more.

Harrods, which started to stock organic beef in January, sells it at 25 per cent dearer than its standard grass-fed Scottish beef. But this is a small price to pay for peace of mind, say its customers.

The store's meat buyer, Harry Hutton, says shoppers are wary of BSE. 'We planned to sell organic meat long before the BSE scare,' he explains. 'Our customers have been saying they want something more natural. People also tell me the meat tastes better.'

Harrods meat carries the symbol of the Soil Association (SA), the first organisation to set standards for organic beef, in 1973. Authentication by the SA guarantees animals have been given no chemicals such as antibiotics and growth promoters, and no medication (sick cattle are treated, but removed from the herd and not sold as organic). Animals are reared on land which has to be passed by the association. This means a three-year period to 'rest' the land if chemical fertilizers, weedkillers and insecticides have been used.

There has not been a case of BSE in organic herds. 'We don't want to crow about it,' says Francis Blake, the secretary of the SA. 'We don't know if BSE can be passed on maternally. If some animals introduced into organic farms are from suspect stock, we cannot tell until it is too late. So we are keeping our fingers crossed.'

The Meat and Livestock Commission (MLC), which is responsible for promoting British meat, says there is no evidence of vertical (maternal) or horizontal (infectious) transmission of the disease. This is seen as highly optimistic by Professor Richard Lacey, a microbiologist at Leeds University, because scrapie, the spongiform disease in sheep, is transmitted vertically and horizontally.

If BSE is passed maternally, it will put a premium on animals born before 1980 when farmers first fed ground sheep's heads as a protein supplement to boost milk production.

Richard Guy, who runs the Real Meat Company in Warminster, Wiltshire – the largest organic meat supplier – is now searching for meat from pre-BSE cattle which he can sell as an alternative to organic beef. He has seen his company's sales of organic meat double each year since he started selling in 1985 with his wife, Gillian Metherill, a pig farmer. They have a shop in Bath, two in London, and supply 40 retailers.

Mr Guy's standards are parallel with the Soil Association's, but he also pays scrupulous attention to animal welfare and taste, winning the approval of the BBC's *Food and Drink Programme* (which voted his bacon 'the best in Britain'), and the RSPCA.

Mr Guy is exploring the possibility of a family tree as a selling point, and has sent questionnaires to the suppliers of his organic meat. '1 found a Welsh farmer who hasn't taken any new stock into his herd of Welsh Blacks since 1921. Unless BSE is transmitted by air, birds or rodents, it's got to be clean.'

He works in conjunction with a Bristol University team which turns up at farms unannounced to carry out inspections. He's currently investigating claims by an Exmoor farmer who says he has bought no new stock this century. 'Farmers who have followed traditional methods all these years,' he explains, 'are beginning to realise there might be something in it for them.'

Safeway is the one supermarket chain selling organic beef, vegetables, fruit, bread and cheese. It was the first to introduce organic foods in 1981, but it wasn't until this year that it started stocking organic beef. The product is available in 13 stores in the Home Counties at prices up to 35 per cent higher than standard beef, but the company would sell more if it could get it.

Building up an organic beef herd can take as long as five years. There may be some short cuts now the demand is there, and farmers are beginning to recognise that they can ask premium prices. Suddenly, traditional farmers are coming out of the woodwork and asking to be registered.

There are also Scottish hill farmers, says Richard Guy, with clean land exempt from the three-year conversion from chemicals usually required. 'Because of weather conditions, they are only able to suckle the cattle. At six months, they pass them on to low land farmers to fatten and finish them.'

If you can't afford or find organic beef, which is the safest to eat? Critics think the Ministry of Agriculture has been too hasty in clearing beef so soon after declaring emergency measures (cattle are still being slaughtered at the rate of 1,000 a month). But even they agree that it should be safe to eat any animal killed before the age of two, since the disease does not develop until cattle are four years old. Younger animals comprise 30 per cent of the beef supply, and your butcher should tell you which meat is which if the price doesn't make it obvious.

The other 70 per cent is from five to nine-year-old cows which are at the end of their milking life in dairy herds. The Commission says there is nothing to worry about now, since animal protein feeds were banned in 1988 and suspect animals are being slaughtered (20,000 to date, with the disease confirmed in 16,000). At abattoirs, those parts which can carry the disease are removed: brains, spinal cord, spleen, tonsils, and intestines.

'In the extremely remote case of anything getting through,' says the MLC, 'the dose would be so small that we don't think it would breach the immune system.' This opinion is not shared by Professor Lacey. 'Some nerve tissues in meat are half an inch thick,' he says, 'and a small dose might be the size of a small grain of sugar. It might take 40 years to show, instead of 10 years – which isn't satisfactory if you're feeding it to your children.'

If you're still worried, you could go vegetarian. Alternatively, you can buy tastier meat from organic suppliers and salve your conscience about animal welfare at the same time.

A Steamboat Full of Eastern Promise

Thai restaurants have produced some of the most exciting new taste sensations of the last decade: spicy, sweet-sour, clean, fresh, uncompromisingly fiery – and exotic. Yet people who might attempt Chinese or Indian cuisine at home are often fazed by the idea of cooking Thai food.

Finding a recipe is one problem, buying the right herbs and spices another. What on earth are kaffir lime leaves, which appeared in a soup recipe offered to *London Evening Standard* readers the other week? The second ingredient was lemon grass, one-foot lengths of grass as tough as bamboo that yield a lemon taste when crushed. They are sold in Chinatown, Harrods, and the odd Waitrose and Tesco.

You can just about approximate lemon and lime flavours, but what about the required teaspoon of Nam Prik Poo? This turns out to be a hot, fishy curry paste; Nam means sauce, Prik is chilli and shrimp powder is Poo.

The dish was submitted by 'guest cook' Philip Harris, owner of London's Bahn Thai restaurant. It was one of the capital's first when it opened in 1982, but now there are at least 100 and as many again in country towns. The success of Thai cuisine is surprising because, unlike Indian and Chinese cooking, it owes nothing to our colonial past. Its attraction lies not in its familiarity, but in its freshness, flavour and appeal to the eye.

The pleasant dream of trying to recreate Mr Harris's formula at home fades when it becomes clear that no shops sell kaffir lime leaves – and if you want lemon grass, you'll have to whistle for it. Other ingredients are more common: green chillies, green coriander (which used to be known as Chinese parsley) and basic prawns and mushrooms. But the soup needs a dash of Thai fish sauce (that's a salty sauce like soy, made from fermented small fish), not to mention the Nam Prik Poo.

Mr Harris, you may assume, is now chuckling to himself as he goes on to suggest you might like to serve it in a steamboat – if you have one. This is a bowl with a central chimney containing glowing charcoal, to keep the dish warm. It is used in his restaurant in Frith Street, Soho, where this delicacy costs £10.30 for two.

By this time, quite a few frustrated readers must have wanted to put Mr Harris on a slow steamboat to Thailand. But it seemed a pity to have to give up, considering there has been such a proliferation of exotic herbs and spices in Britain. So I went to see if he could pass on some tips for getting the taste of Thailand into the home.

Philip Harris is 34, 6ft 3ins tall and a descendant of the Wiltshire family which founded the famous Harris pork sausage company in the seventeenth century. As a child, his mother used to take him regularly on holiday to Bangkok. A smattering of the language came in useful when he set up business selling catering equipment.

His first customer in 1982 was the Thai owner of a new restaurant, The Siam, who immediately offered him a partnership. The Thai lady who came to him for a job is now his wife, thus happily sealing his love of Thai life and culture.

As for his recipe for Hot Sour Prawn Soup, there could be no compromise, he said. Thai food was the most exciting in the Far East, probably in the world, but already it has been corrupted in Britain. Half the restaurants have made do with less expensive or more convenient ingredients. 'For me,' says Mr Harris, 'it is a torture to have to eat Thai food which is not authentic.'

His Hot Sour Prawn Soup, he said, sums up the essence of Thailand, where it is eaten every day in some form. The sour note in Thai cooking is essential, provided by limes, lemons, tamarind (the sour taste in our own HP sauce), lemon grass and the peel of kaffir limes and their leaves.

Fiery heat is also essential, provided by chillies, fresh or dried or chilli powder, paste and oil. The Thais never remove the pungent hot seeds before cooking, as genteel English cookery writers recommend. 'I have an addiction to them,' Philip Harris confesses, 'and I've built up a resistance. But after a spell in Germany where they weren't available, I came back and binged on them. I burnt a hole in my gullet, according to the doctor. It caused some kind of ulcer, and I wasn't allowed to eat them for three months.'

The trinity of Thai flavours, he says, is garlic, chilli, and coriander. Leaf coriander is actually the world's most widely consumed herb. The leaf, chopped stems, pounded root and seeds (toasted whole to release their flavour, then ground) are used in every savoury dish in Thailand. Fresh green ginger root, and its cousin galangal (known to Elizabethan Britain as the medicinal herb, galingale) add more fieriness. Soy sauces, fish sauces and dried shrimp powder contribute intense, savoury saltiness. But even Mr Harris admits that blachan – square blocks of shrimp paste which look like fudge, but smell like last year's rugby socks – break the bounds of gastronomic nicety. Most Westerners give these a miss, and he goes along with that.

In Thailand, soup is not the overture to the meal but the incidental music. It is drunk right through an endless feast of dishes that might start with deep-fried morsels dipped in hot sauces – like skewered satay with its spicy chilli and groundnut dips. Then come hot curries of meat and fish, accompanied by steaming bowls of rice and sometimes cooled with coconut. The meal might also include palate-tingling salads of cold noodles tossed in spicy dressing, with cucumber and lettuce sprinkled with sugar, pineapple dipped in chilli salt, grated peanuts and raw chillies.

With such a wealth of ingredients, where can we go for guidance? Mr Harris says there isn't a good book on Thai cooking, but television cook Madhur Jaffrey has an enthusiastic chapter on Thai food in the BBC's *Far Eastern Cookery* (£11.95) And there's a timely guide to oriental products, *Foods from the Far East* (Century £15.99, published last week), which talks you through unusual herbs, spices, seeds, nuts, sauces, vegetables, dried and preserved foods. Kaffir limes are ugly, knobbly things used for their tangy peel and pungent leaves, never their juice, the book reveals. It is really useful, thinks Mr Harris, except that its Californian author Bruce Cost seems to have omitted kaffir lime leaves from his Hot Sour Prawn Soup recipe.

I put it to Mr Harris that this soup offered such a clean, fresh and stimulating taste that it was surely worth having a stab at it – even without being able to find all the authentic herbs and spices. So here's a recipe suggesting alternative ingredients to try at home. But don't even think about the substitutes if you're having Mr Harris to dinner.

There are four very brief stages:

1. Make a prawn stock – this takes around 15 minutes (otherwise you can use chicken stock).

2. Flavour the stock with hot, sour, spicy aromatics – allow 5 minutes for this.

3. Cook the seafood, adding hot, salty ingredients – this should take roughly 3 minutes.

4. Garnish with coriander leaves.

HOT SOUR PRAWN SOUP

Serves 4-6

1lb raw prawns with heads
    or combination of: 2oz raw prawns,
    2oz filleted white fish and/or sliced squid,
    1 dozen mussels and/or clams

¹/₂ lb mushrooms or 1 can straw mushrooms
2 pints prawn stock (simmer heads and shells for 15 minutes
   and strain) or chicken stock
Aromatics: stick of lemon grass and 3 kaffir lime leaves or peel
   of ¹/₂ lime or ¹/₄ lemon, stripped of its white pith
Sour agent: 2 tablespoons lemon juice
Fiery agent: 1 or 2 whole green chillies, chopped
   or 2 small dry chillies
      or teaspoon chilli or cayenne
Savoury finish:
   1 tablespoon fish sauce
      or light soy sauce or teaspoon salt
Garnish: coriander leaves or parsley

First, make the stock. To flavour it, crush the lemon grass and cut it into half-inch lengths. Add the kaffir lime leaves, or lime or lemon peel, the lemon juice and a crushed, chopped chilli (green or dry red). Simmer for 5 minutes and strain.

Poach the seafood in the liquid and add sliced mushrooms – this will take 2 or 3 minutes for the white fish, 1 minute for mussels or shellfish, 20 seconds for the peeled prawns to turn opaque. Add fish sauce, or soy sauce, more chopped green chilli if you dare, and torn coriander leaves.

The Book of the Dish of the Day

The eating fads of New York may be poised to cross the Atlantic – in hard cover.

We may not be able to scoff at the vagaries of New York food fashions for much longer. It is impossible to suppress a smirk upon hearing that Tex-Mex is out, Californian Chinese is in. Not so long ago a New York food critic announced that French cooking was out. Poor old French cooking. It's been around for four and a half centuries in Europe but it couldn't stay the pace in New York.

It's the same with cookbooks. Each year the big New York bookshops are replenished with the new season's offerings. In Paris the same two shelves suffice – with the odd new book on North African food, or one by the chef who is the talk of *tout Paris*. The difference could be that the French eat with their mouths, the Americans with their eyes.

Could it happen here? Probably. The first issue of *Metropolitan Home* features some fashionably pretty platefuls from Paris. A commentary by the American cookery writer, Colman Andrews explains that *nouvelle cuisine* is out, and modern French chefs are 'mixing French culinary notions energetically with those of Italy, Japan and even America'. He declares that 'subversive simplicity is in' – 'simplicity' as in simple *Pieds de Porc Désossés en Galette au Jus de Truffles*, which is one of the recipes selected; 'subversive' may refer to the price.

Mr Andrews singles out for praise a dish of thinly-sliced tomatoes gratinéed with olive oil and Parmesan cheese, and decorated with basil leaves. It costs £13. He asks 'Where is the art?' and answers, 'the art is in the purity and perfection of the ingredients.' Some might argue that the art lies in the bald-headed cheek of the restaurateur who dares ask £13 for a tomato.

But we have our share of fashion food. A glance at the pre-Christmas crop of cookery publications reveals a high incidence of expensive, beautifully-photographed coffee-table books featuring unattainable dishes created by fashionable chefs. If cookery books are now being designed for the eye, where are the books for the mind?

The person who ought to answer this question is Caroline Hobhouse, who, for more than 20 years, was one of Britain's most influential cookery editors. Although she would never have dreamed of commissioning glossy picture books herself, she has just wriitten *Great European Chefs* (Pyramid, £19.95), one of the most shamelessly sumptuous of the season. It is an extravagant visual record of visits to 18 chefs in Britain, France, Italy, Germany, Spain, Hungary, Ireland and Switzerland.

Ms Hobhouse laughs about this. 'One's either got to be defiant or sheepish.' But as an editor she launched a stream of seminal books, mostly from Macmillan, which she now describes as books written with passion, interest and curiosity, a style which she says the late Jeremy Round of *The Independent* epitomised. Among the first books Ms Hobhouse published were *Poor Cook* by Caroline Conran and Susan Campbell, and Jane Grigson's *English Food*. She also published George Lassalle's *The Adventurous Fish Cook*, Gail Duff's *Fresh All The Year*, Marcella Hazan's Italian books, and Alan Davidson's *North Atlantic Seafood*.

Above all she triggered a cookery revolution when she published a book for slimmers by a French chef. The slimmers were patients at Christine Barthélémy's health spa at Eugénie-les-Bains in south-west France; the young man who devised the recipes was Christine's husband, Michel Guérard. The book, *Cuisine Minceur*, went on to become the most successful chefs' book ever published.

Anxious not to be branded oddball by his peers, Guérard swiftly wrote *Cuisine Gourmande*, about food to eat when you get sick of slimming, like caviare and lobsters. 'The era of the chef as hero had begun,' says Ms Hobhouse. 'Suddenly cooking was about charisma. And above all it became big business. I sometimes wonder what kind of a monster I released.'

She had not only signposted a new style of cookery but opened up a new role for chefs as authors. French masters dropped their whisks and picked up their pens, as they tumbled over themselves to get into print. A stream of chefs' books emerged, initially published by Robert Laffont in Paris, from the likes of the Troisgros Brothers from Roanne, Frédy Girardet from Lausanne, Roger Vergé from the South of France, Jacques Madmin from Nice, and Georges Blanc from Burgundy.

Other publishers jumped on the bandwagon, and with television adding lustre to the stars we acquired our own chef heroes: Albert Roux and his younger brother Michel of Le Gavroche in London and The Waterside Inn at Bray; and Anton Mosimann, the former *Chef des Cuisines* at the Dorchester, owner of Mosimann's in London.

The chefs who cook in the six British restaurants rated most highly by the *Michelin Guide* are all now in hard covers. The Roux brothers, Nico Ladenis of Chez Nico, Pierre Koffmann of La Tante Claire in London, Raymond Blanc of Le Manoir aux Quat' Saisons near Oxford; and south London's new two-star chef Marco-Pierre White of Harvey's, will be dashing on to centre stage next month with *White Heat*.

Ms Hobhouse still admires writers of passion and knows their books will endure for decades, from Elizabeth David through to Elisabeth Luard. On the other hand, she thinks the emergence of the professional cook as a star is the most exciting thing that could happen to food.

'I was talking to Alice Waters [another cook, another book] who runs California's most prestigious restaurant, Chez Panisse, and she was saying how wonderful it was, because we both remember cooks as scruffy fellows of dubious hygiene. Now they are monarchs of all they survey, completely conscious of their status and ability. Cooking will never be the same again.'

Caroline Hobhouse has seen some momentous changes in British attitudes to food since her school days, when Spam fritters were on the menu. Our attitudes will continue to polarise, she predicts. 'The tired mother will cook convenience food in the week, but she will plan for a special party at the weekend. There will be food for special occasions, and fuel food, and we don't mind if it's a McDonald's. We just turn off.'

Inevitably, food in the Nineties is going to be about fashion, she thinks. 'The idea that you had the same food in 1950 that you had in 1910 has changed. From now on, it's never going to be the same two years running.'

You Don't Have to Mortify the Flesh to be a Vegan

If you think you would enjoy eating Imam Bayildi, the Turkish delicacy consisting of aubergine shells stuffed with sautéed onion, tomato, sultanas and pine nuts, glistening with virgin olive oil...

If you find mouth-watering the idea of a moist plateful of tabbouleh, juicy grains of bulgar or couscous, with handfuls of chopped green coriander, parsley, mint and spring onions, dressed with oil and lemon juice... If these delicious dishes appeal, low in animal fats and cholesterol, packed with fibre, vitamins and minerals, you are one who enjoys the food of vegans.

Vegans? But aren't they those aliens with a peculiar message from inner space, who believe you shouldn't abuse your stomach by putting food into it?

It is true that vegans are minimalist vegetarians. They decline to eat flesh, fowl, fish, dairy products or honey, so as not to exploit animals, even insects. Still more minimalist are fruitarians, who believe it wrong to eat the living leaves and roots of vegetables.

Despite these earnest sentiments, vegans have recently been getting a bad press. Alternative treatments for breast cancer at the Bristol Cancer Help Centre – which was named in a medical survey as showing a higher relapse rate than conventional treatment units – were apparently based on a vegan diet. So some have concluded that, far from alleviating the effects of cancer, a vegan diet might aggravate it.

Carnivorous columnists immediately crowed about this apparent failure of a diet which excluded meat. One writer linked the misfortunes of Bristol patients to character defects in vegetarians such as Hitler, and attributed Prince Charles's slow recovery after his polo injury to eating organic veggies instead of British meat.

Dr Alan Long, the celebrated research adviser to the Vegetarian Society, a vegan himself, points out that the Bristol diet was not strictly vegan. In any case, vegans claim no curative powers for their diet, although there are 'anecdotal' reports of successes.

'There is extensive evidence,' Dr Long says, 'that the vitamins in carrots and cabbage in particular prevent disease. And, to coin a cliché, prevention is better than cure. For example, carotenoids – the precursors of Vitamin A – cut down the free radicals implicated in cancer and heart disease. There is now a paper showing that raw carrots can be effective in killing listeria.'

The Vegan Society has 4,000 members, and hundreds of thousands more subscribe to its principles. Dr Long would guess that 70 per cent of vegans thoroughly enjoy their food and live well. But probably 30 per cent of vegans have chosen the diet precisely because it can be meagre, Dr Long suspects. 'People of anorexic disposition are drawn towards it,' he says. 'This may be how some cancer patients feel. They get into a state of self-mortification, have a desire to purge themselves and achieve a catharsis. I myself think that, in cases of cancer, you've got to be gentle. Give the system the easiest run possible, but don't be abstemious, spare or meagre.'

The Vegan Society was founded in 1844. Its chairman, Richard Savage, says it was formed to dispel the view, held by the medical establishment, that anyone on this diet would quickly perish. 'We were told we would all die. So we set out to show that you could live on a compassionate diet. It was never intended to be a miracle cure-all, but we do discover now that our diet has the lowest total of saturated fat – and we are less likely to get diet-related cancers.'

Vegans don't see their choice of food as limited. Basic grains are so varied, from wholemeal and white flours to couscous, bulgar, oatmeal, barley, maize (to make polenta and cornbread), rice and millet. The range of pulses and dried beans is similarly vast, as is the variety of vegetables now that exotic specimens are flown in fresh to supermarkets from all over the world.

Mediterranean, Balkan, Middle Eastern, Caribbean and South American cuisines are full of varied dishes which happen to be vegan. With all these ingredients and with all these cuisines to draw from, a good cook should be able to turn out a feast every day. But alas there is no indication that vegans are better cooks than anyone else, and they are forever toying with meat substitutes, nut rissoles and lentil cutlets. The worst of these must surely be tofu or soya bean curd.

Customer: 'What's this?'
Waiter: 'It's bean curd.'
Customer: 'I don't care what it's been. What is it now?'
What it is now is a bean pretending to be a slice of junket. At the South Bank Polytechnic, a team of food scientists is labouring to produce a bean burger made of tempeh (fermented rice and soya beans). They call it a Shamburger. I call it a shame.

Vegan food is as good as the cook who prepares it, but gastronomy is not what concerns vegans; many of them choose the penance of sticky brown rice and jaw-gumming wholemeal pastries. The conclusion has to be that, to the vegan, choice of food is a moral and religious statement. The following recipe, therefore, is a statement of another kind: Food is Fun.

Guacamole is the perfect first course for a dinner, and it is a good party food as a dip or in tacos. It complements party wine, the oily content protecting the stomach lining from over-fast absorption of alcohol. The texture is bland and slippery, but the seasoning will tingle the most macho of taste buds. And it does not exploit animals, fish, the birds or the bees.

GUACAMOLE

Serves six
2 ripe avocados (buy in advance to ripen)
half an onion
$\frac{1}{2}$lb ripe tomatoes
$\frac{1}{2}$bunch fresh coriander (stalks and leaves)
2 fresh green chillies
juice of one lime or $\frac{1}{2}$ lemon
1 tbsp virgin olive oil
sea salt, freshly milled black pepper to taste

Don't prepare the avocado until the last minute, or the flesh will discolour. An hour or two before serving, place tomatoes in boiling water for one minute, and remove skins under a cold tap. Make four cuts and squeeze out pips into a cup. Chop flesh into small chunks. Chop onion very finely. Chop green chillies finely (Mexicans would leave the seeds in, which makes it hotter, but you can remove them). Finely chop stems of coriander, reserving leaves for garnish. Mix onion, tomatoes, oil, some of the lemon/lime juice, coriander, chillies, seasoning into a bowl, and leave to blend.

Half an hour before you are ready to eat, spoon out the flesh from the avocados, mash with a fork and blend with the seasoned tomato and onion, tasting to check seasoning. Add more lime juice, oil, salt or pepper as required. Cover the bowl with clingfilm and leave in the fridge until serving. Garnish with coriander leaves.

Everything but the Quack

What can you get from a 5lb duck? Many amateur cooks open the oven to find that it doesn't amount to much.

Questions in arithmetic papers have more obvious answers. If a 3½lb chicken can feed four people, how many will a 5lb duck feed? Six is not the correct answer, as anyone roasting one for the first time will have found out, usually while carving for friends at the table.

Only the genius of the Chinese can make a duck serve six or eight. Spicy, crispy duck is one of the great eating experiences of the world; the meat shredded, the crackling skin cut into strips, folded into pancakes with sliced spring onion, matchsticks of cucumber and dabs of sweet hoisin sauce.

The real Peking Duck takes about 24 hours to prepare, but shorter recipes achieve a similar effect; for example, simmer the duck for 30 minutes in water spiced with star anise, peppercorns, sliced green ginger, chopped spring onions and sherry. Let it cool in the liquid another hour, before drying it and painting it with melted malt syrup (which they sell in Chinese supermarkets) or with a solution of honey, sherry vinegar, and cornflour. Hang it in a draught for a few hours to dry out (people have been known to use hairdryers), then deep-fry it in a wok or deep pan for 15 minutes (it may be easier at home to fry it in two halves).

Duck, in some of the world's best restaurants, serves two only. In Switzerland, at Frédy Girardet's three-star restaurant in Crissier, near Lausanne, it comes at you twice, at about courses four and five – after the *amuse-gueules*, after the soup of frogs' legs, after the paupiettes of sole with salmon and saffron and after the Cassolette lobster. The duck is roasted for 30 minutes in a very hot oven, then presented at table, where the breast is carved and served. The legs are returned to the oven and offered to you 15 minutes later, when you may have finished eating the breast.

The Romans prized duck. In the recipes of Apicius they are boiled first, as in the Chinese recipe above, then finished by frying, and accompanied by a spiced sauce with honey and wine. The

Romans also cooked them with turnips, a dish which the French claim they invented.

What the French did invent was *foie gras*. They discovered that when you fattened up ducks and geese you not only produced fine large birds, but also fine large livers. The more you fed them, the bigger they grew. The goose livers that make up the truffled *foie gras* of Strasbourg will weigh around a kilogram each, twice the weight of the liver of an overfed duck. In a normally fed duck, the liver weighs a couple of ounces.

The by-product of these overfed birds are the large breasts, known as *magrets*, which are now the fashion of the food world. Briefly cooked, and served pink, they have ousted fillet steak from the businessman's lunch. The result is that any duck breast, however modest or small, is now described as a *magret* – or on some menus as a *maigret* but that is to confuse a noisy bird with a quiet detective.

Their popularity can be gauged by their emergence in pairs, on plastic trays under clingfilm, in the classier supermarkets. But it is a pity to surrender to this easy but expensive way of buying duck, says Brian Turner, patron chef at Turners in Walton Street, London. Having paraded the *magrets* as stars, he found himself awash in surplus legs, livers, fat and bones.

Since profit in restaurants derives from economical use of ingredients, the livers go into warm liver salads, or pâtés and terrines, the bones are simmered to make rich, succulent stock for soups (the essence of so many excellent soups in good Chinese restaurants). The copious fat is used to impart its delicious flavour to sautéed potatoes.

And the legs, Brian Turner has discovered, lend themselves to confit of duck, a dish which is fast overtaking *magret* as a favourite on his menu. In rural parts of France, the confit is the peasants' thrifty way of conserving unused duck or goose. Once the precious liver has been removed and sold on, the rest of the bird is chopped up, including wings and gizzard, and preserved in its own fat, so that pieces can be retrieved at any time during the winter to add body to a stew or soup, or dropped into a warming cassoulet of haricot beans with pork, lamb and Toulouse sausage.

So, what do you get from a 5lb duck?

Two magrets: weighing 6oz each, easily parted from the rib cage (easier if you cut out the wishbone first).

Two legs: weighing 6oz each with bone (anyone who can dismember a chicken can snap the base bone and cut out the legs).

Liver: a few ounces to be fried up as a treat to serve on toast.

Bones: a box of a rib cage, plus the neck and the heart, which makes a savoury stock.

Fat and skin: when rendered down, it yields at least three-quarters of a pint, which is ample for preserving the thighs.

THE MAGRETS

Trim neatly, and fry in a little fat for two minutes skin side uppermost, then 10 minutes skin side down, so that the fat runs out and the skin crisps. Remove to a hot plate and cover, while you make a sauce, deglazing the pan with a glass of white wine, adding a splash of port when the alcohol has evaporated. Stir in a little duck stock made with the bones, and whisk in a couple of knobs of butter to give the sauce a sheen.

THE DUCK FAT

Cut fat and skin off duck. Chill it, then chop finely or mince it. Put in a pan with a glass of water over lowest heat, till fat has melted. Heat the fat to evaporate the remaining water, being careful not to let the fat colour. Strain carefully to remove impurities.

CONFIT OF DUCK

Rub the thighs with a cut clove of garlic, sprinkle with salt, and leave for 24 hours. The next day, mop the legs dry and stew them gently for $1\frac{1}{2}$ hours in their own fat in a low oven, covered with foil to avoid browning. They are done to perfection when juices run clear when pricked with a skewer. If you have overcooked it, and the meat disintegrates, you have made rillettes. Well done, anyway. Strip the meat from the bones, shred with two forks, press it down in a jar and cover with duck fat.

Back to the confit. Strain fat carefully. Put the legs in an earthenware crock, and cover with fat, making sure they don't touch sides.

If you don't have enough duck fat, make it up with lard. Keep for a week before using, but, made properly, a confit keeps indefinitely in a cold place under its coating of fat. To cook: Roast for 15 minutes in medium oven, finishing skin side down in a frying pan to crisp.

DUCK STOCK

Chop the bones, neck, and heart. Put them in an oven dish. Cover with a chopped onion, a chopped carrot, and two chopped sticks of celery. Roast for 30 minutes in a hot oven. Transfer to saucepan. Cover with water and some glasses of vin de plonk, adding bay leaf and peppercorns, bring to boil, and simmer two hours, skimming regularly to remove fat. Strain. If you want the fine finish of a consommé, clarify by whisking in, away from the heat, one white of egg and two minced field mushrooms, and then bring stock to the boil. Strain through a cloth. Season to taste.

A Little Bite of What You Fancy

The subject of aphrodisiacs never fails to tickle the imagination. You might be inclined to think all the claims are nonsense. But this isn't so. There are drugs, hormones and glandular extracts which do the job, but as their aim is to alter the metabolism they can also be dangerous.

So it is perhaps with relief that one turns to the harmless nonsense of a book called *The Foods of Love* (Dorling Kindersley, £8.99) by Max de Roche. It claims to contain 'the Delights, Vertues, Magickal Properties and SECRET Recipes for all manner of exquisite LOVE POTIONS and proven Aphrodisiacs'. The idea that love's secrets may be distilled into potions has always held great attraction, but food is what really turns the author on.

Food of every kind from seafood and game to figs and pomegranates, from chocolate and nuts to truffles and ginseng and royal jelly. Indeed, it seems that there isn't any food at all that has not been prized as an aphrodisiac by one culture or another.

Max de Roche is the *nom de plume* of William Stobbs, a former principal of Maidstone College of Art. He is now 76, and he has studied the mythology of aphrodisiacs all his life. He says it may not be a coincidence that his wife, Joanna, is 25 years younger than him, and that he fathered the youngest of his children when he was 65. The prime ingredient for a good love life, he maintains, is good basic nutrition. But he's aware that it takes two to make it work.

The perfect meal to arouse desire, he suggests, would start with oysters and champagne, followed by lobster and Chablis, and finish simply with fresh figs (eating them is an orgy in itself, he says) and perhaps a glass of armagnac. The meal would be essentially light, and more than two glasses of wine would weaken the effect.

The dinner table has often stood in as a dramatic metaphor for the bed in films: Albert Finney started it in *Tom Jones* as a young stallion, and recently rounded it off as the middle-aged hotelkeeper in Kingsley Amis's *The Green Man* on television, offering an attractive customer a seductive dish of asparagus *laid* between *sheets* of lasagne.

Food is taken to an orgy of excess in Peter Greenaway's *The Cook, The Thief, His Wife and Her Lover*, and in Ferreri's *La Grande Bouffe* (with its unforgettable milk pudding moulded as a breast). In Itami's *Tampopo* the two lovers transfer a raw egg from mouth to mouth in an unspeakably erotic way.

Puritan sums up British restaurant guides, and British dining out in general. The outrageous exception to this rule is Marco-Pierre White, owner of Harvey's in Wandsworth, which won a second Michelin star earlier this year. He has just been presiding over the publication of his first book, *White Heat* (Pyramid, £16.95), an unambiguous statement about how very, very sexy food can be. He takes the view that 'there's one reason, and one reason only, why a man takes a woman out to dinner.'

So it is no accident that his dishes are composed of frenzied sensual encounters, writhing limbs of langoustine in congress with squids' tentacles, buttery oysters spawning fat grains of caviar. 'Oysters, what are they if they are not sensuous? People who don't see that they are erotic will never see anything. I do squid in a sauce of their own ink, which is orgasmic, it's just like drowning. The liquorice black sauce sticks to your fingers, sticks to your lips.'

Although only 28, he has seen colleagues fall into the trap of nouvelle cuisine only to end up with twee pictures on a plate. Influenced by his Italian mother, he held on to his passion for sensual flavours, smells and textures. 'I do a Tarte Tatin (upside-down apple tart) which is sensuous and decadent, it sticks to your mouth and fingers, it's an excuse to get dirty, wipe your sticky hands on the tablecloth, the napkin, your trousers. Everyone likes an excuse to get dirty.'

Not everyone, perhaps but certainly people like Oliver Reed, who's an ardent fan of Harvey's. 'He's my most sensual customer,' says Marco-Pierre. 'He doesn't give a fig about knives and forks, he eats with his fingers. He has a feast, he doesn't care if the sauce drips on his tie, you know he's really enjoying himself. If you haven't got this passion in you, it's very sad.'

Lobster, crab, oysters, clams and mussels fan this passion. The Chinese will take apart with their fingers a sticky crab in garlic and black sauce and the highly civilised Belgians will don a bib and then bathe in a *waterzooi* of crayfish or lobster. This Green Mussel Bisque is based on a recipe from Seppi Renggli in New York and is as sensual as any, but you don't have to swim in it.

GREEN MUSSEL BISQUE
Serves 4
3lb mussels
$^{1}/_{2}$ bottle dry white wine
1 head of celery, including green leaves
1 onion
1 bunch parsley (or dill, or coriander)
sprig of thyme and a bay leaf
3 cloves of garlic
1 small bulb fennel, with green fronds
olive oil
$^{1}/_{4}$ pint double cream
freshly ground white pepper

Chop half the onion and one stick of celery and put them with the cleaned, bearded mussels in a large saucepan. Cover with white wine, adding a sprig of parsley, the thyme, and the bay leaf. Bring to simmering point, and cook a few minutes, until mussels open. Strain, reserving mussels and liquid. When cool, remove mussels from shells.

Roughly chop the celery, fennel, garlic and remaining onion, and sweat in a heavy pan in a little olive oil for about 10 minutes, stirring constantly, till vegetables are tender. Blend in a food processor, together with the mussels and their liquid, pressing through a sieve with a wooden spoon to extract all juices. Add the cream, reserving a teaspoonful, to the mussel broth, and boil to reduce volume to two-thirds. Season with pepper (and salt if necessary), and whisk in last spoonful of cream before serving. Garnish with the finely chopped parsley.

The Renggli refinement is to cool the broth, divide it between four soup bowls, and cover with circles of puff pastry. Chill 30 minutes more, then brush with egg wash (one egg yolk and one spoonful milk, beaten together) and bake in hot oven 10 minutes, then lower heat another 10 minutes till it browns. As you cut the crust at table the scent explodes in your face.

Designed by Italians . . . Eaten by Everybody

The most sensational pasta shape in Italy was created by Giorgetto Giugiaro, celebrated designer of the original Volkswagen Golf. Pasta designed by a man in the motor trade may seem a strange idea to us, but not to the Italians. Cinzia Ceccaci, an executive with the clothes company Benetton in London, explains: 'The designer in Italy designs everything. He designs the car, then he does the tyres, then he does the people. He starts with the shoes, then he does the underwear.'

And eventually he arrives at the pasta. They can't stop designing, agrees Valentina Harris, presenter of the BBC's recent series on regional Italian cooking. 'It really gets to my heart-strings; they make an art form of pasta, and it's only flour and water.'

Giugiaro's pasta sculpture is called *marille*. It consists of double tubes of macaroni, welded together to retain shape during cooking.

The inside is ribbed to encourage the sauce to cling. In order to scoop up even more sauce, *marille* also has a curved flap, resembling the doors on the De Lorean sports car – the ones which flew upwards. (Yes, that was another of the 70-odd cars Giugiaro has designed.) He was commissioned by Voiella, one of the big pasta companies, and this set a trend. 'All the big companies are commissioning top designers now,' says Buitoni's man in London, Allan Allbeury. 'They release a new shape every year.'

Pasta has never been more fashionable. It enjoys star billing in the trendiest restaurants from Rome to London. It's the food of the Nineties, achieving what our new Prime Minister, John Major, would call social mobility, having been for so long the food of the poor. We're not talking of spaghetti, which is still the most popular shape in Italy, and in Britain too. No self-respecting Italian would go into a trattoria and order Spaghetti Bolognese (unless they were in their home town of Bologna; but that's something else, a *ragu* cooked with 15 ingredients for at least 12 hours).

The pasta revolution is comparatively recent. In the economic boom of the Fifties and Sixties, consumption of pasta went down. Pasta was held in low esteem, pasta made you fat. Then two American dieticians, Ancel and Margaret Keys, wrote a book on the Mediterranean diet, showing that the food of South Italy was the healthiest in the world. 'It wasn't the pasta that made you fat, they said. It was what you put on it – the butter, creamy sauces and helpings of cheese,' says Valentina Harris.

During her researches while writing nine books on Italian food, Mrs Harris (maiden name Sforza) has counted some 652 different kinds of pasta. They accompany Italians from the cradle to the grave. 'An Italian baby gets its first pasta at about the age of eight weeks,' she states. 'You get baby pasta in tiny star shapes and circles from the chemists, beautifully designed, not a millimetre thick. You enlarge the hole in the feeding bottle, and off you go.' And when they see you off, in hospital perhaps, they'll serve you delicate, easy-to-digest pasta in *brodo*, fine noodles in broth.

Valentina Harris recommends making your own or buying fresh pasta from Italian stores, but she deplores the 'blotting paper' sold as 'fresh' in most supermarkets. Better to buy dry pasta.

Pasta is the stuff of mythology. The innkeeper who spied the naked Venus through the keyhole modelled tortellini in the shape of her navel. The tangled form of tagliatelli is said to represent the tresses of Lucrezia Borgia. And the prosaic explanation of the origin of spaghetti (the left-over central stems forced out of the machine making macaroni) is rejected in favour of the tale of a girl taking dough to the bread ovens, and falling asleep. The dough seeps out of the holes in her pannier and dries in long lengths, so the girl boils them instead.

Which sauce goes with which pasta, says Valentina Harris, is a matter of much regional debate – even family rows – but red sauces (tomato) usually go with long pasta, and creamy sauces (with ham, peas, mushrooms) with chunky pasta. But today's trends accommodate everything going, from coloured pasta – tomato for red, spinach for green, squid's ink (and even chocolate) for black – to pasta flavoured with vodka and champagne.

The quality of the pasta is vital. It should have a sheen, a rich yellow colour, hold its shape when cooked, and must be eaten, of course, *al dente*. 'The English cook it too long,' says Valentina Harris, 'which makes it gluey and indigestible and heavy on the stomach.' The off-the-wall test: throw a strand of cooked spaghetti against the wall and if it sticks, it's done. The biggest-selling pastas are Buitoni and Barilla, and they make most supermarket own brands. What fussy Italians buy, however, are the De Cecci or Agnesi brands.

Pasta is the original fast food, ready in 10 minutes. In its simplest form, it can be eaten as a snack at night when you get home with friends. A 'spaghettata' as this is called, is a small serving of spaghetti each, cooked *al dente*, tossed in olive oil and crushed garlic, with a few *peperoncini* (dried red chilli peppers). The most famous quick pasta dish is plain boiled spaghetti, with a knob of butter and parmesan cheese, which is known as *pasta di cornuto* (which means horn). When an Italian husband is served this instead of a slow-simmered, lovingly cooked *sugo* (sauce), he may wonder whether this is the end and he has been cuckolded.

Pizzaiola Sauce

This is the traditional quick tomato sauce, cooked by every Italian Momma in every Italian home, every day. It may seem simple but if you don't do it right, it will be tasteless or bitter, too wet or too dry. Make the sauce while the spaghetti is boiling. You will need four tablespoons olive oil, heated. In it, cook three finely sliced cloves of garlic till brown, then discard. Add 3lb skinned fresh tomatoes, deseeded, or two tins tomatoes, chopped, two tablespoons of tomato concentrate, salt, and simmer gently for five to 10 minutes. At the end, add two tablespoons of dried oregano, stir for a minute, then serve.

Little Ears of Pasta – Orecchiette

This pasta is slightly tougher and more chewy than most, and you need to buy it from an Italian store to get the real thing. Asking for it is difficult, as Italian assistants will not understand you if you don't get it exactly right. Phonetically its 'oh-ray-kee-etty'. Having bought it, make this marvellous dish of contrasting textures, colour and flavours. While buying orecchiette, also get some pancetta ('pan-chetta') which is the rich-tasting, fatty bacon which has been cured, unlike British bacon, without the benefit of injected water.

Serves 4
1lb broccoli, cut into very small florets
12 oz orecchiette, or pasta shells
6 tablespoons olive oil
1 thick slice pancetta or streaky bacon, finely diced
2 cloves garlic, peeled and finely sliced
salt and pepper
grated Pecorino or Parmesan cheese
(salt)

Cook the pasta rapidly in plenty of salted boiling water for 12-15 minutes, till soft but chewy inside (*al dente*).

After 10 minutes add the broccoli, bringing it back to the boil quickly.

Meanwhile, gently fry the pancetta in the olive oil until transparent, then add the garlic. Keep the heat low and do not let the garlic brown. Remove the garlic (unless you don't mind the extra bite, which can be fierce).

Drain the pasta and broccoli and in a warmed bowl, swirl the olive oil and pancetta mixture to coat it well. Sprinkle generously with grated cheese.

Serve extra olive oil at the table.

Treat Yourself to a Belly Full of Roots Recipes

Caribbean food can be so exotic, so exciting, so evocative. Yet only the tiniest handful of restaurants serves a community of over half a million West Indians in Britain. By contrast the Chinese population, which is a fifth of the size, generates an industry of at least 5,000 restaurants.

Why should this be? Chinese restaurants are supported by Chinese customers, says the Trinidadian playwright Mustapha Matura. 'West Indians don't eat out as a habit. But this may change with the growth of the black middle class.'

The generation which came to Britain in the Fifties is not passing on its traditions. 'The children of these immigrants are eating Kentucky Fried Chicken, pizza and burgers,' says Mr Matura. 'The traditional island recipes are beginning to dry up.'

In the minds of West Indians home cooking can summon up memories of their roots. And roots are exactly what summon up the memories – starchy tubers such as cassava, yams and sweet potatoes, plantains (green bananas) and hairy eddoes. They are not really foods to excite the gourmet.

'Starch puts people off,' Mr Matura agrees. 'West Indian food is poor people's cooking, food to fill your belly. But it's also food for enjoyment.'

It is cooking born of plantation poverty, where starchy roots and leaf greens were the main ingredients, and fish and meat the seasoning. The leftovers of salt cod, salt beef and salt pork, imported from Europe by the slave owners, provided meagre bones and scraps, but great skill and ingenuity was employed to make the most of them. Still today, a dish of crab will be enriched with flakes of salt cod. A one-pot stew of fresh meat may also include salted meat. Brined pigs' tails will be added to a stew to lend gelatinous texture.

So there are barriers to Europeans enjoying West Indian food, but they are not insurmountable. On the contrary, Cristine MacKie, who publishes a book on West Indian food in the spring, thinks the day of West Indian cuisine is coming.

The islands of the Caribbean are a stew pot of cultures – African, Spanish, Portuguese, Dutch and even Indian and Chinese (they came to work the plantations when slavery was abolished). Add this combination of cooking skills to some exotic ingredients, and the effect can be explosive.

Most of us who see the colourful displays at Afro-Caribbean counters and shops will delight in the juicy mangoes, canary yellow bananas and scented pineapples, creamy coconuts and tingling limes, golden pawpaw and sweet guava; the pumpkins slashed open to spill their orange seeds, the array of fierce red and green chillies and yellow and red bonnet peppers, and unusual vegetables like okra (ladies' fingers). But in themselves these ingredients give no clue to the exciting dishes they inspire: fish cooked in coconut; clams with lime juice; chicken with lemon and banana; pork with allspice and chillies; fried fish soused in vinegar with chillies. There's the Spanish influence in Caribbean pilau, based on paella, red snapper, oysters, and chicken cooked in fish stock; or the dramatic fish and meat combination in pepper pot made with beef, bacon, lobster and crayfish.

Cristine MacKie says it is the aroma and spicing of West Indian food which is so special. 'If you haven't had coconut rice made from freshly-made coconut milk, you have not lived. The smell is sensational.'

There are cooking techniques unique to the West Indies, she says, such as cooking a couple of tablespoons of sugar in oil till it browns before frying meat in it, so as to develop a caramelised sweetness and colour, before adding water to make a stew.

There are dishes, too, with vegetables unique to the West Indies, such as callaloo, the green tops of the eddoe root. It tastes of spinach but is almost indestructible in the cooking. In callaloo soup it is simmered with fresh crab, thickened with finely chopped okra, spiced with chillies, and sometimes seasoned with salt cod. It is indeed one of God's great dishes.

When the Great Dawn of Jamaican Cuisine breaks, ackee and salt cod will surely feature on the menu. The ackee is a yellow fruit with a slightly burnt, bitter note, which looks like delicately scrambled egg. It is served in a colourful breakfast dish, with a tomato sauce and flaked salt cod, cucumbers, olives, and hard-boiled egg. (You can buy ackee at around £3.75 a can in Caribbean shops, and callaloo at under £1.)

But the most popular everyday dish in the Caribbean is 'rice and peas', in fact rice and what we call beans.

RICE AND PEAS
Serves 6
1 lb Basmati rice
$1\frac{1}{2}$ pints coconut milk (see below)
1 can red kidney beans (or black-eyed beans)
2 cloves garlic
2 sprigs fresh thyme
Salt and freshly milled black pepper

Wash the rice well, put in a pan covered with the coconut milk and bring to the boil. Lower the heat, and use a mat or heat diffuser to prevent burning. When the liquid is absorbed, add the juice from the beans and an equal quantity of water. When nearly soft, after about 20 minutes, gently stir in the beans, the crushed garlic and the seasoning. Add more boiling water as required. Serve garnished with slices of green pepper. Or leave to cool overnight so that flavours blend, and serve reheated the next day.

Reach for the Stars, Inspector Brown

No surprises in the new *Michelin Guide to Britain and Ireland*. No new three-star restaurant. Only a single one-star restaurant upgraded to two.

Not even a launch party or press conference greeted the guide's publication this year which was pushing Michelin's reputation for self effacement further than ever. Surely it owed us an explanation. Perhaps I could track down its anonymous head.

Ever since the British edition of this French tyre company's red guide was launched in 1974, it has been undemonstrative to a fault. It is conservative in its judgements, cautious about recognising new talents, terse in communicating information, anonymous to the point of secrecy. Restaurant critics may resent its continuing position as leading arbiter of excellence in restaurants, but it continues to be the guide that matters to the chefs. A Michelin star, in fact a rosette, is usually the last mile of the road to assured financial success. But its food criticism is non-existent. We never learn what the inspector eats. In fact, it's hardly a restaurant guide at all. It actually claims to be a motorists' guide in the first place (giving singular importance to hotels, petrol stations, up-to-date town maps, and distances by road) and would put itself on a par with the *AA Guide to Hotels and Restaurants* rather than *The Good Food Guide*, The Ronay Guide and The Ackerman Guide.

It seems ridiculous that, having put its inspectors to so much trouble and expense to reduce Britain's acceptable eating places to some 5,500, the guide denies them voice. The only details of food are those which follow an entry for a three-star restaurant, mentioning three of their best dishes. So the intangible magic and mystery of Le Gavroche (three rosettes) in Mayfair is summed up as: *Soufflé suissesse, Assiette du boucher,* and *Sablé aux fraises.*

The head of the British edition successfully maintained total anonymity for the first 10 years of his reign, professing to be a Mr Smith until Paul Levy in *The Observer* revealed that Mr Smith was in fact Mr Brown. Good Heavens.

Derek Brown, publisher of the guide and head of Michelin's map publishing, prefers anonymity but made an exception for *The*

Independent on Sunday. Mr Brown is the image of the Prime Minister, John Major, from the firm specs and curl of the mouth to the quiet poise and tidy suit.

He laughs. 'A man leant over in the Tube the other day, and patted me on the knee. "Doubles," he said. "There's money in doubles, but I knew you couldn't be John Major, travelling alone, on the Tube." Perhaps John Major causes confusion in restaurants: 'Prime Minister? You must be joking. You're the man from Michelin, eating out incognito.'

Derek Brown trained in the catering industry and joined Michelin 20 years ago. The way he was recruited sounds like something out of le Carré. 'I was sent a ticket to Lyons, told to present myself at the airport with a red Michelin guide in my hands, and I would meet one of their inspectors likewise carrying a red guide. I was to follow him.'

He duly made the connection, and accompanied his spymaster to lunch and dinner, on a two-week eating marathon round the region, eating at the best and worst restaurants. Then he was hired.

Some critics claim that Michelin's British inspectorate does not apply the standards required in France. 'This is simply not so,' says Mr Brown. 'All the staff are trained to exacting French standards.' People also assume that our restaurants are not as good as those in France. He denies this strongly. 'The best British restaurants are the equal of the best in France, Germany, Italy and Spain, even if some of our worst are worse than their worst. But they don't get into the guide.'

French bias is another charge made against Michelin. If it's not French, the guide doesn't rate it. 'That's nonsense too. Statistically we have more Chinese restaurants listed than French. Our only criterion is the food: is it good quality or bad, is it prepared well or badly, is it consistent?'

Critics also complain that the British guide has only ever given two establishments three rosettes (Le Gavroche and The Waterside Inn, Bray), both, incidentally, run by Frenchmen (Albert Roux and his younger brother Michel), when other equally good places get ignored.

How is it that they can't acknowledge the evident three-star skill of Raymond Blanc of Les Quat' Saisons, near Oxford, John Burton-Race of L'Ortolan, near Reading, and, in London, Nico Ladenis of Nico's, Pierre Koffmann of La Tante Claire, and Marco-Pierre White of Harvey's?

'This isn't a conspiracy,' says Mr Brown, 'It isn't just a bunch of Frenchmen in dirty overcoats coming here, picking their way through a meal, pulling it apart and saying, "Britain – three stars, forget it." There are four or five restaurants knocking on the door, and they may get a third star in 1992 or 1993. They know what they have to do.'

The line between three stars and two is very thin. 'Consistency is very important because you are paying a lot of money and you have a right to expect this standard every time. Sometimes the bread will let a place down, or something offered free like the *amuse-gueules* before the meal. Or the petits-fours with the coffee may not have been made freshly that day. Or we might not think the wine list quite matches the quality of the food. But it's all about cooking. Comfort has nothing to do with it, although chefs who get the food right will want to provide comfort too. Nobody wants to pay three-star prices to eat in a drill hall.'

Derek Brown wouldn't complain about the quality of British restaurants, but he agrees the price is often daunting: say, £70 or £80 a head for a meal out. 'It is not the cost of food or labour. The cost of buying and cooking a piece of meat is the same in Britain, France, Germany, Italy. It is the enormous overheads of financing. That's how I've worked it out.

'Running a restaurant in Britain is seen as a way of getting quite a serious middle-class income. In Europe it's considered an artisan's business. You can be a greengrocer, cabinet-maker, candlestick-maker or a restaurateur, particularly in Italy where the husband and wife and grandma work together in it. They are like shopkeepers. It's not the same in this country. They are professionals and we are often amateurs.'

People coming from middle-class professions often start under-capitalised, he says. 'Many go in on the basis that friends have told them they are damned fine cooks, so they should open a restaurant. But they need 2,000 friends to come four times a year or it doesn't work. In France and Italy you'll find many restaurants have been in the family for three generations, and there are no mortgages to be paid off.'

Amateurism has its charm, but it loses out on consistency every time. 'I remember in the early days agreeing to meet my team of inspectors at a restaurant,' says Mr Brown. 'We were the only customers for lunch, and the meal was appalling. It was cooked by a man in the kitchen wearing a City suit, evidently the owner. At the end of the meal, as we do, we declared our identity. Like a scene from Fawlty Towers the owner reeled hack, clutching his head. 'Oh no, not Michelin.' Then desperately he cried, 'We're closed.'

Eat Your Way to Perfect Health

Five portions of fruit and vegetables a day can prevent cancer and heart disease, says the World Health Organisation. Sifting through its definitive new report on nutrition, Michael Bateman asks whether healthy eating can be this simple and brings good news for gourmets.

By the year 2000 many people in the world's poorer countries will be eating like rich people. That's the bad news. The good news is that some of us in the world's more affluent countries will be eating like peasants and will be a lot better off for it.

It is now quite clear that the diets of the humbler communities of south-west Europe, the Balkans, the Middle East, Latin America, south-east Asia and Japan have long-lasting health benefits. Ironically, as the people of these countries become richer they quickly drop their good eating habits and assume our bad ones. They adopt our energy-dense diet, with its high volume of saturated fat and sugar, and its low intake of starchy, fibre-containing foods.

As a result, says a report published this month by the World Health Organisation, premature heart disease and preventable cancer will be a major problem 'in virtually every country in the world by the end of this century'.

We have not been ignorant of the scale of the problem in the West. In North America, better dietary habits have helped reduce the heart disease rate by 50 per cent in 20 years; in Britain by 12 per cent. But there are still 160,000 premature deaths a year from heart disease, not to mention the numerous deaths from diet-related cancers.

It is not as if we don't know about healthy eating and cutting down fat. Hardly a week goes by without some St George of the media taking his sword to Dragon Fat. The burly and bearded BBC television cook Michael Barry skewers about three pounds of lamb kebabs, having first explained, panting and puffing like a gardening presenter, that he is paring off the fat.

And most of us do, yes we do. But the World Health Organisation doesn't just advise, 'Hold the fat'. It says, 'Hold the meat', too; we eat far more protein than we need, and what the body does not metabolise it turns to excess fat. The WHO also says cut out sugar completely, if you can.

The trouble is that those of us who are getting the message about what we shouldn't eat have not quite established the pattern of what we should eat in its place. We need to shift our dependence on convenience processed foods and buy more fresh food.

But, the WHO points out, the trouble is we are hearing conflicting messages. 'In North America and Western Europe, health campaigns compete with much greater advertising campaigns for individual foods by food companies. These companies could play an important part in developing new foods with a more appropriate nutrient content.' Food companies don't disagree with the overall message. But each one argues that a 'modest intake of their own product is compatible with a healthy diet'. Instead of eating energy-dense products made of fat, sugar and salt which sustain the food companies' profitability, says WHO, we should be taking more of our calories in the form of carbohydrates. Up to three-quarters of our energy requirements should be fuelled by carbohydrates. In other words, we should eat like peasants and revert to having more potatoes, pasta, rice, and wholegrain bread, and experiment with polenta, bulgar and couscous. We should put back on the menu dishes of pulses, lentils and beans.

Above all, we should eat more vegetables and snack on fruit instead of sweets and puddings, at least 1lb of fruit and vegetables each day. We have known for some time that vegetables provide bulk and fibre that the digestive tract needs. But now epidemiological studies conclusively establish that vitamins A, C and E, contained in fruit and vegetables, play a vital anti-oxidant role in preventing not only heart disease, but cancers too (they scavenge the free radicals caused by fatty acids in the cell membranes).

In America they coined the slogan Eat Five Portions of Fruit and Vegetables a Day. They put it to a poll and found that a quarter had eaten none on that particular day and that half had eaten only one portion. It is no coincidence that in Scotland, which has the highest heart disease rate in the world, they eat fewer vegetables than anywhere else.

It is not so very difficult: we don't need to throw away our old recipe books. I give some examples of favourites from countries which have a famously good heart disease record. So follow these World Health guidelines:

Soups: vegetable soups are a tasty and thoroughly satisfying way to reintroduce vegetables into the diet; tomato, asparagus, lentil soup, big soups like minestrone, cold soups like gazpacho, soups with a potato base like vichyssoise, and especially soups with cabbage, a vegetable packed with vital anti-oxidants.

Salads: give them an everyday role. The French sensibly include a green salad with most meals. Serve raw vegetables as crudités, especially green pepper and carrot, or grated vegetables with a dressing. Raw cabbage is particularly potent, and an ingredient of the famous American coleslaw – except that Americans tend to counteract its healthy benefits by making too creamy a dressing.

Pasta and pizza: southern Italy has one of the best health records in the world, due to high consumption of pasta, pizza and vegetables, and comparatively little meat. Pasta can be combined with tomatoes or vegetables like broccoli to make delicious healthy dishes. The Italian peasant way with meat and cheese is to use them in moderation as flavourings – in meat sauces or grated on pasta.

Quiches and tarts: onion or tomato tarts, such as pissaladiera are tasty, healthy alternatives to put in the repertoire. You could experiment with wholemeal pastry and a cauliflower filling with sesame seeds as an alternative to an energy-dense dish.

Vegetable stews: in the South of France, in Spain and Italy, there are always local versions of ratatouille, the delicious stew of aubergines, onions and green peppers cooked in olive oil. The healthy Balkan people have their vegetable stews too. With an egg, for example, and some bread, they can serve as main courses to provide a substantial meal.

Vegetable side dishes: lentils, pulses and beans – such as black-eyed peas which cook in half an hour – are easily prepared, and are useful alternative sources of protein as well as providing key anti-oxidant vitamins.

Offal: liver and kidneys are rich in Vitamin E, and a tasty alternative to a steak or burger. You can increase their food value and taste by cooking liver with onions, and kidneys with mushrooms, as in Kidneys al Jerez.

Dessert: make fruit after a meal a rule. Oranges and citrus fruits are brimming in Vitamin C; so are blackcurrants and kiwi fruit. Apples and bananas contain Vitamin E (which has the power to reinforce Vitamin C's anti-oxidant properties). Yellow skinned fruits like apricots, peaches and melons are rich in beta-carotene (the precursor to Vitamin A), as are pumpkins, swedes and carrots.

Hasty, Hasty, Very Very Tasty

Fay Maschler is not a short-cut cook; she loves to work to a long, complicated recipe, 'preferably from some recherché book like Colman Andrews' *Catalan Cuisine*'.

On the other hand, putting on a meal in a hurry poses no problems at all. She knows she can stroll into her walk-in larder and come out with an armful of good things: pulses and pasta, cans of tuna and beans, salami and virgin olive oil, spices and herbs; the deep-freeze will yield good bread, ready to spring to life in the oven; the fridge is likely to be stocked with pounds of best minced beef and plenty of tomatoes.

'I'm not of the school that says a spoonful of cream or a dash of sherry turns a tinned soup into a gastronomic event,' she hastens to point out. But these days, easier late-night shopping in delicatessens, Asian shops and supermarkets means you can often put together crispy bacon, or fried pancetta, and some spinach leaves to make a stylish salad: or grill some continental sausage with a relatively high meat content such as bratwurst, and serve it with a salad of boiled potatoes dressed with olive oil, and several kinds of mustard. As long as your oil and mustards are the very best, you have some superbly quick and easy dishes at your fingertips.

It is essential to invest in superlative ingredients for your store cupboard. 'Rather than buying a tired Italian salad which has been sitting all day in a display cabinet, it would be better to make your own from a tin of white haricot beans, a tin of tuna-fish and some chopped onions,' she says.

'Far better than a carton of coleslaw from the deli, which has been sweating in a tub of malt vinegar and inadmissible amounts of sugar, would be a tin of sauerkraut heated up with a little white wine and some additional spices. You could make believe you were in Alsace.'

A simple plate of pasta will jump into focus when you bring out the best parmesan cheese, which you will have stored in a large chunk, double-wrapped in some aluminium foil in the cooler part of the refrigerator.

Fay Maschler is not only London's most celebrated restaurant reviewer, five times winner of the Glenfiddich Award for restaurant criticism, but also the author of some fine cookery books, including the highly-praised *Howard and Maschler on Food*, with Elizabeth Jane Howard (Sphere, £3.99)

The weekly round of reviewing can blunt her appetite at home, but it never dulls her keen passion for the art of cookery. At her home in Belsize Park, north London, cookery books spill from the shelves to form hills on the tables and dunes on the floor. Off the long, high-ceilinged kitchen is a walk-in larder packed with gourmet rations. Dried Hungarian paprika peppers hang from the ceiling beside salamis bought whole on trips abroad. The larder even has its own Chinatown, the province of her friend Owen, a sociologist and serious two-wok cook, who shares the house with her.

Fay inherited her respect for food from her mother, who was brought up in India, so did not experience British wartime food deprivation. But it was not until she was a teenager, during a lonely school vacation in America, that Fay decided to teach herself to cook. She found it to be as intellectually stimulating as it was sensually gratifying.

Her passion for long, slow cooking is against current trends, as is her antipathy to 'healthy' eating. 'When I'm entertaining I usually cook food which people regard as unhealthy. But it's all right to eat it occasionally. When you're entertaining is the right time to make an exception.'

What she most likes to cook is food that is not served in restaurants. 'I like frying. If I have some nice sausages in the fridge, I'll fry up apples and onions together: it's a small amount of effort but it makes all the difference from something pre-prepared from Marks and Spencer. I rather like scattering fried breadcrumbs on things, which is something you absolutely could not get from the cook-chill counter.'

A favourite fast dish is dhal with fried onions and spiced hard-boiled eggs. 'I use small orange lentils (masoor dhal in Indian shops) and they cook in less than half an hour. I grind whole spices and fry them in a little oil, and, this is my own invention, I fry thick slices of hard-boiled egg in the oil until the yolk bubbles and crisps up.' (They develop an unusual mushroomy, fungal flavour.)

This is the kind of food she would share with her sister Beth Coventry, who is a professional cook. But when she wants to entertain friends in the fast lane she is attracted by the thought of quail. 'People love to pick at things. You can buy them in advance, one each (plus a few extra), sauté them in oil, then cook in a covered pan for 20 minutes. I would serve them with savoury rice.'

But since you cannot get quails everywhere, she suggested a speedy alternative, a Gulliver-sized hamburger (to be sliced into six or eight like a cake), stuffed with melting Roquefort cheese, served with spicy dips. It needs to be made with the best quality beef, preferably organic, with some fat – but no onions, other additions or flavourings to distract from the juiciness of the meat. 'I never eat a plain steak. After a couple of mouthfuls it's very boring.' But minced meat, beef, lamb or chicken allow you to create interest with salsas, chilli and onion pickles on the side.

Fay Maschler would put out salami with the drinks, sliced from the whole sausage in the larder. For a first course, she might serve a juicy tomato salad, prepared and left to marinate while the rest of the meal was being cooked. To finish, a sharp lemon soufflé from Elizabeth David, which cooks in 12 minutes. 'Everyone is very flattered to be served a soufflé. People are frightened of making them, I don't know why. This recipe never fails.'

ROQUEFORT GULLIVERBURGER
For six
3lb best minced beef
4oz Roquefort
salt

Take a sheet of greaseproof paper and spread half the minced beef on to it, patting it flat into an 8 to 9-inch round. Slice the cheese finely to cover. Spread the rest of the mince on top, sandwiching the cheese in the middle. It should be at least 1 inch thick.

Fry in a hot pan sprinkled with salt, but no fat, about five minutes each side (more or less if you prefer). Or grill, well seasoned with salt.

Slice into segments, like a cake, and serve with chilli dips, salsas, spicy onion yoghurts and chutneys, Indian pickles, ketchup, preferably with chips and green salad.

Homage to a Taste of Catalonia

Confronted so often with nouvelle cuisine, do you wonder what happened to ancienne cuisine? It's the mark of a modern culture that in order to embrace machines which reduce time and effort in the kitchen, it chucks out time-honoured techniques.

Perhaps it is a romantic notion that ancienne cuisine, food prepared slowly and lovingly, will taste better. But it may account for the continuing success of *Catalan Cuisine*, a cookery book by a

Californian, Colman Andrews, which has become cult reading – a timely antidote to nouvelle cuisine.

Not only is much of Catalan cooking time-consuming, but it does not even look good on the plate, Andrews confesses. 'Much of it tends to be a monochromatic, murky-looking brown,' he says. 'It is food to be eaten, not admired from a few steps back. Its aim is not to seduce the jaded but to fill and please the hungry.'

Andrews has been acclaimed by his peers as a culinary Marco Polo, revealing secrets of the last undiscovered cuisine in Europe. It has certainly remained hidden from the millions who have tramped through the region since the tourist boom. But now Catalan cooking is gaining wider recognition because Barcelona, the region's capital, is becoming one of Europe's most fashionable cities, and is host next year to the Olympic Games. Its cooking is regarded as a symbol of its separate identity from Spain, buried during Franco's 36-year rule.

So it is back, the complete ancienne cuisine, a 2,000-year throwback to the Phoenicians, the Greeks (L'Emporda on the Costa Brava is a Greek city), the Arabs and the Romans (Tarragona was the Roman capital of Spain). From these roots come two of the basics of their cooking; sofregit (see recipe), a long slow-simmered sweet onion sauce, used to start many dishes, and picada, an uncooked sauce of pounded nuts, fried bread and herbs added at the end of cooking as a piquant thickening agent.

This style of cooking is very ancienne, because although a sofregit cooked for one hour is OK, a three-hour sofregit is three times better; and a picada needs to be beaten patiently by hand with a pestle and mortar, because a food processor cannot grind the nuts to a smooth enough paste.

Colman Andrews, who was in London recently, says Catalan cooking is not to be confused with Spanish cooking. Indeed, most Catalans do not consider themselves Spanish, any more than Scots care to be called English. Andrews was fascinated to discover that Scotland houses the only Catalan restaurant in Britain, the Barcelona in Glasgow. 'The owner, Allan Mawn, told me he identifies Glasgow with Barcelona. Both are cultural capitals but not the nation's administrative capital. Both countries are subservient to a dominant country next door. Each country has its own suppressed language. And they have their own, different attitude to cooking. There is a common fondness for offal, such as kidney, liver, tripe, black pudding and poor man's foods such as rabbit and beans.'

Colman Andrews summarises Catalan cooking concisely, but it is his ability to make historical links which pleases scholars of the kitchen. For example, you will learn that the ceviches and escabeches of the Hispanic and Latin-American world, those tempting dishes of marinaded fish, derive from the Catalan, by way of the Middle East. Escabetx, to use the Catalan spelling, is an adaptation of a Persian meat stew called sikbaj in Arabic. (No puns about 'pass the sikbaj, Alice', please.) Recipes for Escabetx first appear in a four-teenth-century Catalan cookbook, *Libre de Sent Sovi*, and as an appetising method of preservation it can hardly be improved upon.

Also unique to Catalan cuisine is *pa amb tomaquet*, no more than a slice of bread and tomato. Exactly how it should be prepared is the subject of fierce argument (such as bouillabaisse arouses in Marseilles), even though it concerns only the toasting of a piece of bread, rubbing it on both sides with a ripe tomato, drizzling it on both sides with strong green olive oil, scattering it with sea salt. It is the subject of a much-quoted essay by Leopold Pomes, entitled *Teoria I practica del pa amb tomaquet*. It is often eaten with anchovies, sardines, herrings, mountain ham or botifarra sausage, white Pyrenean cheese, and occasionally garlic.

Catalan ingredients dictate the style of cooking: olive oil, garlic, tomato, aubergines, salted anchovies, almonds and other nuts, rice more than potatoes, salt cod, eggs, fresh fish and shellfish, poultry and game, pork rather than lamb, and snails.

Five or six sauces, used as seasonings, dominate most dishes and shape this unique cuisine; their mayonnaise, *maionesa* (con-sidered to originate from Mahon in the Balearics), and its garlic-flavoured brother *allioli*, are mixed freely with vegetables, fish and cold meat; romesco sauce, from the old Roman capital Tarragona, is made with pounded hazelnuts and almonds and dried peppers and makes a rich piquant relish for a fish stew, served at table like the French rouille; *samfaina*, which is more like a purée of ratatouille than a sauce; *picada*, used like a pesto; and finally *sofregit*.

'First you make your *sofregit*' is how literally thousands of
Catalan recipes begin. They have been making it at least since 1324,
when it appeared in a Catalan cookery book as a pan of mild sweet
onions fried slowly and gently until dark and almost like jam in
consistency. Sometimes white of a leek was included together with
salt pork, and eventually, with its arrival from the New World, the
tomato.

SOFREGIT

    2 lb onion, finely chopped
    1 lb tomatoes, skinned and seeded, chopped
    2 cloves garlic, crushed and chopped
    olive oil

Cover bottom of a pan with oil to half-inch depth. Heat, and cook
onions on lowest heat, stirring to prevent burning, until light or red-
dish brown. You have to keep an eye on them all the time. Raise heat
a little, add the garlic, and cook for a minute to introduce the
flavour, then add the tomatoes and cook gently until water evapo-
rates, and the tomatoes melt into the mixture.

You could make this the night before, and use for the basis of a
rabbit stew, simmering the jointed rabbit gently in the sauce for one
hour; or a Mediterranean fish soup, adding fish stock and cooking
a variety of firm fish, say pieces of conger and monkfish, for 15 minutes and adding some shellfish at the end: crayfish, mussels, clams.

ESCABETX

    Serves 8-10 as a first course
    2 lb fresh anchovies (or sardines)
    white flour to dust fish
    olive oil for frying
    For the marinade:
    $\frac{1}{2}$ pint olive oil
    $\frac{1}{4}$ pint white wine vinegar
    12 cloves garlic, peeled
    sprig of rosemary and 2 bay leaves
    $\frac{1}{2}$ teaspoon paprika

Gut the fish, wash, dry and flour them, and fry till crispy brown (about five or six minutes). Layer the fish in a suitable container. Put the ingredients for the marinade in a pan and bring to the boil. Pour the hot marinade over the fish, and when cool put in the fridge to stand for three days. This dish will keep for a good month. (A South American cerviche is more likely to be made with raw fish, marinaded in lemon juice and served with finely chopped onion and fresh chillies.)

A Crustacean Worth Shelling Out For

Who would have thought that the salmon, proud king of the rivers, could be tamed? But today for every wild salmon sold, we buy more than 30 farmed fish, the battery chickens of the lochs.

Is it not a short step, therefore, to battery-farmed lobsters? A fortune is waiting for the marine biologist who can crack it, but so far this fierce crustacean has resisted. For one thing, it is an anti-social beast which will kill rather than share lodging. For another, it will need a very patient, listening bank to wait for the first return on investment since a lobster takes at least six years to reach maturity at a very modest weight of one pound.

But there's nothing quite so weird and wonderful in the ocean as the lobster. And there are none that taste so good as British lobsters, whose season has just started, a good month early this year. At £8.50 to £9.50 a pound, lobster is always going to be a luxury item – although that's no more than you pay for a bottle of good wine. But it is a cheaper luxury than foie gras, caviar and truffles – and it is British. Scottish lobsters and Channel Island lobsters are good, but connoisseurs rate the Harwich lobster best.

The North Sea is particularly cold here and the lobsters never seem to grow very big. But perhaps because of their feed, the taste is delicate and the colour exquisite, a deep fiery orange, with speckled ruby flesh when cooked. Chris Oakley, chef at The Pier seafood restaurant at Harwich, enthuses: 'They are nutty, sweet, light and moist.'

He buys his lobsters from the Bennett family – John and Joan, and their three sons. Their fathers and grandfathers were fisherfolk before them, crewing the cod smacks on the Dogger Bank. When John Bennett was a boy Harwich boasted a fleet of 30 shrimp boats, but the tiny plankton on which the shrimps fed were destroyed by detergents, and they are no more.

In the Thirties, when John left school at the age of 14, there was no demand for lobsters. They caught crab, whelks and cockles, or at night they would row up the River Orwell to catch river eels. Even in the Forties when he came back from the Navy there was still no interest in lobsters, although there were plenty about. 'You couldn't sell them for more than one and six a pound,' says Mr Bennett.

Then, in 1950, a Dutchman came over and said he would buy all they could catch if they could get them to him alive in Holland. A year later a French dealer moved in and set up a tank to keep the lobsters alive. 'Up and up went the price, until the place was over-fished and now lobsters are scarce again.'

In the early days, Mr Bennett caught the lobsters with bicycle wheel frames, with a net strung across them. As bait he fastened a gamey, but not rotten, piece of fish to the centre and knotted a rope in three places to the wheel, lowering it to the seabed, some 12 to 30 feet below. 'There was no expense. You needed 20 old bicycle wheels and a ball of string.'

It would take half an hour to set them down; half an hour later he would pull them up, using boats to work the hoops at high and low tide, taking the feeding lobsters with a sudden snatch. It was laborious work, so John decided to build his own lobster pots. They were hooped frames with netting, with passageways leading to a parlour. 'The lobsters would catch themselves, and you could come back 24 hours and find them still sitting in the saloon bar.'

Lobsters take on the colour of their surroundings, explains John Bennett. In Harwich most are coal-black when you catch them, but some are rust-coloured. 'They live in a patch of rocks or rusty ship-wrecks,' he says. 'If you look at a pilot's map you'll see all the wrecks marked. In the war this was called E-boat Alley. There are about 70 or 80 wrecks in the approaches to Harwich alone, mostly sunk by mines.'

Shipwrecks make extremely desirable residences for a decapod (in France fishermen create lobster housing estates by chucking old cars over the cliffs). They provide the security which is essential in the spring when lobsters change shells and are at their most vulnerable, especially from their shark-like enemy, the tope.

Lobsters are lethal to gather. You must tie the murderous claws with thread to prevent the lobster savaging its neighbours, and it is impossible to avoid getting a nasty nip from time to time. It has two claws; the larger one is called the damper, or sometimes the thump or dump claw, which it uses to hold food as it feeds. The smaller claw has saw-edged cutting teeth, and being gripped with this will be very painful. 'It's like dragging your finger across a saw,' says John Bennett.

Yet, fishermen, fishmongers and chefs, everyone who works with lobsters, love these strange, slow and apparently clumsy creatures. They are not so slow when it matters, however, if a lobster is feeding on a hoop and feels a pull on the cord before you snatch it, it will flick its tail and push off.

'I've been told a lobster can move at 100 miles an hour for just a foot or two,' says Chris Oakley. The tail fans out into five blades, and under it four pairs of paddles provide lift-off. The articulated shell winds up to an extraordinary tension, and it suddenly propels itself forward like a rocket, out of harm's way.

Oakley most prizes those rusty lobsters which match the mangled metal of their habitat; they cook to a delicate pale rose colour. The tenderest meat comes from lobsters weighing between one and one-and-a-half pounds. At that point they are about six years old, though some are known to live 40 or 50 years, growing to a metre in length and weighing over two stone.

It seems a pity to eat them, but if you want to you should buy them live. It is a measure of the veneration in which we hold these ancient monsters of the deep that the death of one lobster dropped into boiling water provokes the anger of animal activists, while the fate of billions and billions of shrimps and prawns despatched exactly the same way does not.

Which is the kindest method of killing? There are several myths: that you should start cooking it in cold water so that it is lulled to sleep as the water gets warmer, but this isn't so: that it screams when dropped into boiling water, but this is the noise of air being expelled by the sudden change in temperature. In fact, the Universities Federation for Animal Welfare has declared the latter method the most humane, and it is also considered by chefs the best way for retaining flavour.

How to cook lobster

To each litre of water add four ounces of salt, bring to the boil, drop in the lobsters, and cook for 11 minutes per pound (a little longer for a one-pound lobster) and then remove to ice-cold water. Tear off the claws, which you must crack to extract the meat, and cut the shell vertically down the back. Serve it with no more than a simple home-made mayonnaise and salad. The shells are too good to throw away and should be crushed, roasted and used to enhance a fish stock, or to make lobster butter, which you can freeze and keep to serve with grilled fish.

Lobster butter

This recipe is from Anton Mosimann, the distinguished chef-patron of Mosimann's Belgravia, and works equally well with shells of crayfish, crabs and other shellfish.

> $1/4$ lb of lobster shells
> 6 oz butter
> splash of brandy
> salt and freshly ground pepper

To intensify the flavour of the shells, roast them in a moderate oven (350F/18OC/Gas 4) on a baking tray for 15 minutes. Cover the shells with greaseproof paper and crush them with a rolling pin or mallet, then beat into the butter. Heat in a saucepan, skimming off the froth. Fill the pan with water, strain the liquid into a bowl and leave to cool. The lobster butter can be lifted off the top. Reheat the butter to simmering, add seasoning and brandy and strain through muslin into a small bowl. Refrigerate or freeze until required.

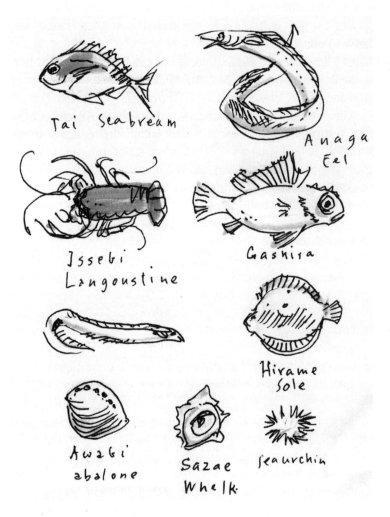

Tai Seabream

Anaga Eel

Issebi Langoustine

Gashira

Hirame Sole

Awabi abalone

Sazae Whelk

Seaurchin

Grey Mullet for Grey Matter

Soon we'll all be getting fed up with admonitions to eat healthily. Then what? It is a sure sign that a message has reached its sell-by date when both main political parties embrace it simultaneously.

The Government has just committed itself to a huge public health programme, part of which is a putsch on diet. And the Labour Party, in a 30-point health plan, promises to encourage production of healthy foods and discourage subsidies for unhealthy foods.

This is all very well, says Professor Michael Crawford, director of the Nuffield Laboratories of Comparative Medicine, but these measures only take account of the body. The next priority should be research into how to improve our minds.

And what his own nutritional research shows is that granny certainly knew best: eat up your fish, it's good for the brain; conversely, if you don't eat fish, your brain won't develop.

For the last 10 years, Professor Crawford has been analysing a series of worldwide studies on nutrition in pregnant mothers to see how diet affects a baby's birth-weight. He concludes that brain growth is retarded unless there is a ready supply of the essential fatty acids (EFAs) which are so abundantly provided by fish. He accepts that more research needs to be done, but given the findings on what low intakes of EFA do to us, he finds it fascinating to speculate how much a high-fish diet might improve brain-power.

Not entirely tongue-in-cheek, he instances the Japanese, who eat five times more fish than the British. Throughout evolution, good nutrition has contributed to the survival of the fittest, and he argues that there are few people fitter than the Japanese. 'One could use the quantitative measurements of the financial markets, exchange rates, trade surpluses, business drive and financial intelligence. Based on the USA's growing budget deficits since 1981, Japan could just about buy out America by the end of this century.' Isn't it possible that nutrition has played a role in the shaping of nations, he asks?

Professor Crawford's starting point is the beginning of life on the planet. He says you can chart the growth of both body and brain of all species according to their access to nutrients, essential vitamins and trace elements, and he's certain that it is the marine food chain which provides the best nutrients for the development of the brain and nerves. 'The origin of brains and nervous systems first occurred in the sea,' he says. 'So it's not surprising to think that we still owe an allegiance to that nutrient chain.'

Where there is a deficiency of marine nutrients, he says, degeneration follows. 'When cretinism was discovered among people living in the mountains of Europe at the beginning of the century, it was found to be due to deficiency of the trace element iodine, which is derived from marine sources. Without iodine, the brain degenerates.'

Professor Crawford believes that apes are a degenerate form of *Homo sapiens*' common ancestor, because they lived away from the rich sources of marine foods which human kind has enjoyed. There was no need to tell early man to eat up his fish, since his advanced brain recognised that the best source of food was by the sea, in rivers, and especially estuaries.

Professor Crawford accepts that it may be 10, 20 or more years before scientists can recommend nutrient levels for the brain and nervous system. Scientists don't even fully agree on precise levels for body growth. They have not started on the brain. Within the last 10 years nutritionists have universally accepted that the essential fatty acids in blue fish (tuna, mackerel, herring, sardines) and in cod liver oil are marvellous for the heart. But the exhortation to eat more fish couldn't come at a worse time, just as we are busy polluting the estuaries, the starting point of the marine food chain. Professor Crawford suggests the next priority for the political parties should be a commitment to cleaning up our waters.

The latest political initiatives on health, recognising that we are what we eat, comes some 15 years after the first committee reports urged us to improve health through a better diet. Perhaps we may not have to wait as long for the powers that be to get the message about fish. Considering that Britain, like Job's Egypt, has been visited by a series of plagues over the last few years (food poisoning reaching the highest levels ever, doubts about eggs, soft cheeses, not to mention the anxieties that accompany additives, food irradiation and pesticides), fish is finding its own way back onto the menu. It offers good value, quality, nutrition, it's healthy, it's delicious, and if it's not fished in the estuaries, it should still be safe. What a bonus if it improves brain-power too.

PESCADO AL HORNO

Baked fish must surely be the best for the brain since none of the essential nutrients, EFAs and iodine, are lost in this process. The flavour of the fish is not only enhanced by the vegetables, but the bones yield up a glutinous richness to the juices.

Serves 4

2 lb grey mullet or sea bream or 4 steaks of cod, hake or firm white fish
1 lb onions, finely chopped
2 tins of tomatoes, chopped
2 red or green peppers, deseeded, cut into strips
3 cloves of garlic
1 dry red chilli, crumbled (or pinch of cayenne pepper)
6 black olives, stoned and cut small
2 oz sultanas
1 oz pine nuts
2 glasses dry white wine
4 tablespoons olive oil
parsley, chopped
salt and pepper

In a heavy flying pan, heat the olive oil, and on a high heat cook the onions for three minutes with a lid on, shaking to prevent burning. Lower the heat and let the onions cook gently for 20 to 30 minutes till soft and golden. (Taste them to check that they are sweet.)

Add the chopped peppers and cook for another 10 minutes. Then add the garlic and chilli. Raise the heat, pour in the white wine and cook till bubbling. Now add the chopped tomatoes, olives, sultanas, pine nuts, salt and pepper, and cook for a few minutes till blended. This sauce can be made well in advance and kept in the fridge overnight if necessary.

Pre-heat oven to 350F/175C/Gas 4. Lightly oil an oven dish and place the fish in it; pour the sauce over. Cover with aluminium foil and bake for 20 to 30 minutes, testing with a skewer for doneness – the flesh should flake away from the bone.

Sprinkle with parsley and serve with rice or boiled potatoes to mop up the sauce.

A Great Tradition Goes up in Smoke

Was I the only one to squirm when MPs sprang to defend the Great Britsih crisp? British it may be, but great? It's laughable.

No fewer than 50 MPs, among them an ex-prime minister, Lord Callaghan, signed a motion calling on the Government 'to save the Great British crisp', threatened as it was by a directive from Brussels. The directive actually concerned Great British flavourings such as malt vinegar, bacon, chicken and cheese. As a feat of food technology, British crisp-making is certainly great; the process successfully converts £1-worth of potatoes (retail) into £13-worth of crisps (you can work it out – a 30g packet costs 20p).

But of course MPs weren't defending the crisp on gastronomic grounds. It was the industry they were fighting for, and the jobs which depend on an annual market which has grown over the last 15 years to £17m.

Now we do have some great foods in Britain well worth defending. Let's hear it for the York and Bradenham hams, Stilton, Lancashire and Lanark Blue, Dundee cake, shortbread, Welsh lamb, Angus beef, marmalades and jams, chutneys and pickles, and our wonderful smoked foods – smoked salmon, Arbroath smokies, Loch Fyne, Craster and Manx kippers.

And it just so happens that Brussels has already got its beady eye on our kippers. It has served notice on the industry that production of kippers by the traditional method of hanging them on wooden hooks will have to cease on safety grounds. If a satisfactory hygienic method cannot be found, they will have to go.

The humble kippered herring has been having a bad time at the expense of its socially superior cousin, smoked salmon. But it would be a shame to see it vanish. Salting fish, and then smoking it, is a peculiarly British phenomenon, the two processes combining to confer a high degree of preservation. The salt excludes oxygen, thus retarding decay, and the smoke partly dries the surface and gives it an oily seal.

In the past, herring was heavily smoked: the red herring for several days, and the Yarmouth bloater (the unsplit fish) for a day or two. In *Kettner's Book of the Table* (1877) kippered salmon from Scotland was considered so salty that 'few can eat more than a very thin slice of it, grilled with exceeding swiftness'. It was a coarse product. Today's lightly salted, lightly smoked product is an anachronism, because the process is irrelevant, refrigeration being the modern agent of preservation.

In fact, if brining and smoking were introduced as new processes today they wouldn't be licensed. In the Sixties there was a cancer scare associated with ham and bacon curing, because in the process the nitrate salts converted to nitrites, which reacted to form potent carcinogens, nitrosamines. The curing processes have been modified, and scientists claim that most of the nitrites we ingest today are those present in our own saliva.

Carcinogens also surface in the kippering process, in hydrocarbons deposited by 'hot smoking' at temperatures of over 70C. It is now general commercial practice in the modern stainless steel kilns to reduce the cancer-forming compounds by generating smoke outside the kilns, and purify it with water sprays before passing it over the fish.

Food technologists have developed a distilling process to make 'liquid smoke', a flavour essence in which the most dangerous compounds have been removed. How does the finished product compare? I suspect it requires even greater kippering craftsmanship than the traditional methods.

I bought two kippers, a heavily smoked Isle of Man kipper from fishmonger Phil Diamond of Turnham Green, in west London, and a conveyor-belt kipper in a plastic pack from a supermarket. There was no contest. In the red corner, in a glittering cloak flashing gold and bronze, was the proud Manxman, potentially dangerous. In the blue corner, limp and lifeless in a dull brown cape, the tame

Technokipper. Seconds out of the ring and they were in for a real grilling. At the end of the round the Manxman was glowing, in splendid condition and perspiring slightly, exuding a taste of aromatic oils. In the mouth it was luscious and moist, tasting complex, smoky, sweet and salty. One hundred points. Technokipper was a pithy, saline sponge, with irrelevant colouring and no discernible smoky taste. Nul point.

So much for the appliance of science. I suspect the Technokipper will meet with the approval of Brussels and the Manx kipper will not. It may be unrealistic to expect officials in Brussels – the city which, in the thirteenth century, gave us the chou de Bruxelles, the Brussels sprout – to satisfy the demands of gourmets. I wish they did.

What they do, and very energetically, is concern themselves with making consumers aware of exactly what is in our food and drink. That should generally be welcomed. I have compiled this list of EC initiatives on safety and quality control with the help of *Which?* magazine.

Lager and beer: Labels will have to list ingredients. You'll find, perhaps to your surprise, that they include not only barley, but maize and wheat flour, yellow and caramel colouring. Caramel refers to the colour and not the sauce. It is not made from burnt sugar as you would imagine, but from coal-tar dye, to which some people are allergic. The labels will also show that most beers and lagers contain preservatives like sulphites and seaweed-derived extracts to hold the head in place.

Additives: The range of permissible additives will increase from 350 to 450. Artificial sweeteners will be listed as E numbers (E stands for Europe). Saccharine will be E954 and Aspartame will be E951. Cyclamate, another artificial sweetener which was banned in Britain, will be reintroduced via the EC in 1992.

Pesticides: Limits for pesticide residues on salads will be established. Post-harvest treatment of potatoes and citrus fruits with chemicals that increase shelf-life will be acknowledged on labels.

Proportions: Ingredients will be shown in proportion to each other. How much sugar, the ratio of apple to pie crust, the amount of egg in mayonnaise, and tomato in tomato sauce.

Quality: The EC would like to produce a quality labelling scheme like the French *Appellation d'Origine Contrôlée* (AOC) which covers wines and some cheeses such as Roquefort, Camembert, Franche-Comte and Savoie. A strong case will have to be made for the unique character of the product. For example, the Scottish smoked salmon industry will lobby hard to protect its product from imitators. It's too late for Cheddar cheese, on the other hand, because the name is already too widely used now for it to be limited to cheese produced in a valley in Somerset. But Britain's growing cheese industry might plead the case for certain products; old ones too, like Stilton.

Sophie's Choice

Sophie Grigson is by nature a snappy cook. When she got home the other night at 8.30 pm after an early film, she was tucking into a superior snack within 10 minutes.

'I needed supper and there wasn't a whole lot in the house. Some celery, chicory, a red pepper, a tomato, a jar of black olives. Some granary bread. I toasted a slice in the grill, dribbled olive oil on to it, shaved slices of Spanish manchego cheese on top, covered it with a mixture of chopped vegetables and olives, put more oil on top and grilled it a second time.'

The *cognoscenti* will recognise that Sophie is talking *crostini*, which are madly fashionable in restaurants in Italy these days as appetisers: little pieces of toast topped with vegetables, or aubergine purée, or chopped mushrooms, or a spread made with black olives, garlic, anchovies, capers and olive oil.

Sophie points out that it has to be decent bread – like Italian *ciabatta*, Greek or a peasant variety. 'A slice of Mother's Pride is not the same. Bread is tremendously important, especially when you're entertaining. If everything else is a disaster, people can tuck into the bread and cheese.'

Sophie Grigson is the youngest of the cookery writers, standing out on television with her punkish blonde hair and junk earring (from a collection of many hundreds). Her cooking style is so very direct it is easy to forget that she is the daughter of the late Jane

Grigson, the admired cookery writer whose work combined literary, academic, romantic and practical appeal.

Sophie's cooking is in the fast lane, and she is of the first generation to embrace microwave ovens; older cookery writers tend to be disdainful about them, as if they debased their profession. 'I *was* a bit snotty about microwaves,' she confesses. 'Then I tried one out.' Essentially the microwave is good for foods which you might otherwise steam, she believes, such as fish and vegetables (it retains the flavour in globe artichokes, spinach and new potatoes, though asparagus is less appealing). It is hopeless, she says, for pastry, pasta or lumps of meat (although a chicken casserole is good). It is fantastic for a 20-minute chicken stock, for dissolving gelatine in water, melting chocolate and drying herbs or orange peel.

Sophie's cooking is very modern, with an emphasis on freshness, flavour and texture. For the fast meal she devised for us she uses a microwave to cook globe artichokes, saving the trouble of boiling a huge pan of water. The way she cooks the fish is inspired; it requires three minutes only in a very hot oven, since the slices of fish have been shaved to the thinness of a ruler. The salsa (sauce), which is the key to the new generation's cooking, also takes no time at all.

How to Make the World of your Oyster

At last there's an R in the month. Ever since May, oyster-lovers have been waiting to indulge in native oysters again. The breeding season over, their flavour will improve, and soon they will return to their incomparable quality which makes them quite the best in the world.

Best of all are those from Colchester. The Romans recognised the quality of the feeding grounds here, in the rich ooze of the West Mersea waterscapes, and sent the fattest back to Rome slung in nets from their boats. The first of the season will be dredged this month; then, on 25 October, the Mayor and councillors will assemble in the Moot Hall to celebrate the charter of 1196 when Richard I granted them rights to the oyster beds. They will eat themselves silly, consuming some 2,000 oysters at one sitting.

Natives may be the best, but they are by no means the most common. Rock oysters (also known as the Pacific or gigas oyster) outsell them by 20 to 1; unlike the natives, they do not have a close season and are sold throughout the year. But to me they taste less pleasant in the summer months, with their rather creamy consistency.

There is frankly a snobbery about preferring the broad, flat, native oyster, *ostrea edulis*, though there's no denying that they are satisfyingly buttery, firm, sweet and nutty. They are also expensive – the largest of the seven sizes, the Number Ones, retailing at £1 each. But the cheaper rock oyster, selling at 40p or 50p each, with its shell like the sculpted skirt of a flamenco dancer, can also make excellent eating.

Few of us Brits, however, eat oysters at all. (The French eat over a billion a year.) It takes some bravado to place these living, quivering morsels in the mouth. As Jonathan Swift said: 'He was a bold man that first ate an oyster.' It was Auguste Escoffier, the French chef who codified *haute cuisine* at the turn of the century, who dictated that oysters should be eaten raw, displayed in their opalescent marbled shells sitting on a bed of crushed ice, with nothing but a few wedges of lemon.

But, it wasn't Escoffier who popularised the raw oyster, rather its eighteenth-century reputation as an aphrodisiac. Casanova was said to have eaten 11 dozen at a sitting. Now there is some modern scientific support to the idea that they aid the libido. Professor Derek Bryce-Smith of Reading University reported last year that oysters have the highest zinc content of any food, zinc, he says, being associated with a high sperm count.

There are drawbacks to oyster-eating, however: cost (Claridges charge £16 for half a dozen best British natives); the connoisseur's insistence that they should be eaten raw; and the difficulty of getting them open. The conventional method is to prise the oyster open where it is joined by a hinge. In a restaurant kitchen there is a team of chefs working dangerously with those broad, short oyster knives. But a knack rather than brute force is involved. Wrap a teacloth several times around the oyster, the deep cup-like shell underneath. Expose the hinge, an indentation as long as the nail of your little finger concealed in the narrow end of the oyster. You don't need a special knife, any short-bladed one with a sharp point will do. Prod firmly, digging this way and that, twisting the blade till the hinge loosens. Slide the point of the knife inside the upper shell, and sever the top muscle locking it to the shell. Lift off the top shell, taking care not to spill the juices in which the oyster sits. Slide the knife under the oyster and sever the second muscle. For tidy presentation, turn the oyster over with your knife to show its smoother side.

The Big Apple

You may well be baffled by the unexpectedly large range of apples in the shops this autumn. Until this year the range of British apples has been restricted to mainly Cox's Orange Pippins, Egremont Russets and Bramleys; these represent 80 per cent of the home grown market and they have been competing with imported apples such as South African Granny Smiths, and New Zealand Braeburns.

Suddenly there has been a revolt, almost as dramatic as that against sliced white bread. The supermarkets have finally decided we are entitled to buy apples with more character and flavour. And this autumn no fewer than 60 varieties of home-grown apples will be on sale, some of them traditional 'old-fashioned' varieties, such as Charles Ross, Blenheim Orange and Chivers Delight, others more modern, developed in British research stations but ignored until now because they did not conform to perceived commercial appeal.

The revolution may have taken a long time, but the seeds were sown all of 10 years ago, when fruit farmers woke up to the fact that they had been outflanked by the commercial apple-growers of North and South America, South Africa, Australasia and France – especially France, whose Golden Delicious (hardly regarded at all in its own country) has grabbed a larger slice of our market than any other single apple.

The French took our markets by storm in the early 1980s, to the despair of British growers, some of whom responded by grubbing up acres of traditional varieties and planting Golden Delicious. This turned out to be folly, since the French apples ripen weeks before ours. For British growers it was the start of a very long fight back, led for the most part by Lord Selbourne, whose Blackmoor Estate in Hampshire is one of the three largest nurseries in the country, providing stock for the growers. The supermarket buyers told him that uniformity, durability and shelf-life were prime requirements. They added that most customers bought with their eyes, valuing colour and appearance above taste and flavour. Lord Selbourne knew from his own experience that the growers wanted varieties which offered the least problems, were disease-resistant, and high-yielding from the first year – precocious, as they call these trees.

For a while it seemed that his dream of bringing back vanishing species was unrealistic. Then he found an ally in Marks & Spencer, which last year introduced a range of a dozen 'old-fashioned' varieties with great success. One of them was Chivers Delight, a deliciously sweet, slightly acid apple, first grown by John Chivers (of the jam family) but never commercially because it was thought too temperamental. Now it is grown by his great-granddaughter, Caroline Chivers, alongside her main crop of Cox's Orange Pippin.

This year Marks & Spencer will be selling 18 old English varieties, and they expect to sell 5 million before Christmas. Safeway have gone further, and are selling 40 British-grown varieties, not only traditional, but modern ones too, which have never been given the chance to shine before. Sainsbury's are putting out 20 varieties, Waitrose 17, and Tesco 13.

Are we ready for this? We have become accustomed to the sturdy, one-note character of supermarket apples – the equivalent of plonk, in wine terms. Dr Joan Morgan, the apple historian, says that the Victorians paid as much attention to defining the taste of their apples as modern connoisseurs do to fine wine. In the applespeak of their day, for example, they would describe the Cox's Orange Pippin as 'a perfectly-balanced and subtle harmony of complex flavours, tasting of pears, nuts and a hint of spice'. We just think of it as an apple.

The Victorians delighted in the traditions of their ancestors who chose lovely names for apples, evoking 'merrie' England: Cornish Gilliflower, Worcester Pearmain, Devonshire Quarrenden and Norfolk Beefing. The art of apple culture reached a sublime peak at the Apple Congress of 1883 in London when no fewer than 1,500 different varieties went on display. Today, there is a register of apples that lists over 7,000 varieties around the world.

The British apple may be on the way back, but it has been a close-run thing. It might not have survived at all if the government had had its way: two years ago there was a blaze of publicity when the Ministry of Agriculture, Fisheries and Food (MAFF) announced it was closing down Brogdale National Fruit Trials in effect, consigning the British apple to the compost heap, since it would mean the destruction of the unique national fruit collections, the seedbed of our priceless heritage.

To anyone who loves apples, the sight of Brogdale orchards in autumn is nothing short of thrilling. The branches of several thousand trees bend low under the heavy fruit which glows in nearly every hue, from ruby red, apricot and emerald to beige, russet and gold. Brogdale grows no fewer than 2,300 different species. The 150-acre site also houses the national pear collection (450 varieties), the plum collection (350), the cherry collection (220), as well as currants, gooseberries, nut trees and old English quinces and medlars.

This story has a happy ending thanks to the Prince of Wales: through the Duchy of Cornwall he contributed 75 per cent of the cost of buying the fruit station from the government. In May, he presided over its rebirth as Brogdale Orchards, a commercial concern servicing fruit-growers and embracing a new charitable body, the Brogdale Horticultural Trust, which is an educational centre. So Brogdale becomes a living museum to the fruit which the British are best at growing, and which also happens to be Britain's favourite (we spend £550 million a year on it). It would be ironic if the new Brogdale eventually turned out to be of more inspiration to growers and the general public than the old one ever was.

The Brogdale Horticultural Trust, Brogdale Farm, Faversham, Kent ME13 8XZ (Tel: 0795-535236).

60 Varieties

Many of these apples, some traditional, but others the fruit of modern research, have never made it to the greengrocer's before. Now they may surface at a shop near you.

ALKAMENE: Green and orange-red, crunchy

ASHMEAD'S KERNEL: Green-tinged flesh, rich and juicy

BAKER'S DELICIOUS: Pale yellow in appearance, firm, crisp, aromatic

BLENHEIM ORANGE: Dry taste, slightly winey, crisp

BRAMLEY SEEDLING: The most famous English cooker, large, green, irregular size, truly sour

CHARLES ROSS: Yellow flushed with red stripes, coarse texture, juicy and sweet

CHIVERS DELIGHT: Golden yellow, crimson flush, sweet and acid balance, juicy, with fine texture

COX'S ORANGE PIPPIN: Our most famous apple, good balance of sweet and acid, aromatic, nutty flavour

CRISPIN: Originated in Japan as the Mutsu. Like a large Golden Delicious, honeyed, crisp

DISCOVERY: Hint of raspberry, crisp but ripens to soft

EGREMORT RUSSET: Firm, crisp, rich, nutty flavour

ELLISON'S ORANGE: Similar to a Cox, though the fruit when ripe develops an aniseed flavour

ELSTAR: Crunchy texture, fresh flavour, juicy

EPICURE: Cross between Wealthy and Cox. Firm, juicy

EXQUISITE: Firm, crisp, juicy, aromatic

FALSTAFF: Yellow with red stripes, good acid and sugar balance, crisp and juicy

FIESTA: Modern cross, bred from a Cox's Orange Pippin with some of the Cox flavour. Crisp, juicy

GALA: Another modern cross, sweet, crisp, juicy

GLOSTER 69: Green-tinged flesh, fine texture, juicy

GRAVENSTEIN: Enormous, uneven fruit weighing up to a pound. Coarse texture but very juicy

GRENADIER: Cooking apple. Pale yellow with russet speckles, crisp, pleasantly tart

GREENSLEEVES: Crisp, mild flavour, refreshing

HOLSTEIN: Similar to Cox, aromatic

HOWGATE WONDER: Very large cooking apple, firm until cooked when it breaks up completely

IDARED: Pink-tinged flesh, crisp and juicy

INGRID MARIE: Greenish-yellow with crimson flush, crisp,

fine-textured, juicy
JAMES GRIEVE: Fine-textured, soft, juicy
JONAGOLD: Large, creamy white flesh
JUPITER: Greenish-yellow, aromatic
KATY: Pale green skin ripening to yellow
KENT: Creamy white flesh, juicy
TODD'S ORANGE RED: Small firm, crisp fruit
LAXTON'S FORTUNE: Cinnamon-russet stripes, tender but firm flesh, sweet-scented
LAXTON REARGUARD: Yellow, flushed red and russet
LAXTON'S SUPERB: Very sweet when ripe
LORD DERBY: Cooker, stays intact when cooked
LORD LAMBOURN: Greenish-yellow, red stripes, sweet
MERTON BEAUTY: Golden-yellow, flushed with red, fine-textured, firm flesh
MERTON CHARM: Golden-yellow with creamy white flesh, tender, sweet, juicy
MERTON JOY: Creamy flesh, juicy, nice acid balance
MERTON KNAVE: Pink-tinged creamy flesh, sweet
MERTON WORCESTER: Firm, juicy, sweet
MICHAELMAS RED: Suit, juicy, with sweet aroma
NORFOLK ROYAL: Green-tinged flesh, crisp, firm, juicy
PITMASTON PINE APPLE: Juicy, distinctive rich flavour
RED JONAGOLD: Very honeyed, keeps well
RIBSTON PIPPIN: Lovely acid-sweetness balance
ROBINSON'S 13: Greenish-yellow with a quarter striped orange-red, firm, creamy flesh, juicy
ROSAMUND: Highly coloured form of James Grieve
ST EDMUND'S PIPPIN: Very rich flavour when fully ripe, crisp and juicy
ST EVERARD: Greenish yellow, almost completely flushed with dark crimson. Sweet, juicy and aromatic
SPARTAN: Turns to a deep purple-maroon colour
SUMMARED: Very crisp and refreshing, soft, white juicy flesh
SUNSET: Almost orange, sometimes flushed with red, Cox-like flavour, crisp, white flesh, aromatic
SUNTAN: Golden-yellow with grey russet patches, acid tang,

creamy-white flesh, quite juicy
TYDEMAN'S EARLY WORCESTER: Raised by the famous breeder in 1929. Particularly crisp texture, lovely scent and aroma
WEALTHY: Hardy, crisp, juicy with a hint of strawberry
WINSTON: Creamy white flesh, firm texture, juicy, notably sweet, good aroma
WORCESTER PEARMAIN: Greenish-pale yellow, sweet and juicy
ZABERGAU RENETTE: Greenish-yellow, overlaid with russet, firm and acid

Cappuccino Crazy

The craze for cappuccino which is sweeping the country is mystifying to Italians. They don't understand how we can drink it all day – with lunch, at tea-time, after dinner while in Italy it is only ever drunk in the morning.

Nor would Italians ever dream of making it at home, so they are astonished to learn that committed members of the cappuccino cult actually install semi-industrial espresso machines (costing up to £300) in their homes, and are likely to be as proud of the fine tooling on their Gaggias and Pavonis, their Krupps and Mokas, as motorists are of their Alfa-Romeos, Maseratis and Lamborghinis.

Dedicated followers of the cappuccino fashion instantly reject a restaurant which does not offer their preferred brew. No trendy new eating place hoping for a young clientele would think of starting life without a Faema Supertronic, Cimbali Bistro M30 or Gaggia Thermo Reserve.

The Red River Café was due to open in South Kensington last week, with a gleaming new industrial coffee machine duly installed and espresso cups stacked on top, when someone saw there were none for cappuccino. The correct wide-brimmed cups were bought immediately, and disaster was averted. But the Red River Café is not a brasserie or a trattoria: it is a Vietnamese restaurant.

A coffee machine by itself, however, is not enough. Howard Malin, who owns several London restaurants including Tall Orders in Fulham, says you tend to be judged by the quality of your cappuccino: 'It's the last thing people have at a meal and it's what you are remembered by.'

It's a costly business, he says, citing the film *Queen of Hearts*, in which a Soho restaurateur installs a machine costing more than the lease on the café. 'As customers have become more sophisticated in their tastes,' he says, 'so has the machinery.'

To make espresso you force hot water through compacted ground coffee at intensely high pressure. The first machines were purely mechanical (the process was invented by Gaggia in 1949), but to meet the rising demand for this kind of coffee, manufacturers have now produced advanced electronic push button machines. At a cost of many thousands of pounds you can buy machines which pump out hundreds of cups an hour, filling, emptying and refilling the coffee scoops automatically.

The machines must be nursed as carefully as any old-fashioned steam engine, which in some ways they resemble. 'You need to know about blow-back. If you don't blow off the steam at night, it creates a vacuum. In the morning it will suck back milk into its innards, all through its coils. You can't get it out, so the whole machine has to be dismantled.'

As the cappuccino tide swells to a flood, everyone wants a piece of the action. In July this year Nestlé launched instant Nescafé Cappuccino and they have sold 30 million sachets. But it hasn't been to everyone's taste. Restaurant critic Fay Maschler observed that the Nescafé people had 'rendered an Italian speciality about as exciting as going to bed with a leaky hot-water bottle.'

She noted that although cappuccino is de rigueur in the modern restaurant, the trend is for a weaker and milkier product than any acceptable in Italy. 'It seems to have been transmuted into that favourite comforting item of the British, a hot milky drink. Any taste of coffee, that fundamentally foreign, and riskily bitter commodity, is diluted and blanded out.'

What is the definition of the authentic cappuccino? Pietro de Panizza, food and beverage manager of the Hyde Park Hotel, describes it as a double dosage of strong, high roast, espresso coffee, filling one-third of a large wide-brimmed cup, which is then filled with frothed-up milk. 'No cocoa on top or any of that nonsense.'

In Italy cappuccino is drunk in the morning, he says, so he thinks Britons have confused the Italian way with the Austrian: the 'melange', taken in the afternoon with pastry at the equivalent of the British tea-time.

The melange, sometimes called a 'floater', consists of freshly-made black coffee, with whipped cream sitting on top, usually dusted with cocoa or cinnamon.

Where has he found the best cappuccino in Britain? 'Only in places run by Italians,' he says, 'though the French and Spanish understand coffee. You can't leave it to an automatic machine, because it must be made with love.'

Lesley Forbes, the broadcaster, artist and writer who has lived in Tuscany, deplores the British way with cappuccino. 'It may be very snobby of me, but I think we drink it incorrectly. We are actually following the Americans, who drink coffee with their dessert, not after it. Drinking cappuccino at the end of a meal is like having it as a dessert: it's sweet, filling and cloying. A black coffee clears the sweetness.'

Derek Brown, the editor of the Michelin guide in the UK, has been watching the cappuccino craze spread like wildfire, not only in London but in some of the increasingly stylish provincial capitals, like Newcastle, where Tom McMullen, manager of Cafe Procope, says it started in the summer: 'People have being going berserk for cappuccino.' Peter Ferry, of Newcastle's Melbourne Diner, agrees: 'A cappuccino is easier on the stomach than a water-based coffee. I'd walk a long way for a good cup.'

Derek Brown says it is mainly a young person's drink: 'It's chic, it's fashionable, stylish . . . Italian . . . *ciao*. Cappuccino sounds sexy – milky coffee doesn't.' He suspects it is a passing phase. 'I hesitate to say it, but we've seen it all before in the coffee bars of the late Fifties and early Sixties.' Memories are made of this – Lonnie Donegan, skiffle and espresso, Tommy Steele, Soho coffee bars, cappuccino.

But there are some parts of the country where cappuccino was never a fashion, because it was a living part of the culture. The Italian immigrants who brought it with them at the turn of the century must wonder why it has taken so long for their coffee habits to filter through in those parts of Britain where Italians first settled – the west of Scotland and South Wales. They were people who later made a big mark on British catering, for the Fortes sprang from Scotland, and the Bernis from Wales. Even before the First World War most of the catering staff in Largs, the Clydeside resort, were Italians. And one of the luxuries they dispensed to their summer visitors was cappuccino.

It was the same in Wales. Up and down the valleys of South Wales it has always been possible to find good cappuccino, because the cafés are run by Italians. 'The Italian cafés were cultural and political centres when I was a boy,' Tony Heath, a journalist, says. He remembers that in Tredegar, Labour's political giant, Aneurin Bevan (his milkman father was known as Bevan the milk), cut his political teeth debating issues with friends in the Italian café. Over a cappuccino.

MIXES AND MACHINERY
Cappuccino: The blend
There are two basic kinds of coffee, robusta and arabica. Robusta is heavy-cropping and grown at sea-level on trees rather than bushes. Arabica is more expensive (two and half times dearer), fine-flavoured and grown on bushes at heights of 5,000 ft and more.

For cappuccino you need a high roast coffee, ground to icing sugar fineness but not quite to powder. (Cafetière coffee is gauge 9, espresso should he gauge 3.) An espresso blend usually contains a high proportion of robusta coffee for strength, but it needs a little arabica to give acidity and character. The subtle flavour of arabica is considered to be wasted on espresso, although the Marks & Spencer espresso coffee (£1.49 for 227g) is 100 per cent arabica, a dark roast, said by aficionados to be rich and chocolatey.

Cappuccino: The drug
Jean-Anthelme Brillat-Savarin, the French philosopher gourmet who wrote *The Physiology of Taste* in 1825, commented: 'It is not to be doubted that coffee induces a high state of excitement in the brain ... I once saw a man in London crippled by immoderate use

of coffee ...'

Caffeine is the effective drug in coffee. A 150ml cup of a normal coffee blend contains 100-150mg of caffeine, two to three times as much as a cup of instant coffee, a cup of tea, or a 330ml can of a cola drink. But an espresso will contain twice as much caffeine again (this we recognise by drinking it in smaller quantities).

Excess caffeine (more than six to 10 cups a day) leads to restlessness, agitation, palpitations and insomnia. Evidence about the effect on the heart is inconclusive but advice to avoid long-brewed, reheated or long-stewed coffee is also welcome on aesthetic grounds.

More Than One Way to Souse a Herring

Could the increasing popularity of gravad lax signal a subtle shift in the national palate? In restaurants and supermarkets across the country this rich, sweet Scandinavian salmon cured with dill is beginning to challenge smoked salmon.

It would be only a short step to embrace more assertive fish dishes from the Swedish and Danish smorgasbord, such as the many delicious kinds of pickled and cured herring. But they would have to be up to Scandinavian standards. We're not talking of British-made rollmops, herring fillets steeped in fiery malt vinegar, or in non-brewed spirit which is to the mouth what caustic soda is to a sink.

This may take time. It is 15 years since the Swedish restaurateur Anna Hegarty, of Anna's Place in north London, first introduced gravad lax to her customers. They listened patiently while she explained how the salmon (lax) was buried in its grave (gravad) in a marinade of sugar, salt and chopped dill fronds, left in the fridge under a weight for 24 hours, then sliced thickly and served with sweet mustard mayonnaise. They would shudder and say, 'No, thanks.'

She refused to give up. 'It seemed to me that gravad lax was much tastier than smoked salmon. But I had to be persistent.' Soon it was appearing in specialist food shops and delicatessens; it finally passed into the national food consciousness when Marks & Spencer, the country's leading fishmonger, added it to its repertoire.

That was salmon. For people to be convinced that herring is a gourmet food may take a bigger leap of faith. But a battle plan is taking shape in London's Savoy Hotel, where chef David Sharland, who worked in Sweden, offers no fewer than nine traditional pickled herring dishes in the Upstairs Bar: mustard herring, akvavit herring, beetroot herring, herring with chives and sour cream, rollmops, glassblowers' herring (in a sweet marinade with onions and carrot), *matjes* herring, made from the virgin fish, and so on. Chef Sharland is expecting reinforcements for his kitchen from Stockholm's L'Escargot Restaurant for a Swedish fortnight. This will be an opportunity to taste authentic herring dishes and other features of the smorgasbord at their best.

The tastes of Sweden may stir atavistic memories. Anna Hegarty reminds us that Britain and Sweden have ancestors in common and a similar food history. We competed for the same fish, and before refrigeration, we both preserved it by brining and smoking. Not until after the Second World War did our paths diverge, when the British embarked on a romance with Mediterranean cooking. We swapped the swedes, turnips, parsnips and beetroots of northern Europe for the green peppers, courgettes, aubergines and olives of the sunny south.

And we exchanged the assertive flavours of juniper berries, bay-leaves, horseradish, mustard and dill for the heady perfumes of garlic, rosemary, thyme and fennel. But experiencing these flavours at Anna's Place, you are reminded how well mustard, horseradish and aniseed-flavoured dill combine to lift oily fish, like salmon, mackerel and herring, on to another plane.

'In Sweden, perhaps because there is so much space, you feel you are closer to nature,' says Anna. 'We would feel guilty about wasting anything which the earth so generously produces. We'd pick the ceps in the woods, for drying; rowanberries to make jelly; cloudberries for jam, wild lingonberries which we serve as a sauce with fish or meatballs; and tart, wild rose-hips, to make into a juice, or to be dried and stored as powder to make a tea strong in Vitamin C, or rosehip soup' (served thickened with potato flour as a pudding).

Fish was eaten several times a week, herring or cod. 'In winter we'd cut a hole in the ice and one of us, it wasn't very pleasant, would have to stand by it with a piece of string. If you caught a cod, it was so firm, as stiff as a rod.'

The cod would be cut into chunks 2½ inches thick, poached with the head and tail for 8-10 minutes, in a *court bouillon* – boiling water with chopped leek, carrots, onion, parsnip, bay-leaves, white peppercorns and salt – then allowed to stand in the liquid while a white sauce was made with some of the liquid and milk, heated and thickened with *beurre manié* (lumps of butter rubbed into equal amounts of flour) and then finished with cream. Just before serving, a few mustard seeds were crushed in milk and left to swell, then swirled into the sauce with a knob of butter.

Potatoes were the staple food, eaten every day, and celebrated in the teasingly entitled Jansson's Temptation, a dish of sliced potatoes, chopped onions, and salted anchovies, baked with cream. It was by no means peasant food.

On special occasions there was the smorgasbord, a ritualised buffet of cold and hot dishes taken in irreversible order: first, the salted and pickled herrings and many kinds of bread; second, prawns, smoked salmon, eggs stuffed with caviare, and ham with melon; third, cold meats such as tongue, brawn, cold beef, smoked reindeer, salami, sausages, liver mousse, pigeon pâté and pickled cucumbers; fourth, hot dishes, such as sautéed kidneys and meat stews, their famous meatballs, meat dumplings (*frikadeller*), and boiled potatoes. And fifth, fresh fruit, fruit salads and desserts.

Rio is Cooking

Brazilian food generally inspires only the very haziest of associations here in Europe. We think perhaps it might be fruity, like Carmen Miranda, or ostentatious, like Carnival; maybe startling, like their football, or pulsating, like their samba.

In fact, it's many of these things. Brazil is a country of enormous size, comparable to the United States in area and with the fifth largest population in the world. The humid rainforests of the north and the arid deserts of the north-east are in total contrast to the green farmlands of the temperate south, and it's a fact that people at one end of the country will never have tasted the everyday dishes of the other end, and vice versa.

In the south, there are cowboys who eat grilled meat daily, like their neighbours in Uruguay and Argentina. In the north, they enjoy the unusual fruits and vegetables of the tropics. In the north-east, the focus is on seafood and shellfish. In São Paulo, one of the largest cities in the world, with a population of 17 million, the food is different again, influenced by waves of immigrants, first the Italians in the 1880s, and more recently the Japanese (the city has the largest Japanese community outside Japan). They boast that you'll find better pizzas here than in Naples, better sushi than in Tokyo.

But Rio de Janeiro has to be the ideal place to explore the wide range of Brazil's cooking styles. Rio continues to be one of the world's most spectacular destinations. You drive from the airport past hillside shanty towns called favelas to arrive in a city whose fabulous setting is on a par with San Francisco's Bay, Sydney's Harbour and Cape Town's Table Mountain. The heart quickens as you pass the palm-lined, white-sand beaches of Flamengo, Copacabana and Ipanema. Vistas of Sugar Loaf Mountain and Corcovado, surmounted by Cristo Redentor, the giant statue of Christ, open up on every street corner.

The former Portuguese capital of Brazil, Rio, is a sophisticated city with a colonial history that is reflected in the splendour of its public buildings. It glories in a blazingly hot climate with coconut palms offering some shade (the best escape from the sun is to be found in the dense, tropical Jardim Botânico, where the lily pads on the ponds are seven feet across).

As a visitor you won't feel too far from home, since much of the population is of European descent. And you'll quickly find yourself embraced by the city's noisy rhythm, a syncopated samba of sound, with non-stop hooting traffic, accelerating cars, the crashing Atlantic breakers, the cries of beach hawkers selling food and trinkets, and beach footballers in rowdy competition.

Half the population is in transit between office and beach, the latter never more than a few streets from the central areas of the city. From seven in the morning, when hundreds of joggers take to the promenades, until night, when the city lights sparkle like precious jewels, *Cariocas* (as residents are known) are on show. Unashamed and unselfconscious exhibitionists, they have created the biggest street scene in the world.

Cariocas have an immense appetite for sun, fun and (especially) food. They eat and drink on the move, stopping at a *barzhinho de praia* (beach bar) to buy a drink of fresh *água de côco*, sipped with a straw from the freshly severed coconut, or a tender cob of boiled sweetcorn. Or they pop into one of a hundred little bars (*botecos*) with a few stools at a counter to buy *empadinhas*, baked or deep-fried pastries stuffed with spiced beef, pork, ham, chicken, melting cheese, vegetables, *bacalhau* (dried cod) and potato.

There is always a choice of tasty desserts, too. Brazilians are notorious for their sweet tooth and desserts are the unsung glories of the Brazilian table. Many of them have evocative names, such as *sonhos* (dreams), *saudades* (longings), *beijos* (kisses) and *papos de anjo* (angels' cheeks) and they are mostly made with egg yolk and sugar and flavoured with coconut milk. The universally popular *quindim* and *quindão*, which are like thick, sticky, sweet yellow custards, are also flavoured with coconut milk. Everyone loves the sweet, milky desserts *doce de leite* and *manjar blanco*, and a big favourite with children is *olhos de sogra*, mother-in-law's eyes, prunes stuffed with coconut paste with a clove for the pupil.

Every other bar is dedicated to meeting the *Cariocas'* eternal need for a cool drink: some sell only *refrescos* (soft drinks), of which the national example is *guaraná*, an addictive, sugary, caffeine-based drink flavoured with the essence of an Amazonian jungle berry. Others sell *sucos*, freshly squeezed juices such as passion fruit (*maracujá*, the most popular), guava, pineapple, mango, papaya – every tropical fruit you've ever heard of and some you haven't. Or there are fruit juices mixed with milk, like milkshakes, known as *vitaminas*. Mixed with *cachaça* (white rum), they are known as *batidas*. Delicious, but overwhelming.

Brazil has some respectable bottled beers, but many people prefer a cooling draught Pilsner known as *chopp* (pronounced 'shoppee'). *Cariocas* tend to look up to imported beers, but their own are good. Try Antártica or Brahma; even better are Bohemia and Bavaria, found in the smarter bars. And look out for the unusual Xingu, which is sweet and black.

Where to eat in Rio? Many a Brazilian office worker will have lunch in a *lanchonete*, a cheap and cheerful help-yourself bar. I tried out one called Chamusco, which I found in Centro, off the Avenida Rio Branco, the main drag downtown, where I had spent the morning exploring the silent, rather grand art galleries and chaotic, crowded bookshops.

A long central unit offered more than 50 dishes, including a dozen varied and tasty salads with avocado and chayote (they call it *xuxu*). There are Brazilian titbits such as *bolinhos* (deep-fried balls of fish, meat or vegetables), *empadinhas* and *croquettes de frango* (chicken), as well as dishes of beef, pork and chicken, stewed vegetables (okra is a favourite in Rio), and pasta in sauces. This was more than adequate, so it was a surprise when a waiter arrived offering excellent grilled chicken skewered on a blade. He returned several times, with roast lamb and pork, cutting off any morsel you requested. Finishing with *quindim* and *manjar blanco* this 'office lunch' had turned into a feast. The cost, including a couple of beers, was less than £12 a head.

Meat-loving *Cariocas* patronise restaurants advertising them selves as *churrascarias* (the word for a barbecue). This is as typical as Brazilian eating gets, since it's the everyday food of the south. Highly recommended examples are two restaurants going by the name of Porcão, one in Ipanema, the other in Barra da Tijuca, which are huge, lively, busy, extrovert temples to the carnivore's creed. In *churrascarias*, the meat is served *rodízio*-fashion (*rodízio* being a wheel in Portuguese), the waiters circling the room with grilled meat skewered on swords.

If you're looking for a comfortable restaurant, there are plenty of guides you can consult; I followed one which had been highly recommended, called *Guia Danusia Barbara*. I discovered that among the 200 top-rated restaurants in Rio, very few specialised in Brazilian cooking as such. Steak restaurants and seafood restaurants are evidently the most popular, and the most prestigious are those offering French cuisine.

Rio is famous for one important dish, *feijoada*, a bean stew. As the country is the world's largest grower of beans, most Brazilians eat them in one form or another most days. *Feijoada* is bean stew in its Sunday best, and it's the national dish.

And the best in Rio? Probably the one served at the Casa da Feijoada, a cosy, relaxed restaurant in a fashionable, quiet corner of Ipanema. When we visited, the temperature outside was in the mid-30s, and climbing. A cool salad might have been a more sensible choice, but no; shivering in near-zero air conditioning, we tucked into a rib-sticking *feijoada*, as heavy in its way as that famous provincial French winter warmer, a *cassoulet* from Toulouse, loaded with rich meats and sausage. The Brazilian will cheerfully eat this at any time of the year (there isn't a cold winter in Brazil; the weather's either hot, very hot or an inferno).

In Rio de Janeiro, and throughout Brazil, *feijoada* is offered as a special dish on Wednesdays and Saturdays, though Saturday is the favoured day to eat it, since people don't have to get back to work. They'll get to the restaurant from 11.30am onwards and devote three or four hours to celebration. The national white rum, *cachaça* (distilled from cane sugar), also plays an essential part in this ritual.

So it was that, before we could make our order at the Casa da Feijoada, we were offered a *caipirinha*, Brazil's greatest gift to the world of drink, and the only aperitif fit to preface a *feijoada*. This is a rum sour made with crushed sugar, limes and *cachaça*. One restaurant in Rio, the Academia de Cachaça, has 2,000 different examples of *cachaça*, the oldest dating back to 1875, a *Fazenda Capão Grosso*. The Academia is something of an institution and over 11 years it has become a great visitor attraction and a source of pride to the *Cariocas*. It has a wonderful tiny restaurant tucked away, where you can enjoy specialities such as shredded beef with a cassava cream purée or a melting cheese sauce, or fillet steak sliced and cooked with ginger, or a mousse of sweet yams, followed by a hot guava tart with Minas Gerais cheese (like ricotta). At weekends, naturally they cook a *feijoada completa*.

Barmen in Rio have developed the preparation of a *caipirinha* into a serious craft, usually performed in front of you. At the Casa da Feijoada, they bring a wooden chopping board to your table with tumblers, crushed ice, caster sugar, limes and a wooden pestle and mortar. It takes about five minutes to conjure one up, and it's so good, you might as well order your second the moment the first is ready. Before your meal arrives, you are also brought a 'cover': olives, little pieces of hot spicy sausage (*linguiça* and *chouriça*) and a purée of beans. (Beans to eat before a bean dish?)

When the *feijoada* arrives, it is bubbling and black in its terracotta casserole. It is made with small black beans (*feijão preto*, which we know as turtle beans) which have been simmered until tender with at least six different cuts of beef and pork, some salted and some dried (*carne de sol*), together with cured sausage.

Our host explained that the stew owes its rich, gelatinous texture to the addition of pigs' trotters. Picking out the pieces of meat, it's impossible to tell which is which, so the owner came over to explain: this is the ear; this is the snout; this is the tail. Ah. Without these delicacies, he told us, it would not be deemed authentic, for *feijoada* has its origins in the slave plantations, such morsels being the scraps the master did not want.

The dish comes with a colourful accompaniment of finely chopped greens (*couve*, a kind of kale), circles of orange, white rice and a saucer of toasted, buttered *farofa*. This is made from cassava meal and resembles fine breadcrumbs. It is served with almost every meal in the province of Bahia in north-eastern Brazil and is used rather like a condiment, sprinkled on to dishes to soak up the sauce.

Feijoada itself may not be spicy or hot (this is true of most Brazilian food) but the sauces at the table most certainly will be. These are freshly made pots of *malagueta* peppers pounded with oil, or sometimes with lime juice or vinegar, or some of the stock from the bean stew, or even with *cachaça*.

The *feijoada* is, in a way, an introduction to what many regard as the real cooking of Brazil: *cozinha Baiana*. This is the cuisine of Bahia, a region where more than 90 per cent of the population is of African origin, descendants of the four million slaves shipped in by the Portuguese to work on the sugar plantations. I was introduced to this cuisine by Brazilian friends some years ago on a visit to

Salvador, the historic first capital of Brazil (a city that boasts some
365 baroque churches, one for each day of the year). So I knew what
to expect when I made my way to one of Rio's best Bahian restaurants, the Siri Mole & Cia (*siri* is a crab and *mole* means soft – soft-
shelled crab – and *Cia* is short for *Campanhia*, which means company).

The names of the dishes on the menu brought back happy memories and were enough by themselves to get my tastebuds tingling
and my digestive juices flowing: *moqueca* and *pirão*, fish casserole
and fish sauce, *quiabo* and *caruru*, dishes made with okra; *xinx-
im*, a shrimp and chicken stew.

To start, we ordered *acarajé* with a *vatapá* sauce. In Bahia,
acarajé is a bean fritter, much like a Middle Eastern falafel, a street
food sold by women dressed in white turbans and long lace dresses
and dripping with necklaces. It is made from pounded black-eyed
peas, chopped onion and dried prawns, deep-fried and served with
vatapá, a thick yellow prawn sauce made with coconut milk and
thickened with ground nuts. To follow, we had wonderful stuffed
baked crab (*casquinhos recheados*) with *bobó*, a yellow purée
made with cassava meal and prawns.

Special to Bahia is the use of certain ingredients: limes, chillies,
coriander, coconut milk (not *água de côco* – the refreshing water
inside – but an infusion of grated coconut flesh). Cassava root provides the starchy base of their diet in the form of farofa meal and
manioc flour (*farinha*). The cooking oil used in Bahia is unique
too, a thick, yellow, palm-nut oil called *dendê* that both colours and
flavours dishes.

Seafood is the glory of Bahia – fish grilled over wood fires and
seafood stews called *moquecas*. All these were on offer at Siri Mole
& Cia, if in expurgated form (no bad thing: in Bahia, you may wish
to pour off half a pint of oil from your *moqueca*).

Recipes in Bahia pass down through families and are altered
very little, for many have religious significance. Some foods have
allusions to Candomblé, the Bahian form of Macumba, the African
religion with voodoo-like rituals which were brought over on the
slave ships and which African-Brazilians have kept alive.
Candomblé is characterised by ceremonies in religious houses

called *terreiros* in which participants hurl themselves into trances to the accompaniment of hypnotic drumming. Even in Rio, some 800 miles south of Bahia, Candomblé rituals are observed. On the beach, you may stumble across the remains of some ceremony: burnt-out candles, fading flowers, glasses, the charred pieces of a sacrificial chicken. Food plays an important role in Candomblé, with white foods dedicated to Oxalá, god of creation, and others to his three wives: red foods (such as pepper sauce) to Iansã, goddess of winds and tempests; yellow foods to Oxum, goddess of beauty; and fish to Yemanjá, goddess of water.

My last, and possibly my best, experience of Brazilian food was at Café de la Paix at Le Méridien on Copacabana beach. A hotel may not be everyone's idea of a good place to eat, but happily this can be the exception in Rio. Perhaps this shouldn't have come as such a surprise, since the worldwide chain of Le Méridien hotels has built its reputation on good cooking.

There is a saying in Brazil: the blacker the cook, the better the food. Le Méridien's executive chef is a Frenchman, Jean-Yves Poirey, but I quickly discovered that his wife is from Bahia and that he himself had spent three years in Nigeria, heartland of the Yoruba Africans, ancestors of the Bahian people. Jean-Yves took me into the kitchens at Le Méridien, and yes, the cooks are mostly from Bahia. 'They are very poor there and they have no education, so the only jobs they can get are as kitchen porters and cleaners,' he told me. 'But they watch and they have a feel for cooking and soon they are helping out.'

Now the excellence of Le Méridien's breakfast table became clear. Not only were the fresh tropical fruits sublime, and the dried fruits, the cereals, the savoury choices of hams and salamis and eggs and the crumbly young white cheese from Minas Gerais, but so were the maize and fruit breads, conserves of carrot and beetroot, papaya (called *cocadas*), and cakes and sweet desserts, as authentically Brazilian as could be, and the coconut-flavoured *quindão*, *manjar blanco* and *pudim de caramela*.

Jean-Yves explained that Brazil owed its rich tradition of dessert-making to its Portuguese ancestry. The first nuns who came to Brazil brought with them cake-making skills from their convents in Portugal, a craft that had been learned in turn from the Moors during their long occupation of the Iberian Peninsula. In Europe, he told me, these cakes and desserts had been made with almonds, but the nuns who taught the slaves how to make them substituted grated coconut, peanuts or cashew nuts.

Having now become hooked on Le Méridien's breakfast, we advanced to lunch, and there, sandwiched between other styles of cooking designed to please an international clientele, we found a proud exhibition of Brazilian cuisine at its best.

There was creamy *pirão* which is a fish soup: *bobó de camarão* (prawns in a *farinha* purée flavoured with palm-nut oil and cashew nuts) and a consummate *moqueca* with three or four kinds of fish in it. There was an egg dish with shredded dry beef. There was pork in a creamy sauce. And all this was followed by wonderful tropical fruits and rich, eggy custards, cheesecakes and desserts. It was authentic cooking by Bahians, the dishes tweaked by a Frenchman. Who could wish for anything more?

Caipirinha white rum sour

The most famous of traditional Brazilian cocktails, drunk before a meal to give you a kick start. The ice is cooling, the freshness of the lime arouses the appetite and the concentration of alcohol animates conversation. Caipirinha actually translates as 'yokel' or 'country bumpkin', perhaps indicating the rough-and-ready way the limes are chopped into the drink.

Serves 4
300ml (half a pint) *cachaça*
16 ice cubes
4 tsp caster sugar

With a sharp knife, cut the limes into quarters, removing the coarse central pith. Slice the quarters into smaller chunks. Crush the ice. Combine the limes and sugar in a mortar (skillful barmen do it in each glass in front of you) and pound them together. Put into a cockail shaker and add the *cachaça* and ice and shake well. Don't use a blender: the pieces of lime must be shredded. Serve in glasses that have been chilled in the freezer.

Feijoada

The national dish of Brazil. If served *feijoada* in a rough café in São Paulo, you will rightly guess – as you dig out of the pot of gooey beans a gelatinous, salted, pig's tail, (unmistakably) the ear of a pig, and one of the animal's trotters – that the dish comes down from the slave plantations. However, in a private home, or smart restaurant, tremendous attention is paid to the shopping, preparation, cooking and presentation of *feijoada*. The meats are taken from the stew carved, and beautifully arranged on a platter.

It is the black beans, so typical of South America, that give *feijoada* its authentic depth of colour and richness – but you can use red kidney beans. Note that before soaking you should fast-boil all dried beans for 10 minutes and then throw away the water, to remove the toxins.

Serves 6
1½ lb black beans (or red kidney beans) soaked for 12 hours
1 lb salt beef, also soaked for 12 hours
½ lb smoked pork (or knuckle of bacon)
1 pig's trotter (for texture)
½ lb cooking sausage (Spanish, Italian) cut into small pieces
1 onion, finely chopped
3 deseeded green chillies, finely chopped
2 cloves garlic, chopped
Salt, pepper, olive oil

Drain the beans and salt beef.

Put the beef, pork (or bacon) and pig's trotter into a saucepan, cover with warm water, bring to the boil and simmer for 1½-2 hours, until they are tender.

In another pan, cover the beans with water and cook for up to 2 hours, until they are soft enough to mash.

Now combine the meat and beans, and cook them together gently to combine the flavours.

In a frying pan, cook the onion in oil until it starts to colour.

Add the cooking sausage, garlic and chilli, and heat through.

Add a cupful of cooked beans and mash them in the pan with enough liquid to make a thick sauce. Season with salt and pepper.

Cook for a few minutes, then stir into the meat and beans and cook till well blended.

Serve with plain rice.

A classic touch is to add a pint of fresh orange juice to the water in which the meat is simmered.

Some Like it Hotter

Paprika powder doesn't rank very high in the ever-expanding British spice rack. It's surely not up there with whole black pepper-corns and mustard, or chilli powder, ginger and cinnamon or even coriander seed, cumin and turmeric. It doesn't make much of a contribution to the modern, explosive taste revolution.

If anything, this pleasant, rust-coloured powder is dismissed as a food cosmetic and colouring. A pinch of it adds a speckled effect to the white blobs of yoghurt or sour cream you dribble onto soup to improve its appearance. But there is a country in Europe that knows better.

Paprika has been the single most important ingredient in Hungarian cooking for more than two centuries. Hungarians consume 6,000 tonnes a year, half of which goes into food processing (to give that rosy glow to Hungarian salami). The rest is used in the home. There are dozens of dishes which begin with onions being sizzled in lard followed by two heaped tablespoons of red paprika.

The most famous dish is undoubtedly Hungarian goulash (which is, in fact, the British pronunciation of *gulyas*, the Magyar national soup). In Britain, though, it has become a debased commodity, associated more with a factory canteen than with the menu of a fine restaurant. Perversely, the British version of goulash – which is more like a dull tomato and beef casserole than a soup – is one that Hungarians wouldn't recognise at all. In Hungary, the authentic colour of the soup – that of a deep red sunset – is due entirely to the abundant quantities of high grade paprika used during cooking.

Because Hungarian paprika is a premium spice, it fetches the highest prices, even though it represents only 10 per cent of the world's supply. The result is that most of the paprika you buy will be the cheaper stuff from Spain and Israel. Even non-experts should be able to tell the difference between ordinary paprika and Hungarian paprika by its colour and aroma. But it takes a gourmet of rare insight to distinguish between the various Hungarian grades, from Pungent Exquisite Delicate and Noble Sweet, to the orange-coloured Rose, and fiercely hot Eros.

These distinctions are something I learned about only recently, following a visit last year to the town of Szeged, to see the paprika harvested first-hand. Szeged sits on the River Tisza, which cuts through the hot, southern plains of Hungary, where there are, on average, 2,000 hours of sunshine a year – ideal conditions for ripening the fruit to rich, red perfection.

My education begins when I meet Mr Paprika himself, Tibor Huszka. In his mid-forties, Tibor is the technical head of Szegedi Paprika Rt, a firm which dates back to 1748. Passionate about paprika, Tibor is also laboratory scientist, miller, marketing chief, nurseryman and grower.

Paprika, Tibor believes, was introduced to Hungary in the 17th century during the Turkish occupation, when it was known as Turkish pepper. Hungarians were forbidden to grow it on pain of death, but once they'd sampled its warmth and piquancy, many did grow it, illegally grinding the dried peppers to a powder that could be preserved.

Tibor whizzes us off to the paprika fields to see the harvesting. Paprika-growing has changed little over the centuries, he says, and remains essentially a family occupation. Every family has a little plot and, at harvest time, everyone works together, youngsters picking the peppers, grandmothers grading them for drying.

We are met by a local dealer, Josef Vaslag. Josef, now aged 70, is as committed to paprika as Tibor, and 25 years ago won Ireland's Golden Harp award for his short documentary about the paprika-pickers of Szeged. These days he rents a disused Texaco petrol station to use as a temporary grading shed. Mountains of the conical red peppers are piled up under the canopy where the women, who are mostly in their sixties and seventies, sit comfortably on mattresses and straw pillows, their legs stretched out in front of them. Using 10-inch metal needles they laboriously stitch the stems of the peppers together to create strands three metres long.

The Hungarian pimento is sharp and pointed, rather like a chilli, and is between four and five inches long. It is thick-fleshed, tough and leathery. In Hungarian folklore, explains Tibor, it is represented as a phallic object and, on cue, Josef offers to bring out his fiddle and leads the 'girls' in a rendition of a ribald folksong. 'The fruit is full and ripe tonight,' they sing. 'Oh, where will we sleep tonight? At your home, sweetheart, on your soft bed . . . That's where we'll sleep tonight.'

As the brilliantly colourful garlands are finished, they are hung out to dry under the eaves of houses, on fences, anywhere there is space. Within three weeks, they will become so brittle they will rattle in the wind.

This drying period is very important because pigmentation doubles during this time. To complete the drying process, the peppers are taken to a factory where they spend a few days in kilns at 50C. Then they are crushed, ground between millstones and sieved to form an orange-red powder.

Enhancing the colour is the most important function of the miller, says Tibor. And it is the seeds, which are 40 per cent oil, that help to sustain the texture and colour. 'Without the oil, the spice will be dead and lifeless,' he says. The milling process generates friction, and the heat begins a gentle process of caramelisation. You can smell the sweet, almost malty aroma. Using his judgement, Tibor will add water to lower the temperature and prevent drying out. There is a fine line between slight caramelisation, which produces delicate sweetness, and overheating, which causes bitterness.

In Hungary, there are at least seven grades of paprika for sale. The premium powder comes from the best hand-picked peppers, which are carefully selected for their purity and depth of colour. Hungarians rate the very mild *Különleges* (Special Quality) above all others, because it is the richest in colour. Also mild is the light red *Csipmentes* (Delicate); *Csemegepaprika* (Exquisite Delicate) is similar, but a little spicier. The most widely exported is

Édesnemes (Noble Sweet), which is brightly coloured and mildly spicy. Hotter grades of paprika include *Csipös Csemege Pikáns* (Pungent Exquisite Delicate), *Félédes* (Semi-Sweet) and the spicy, pale orange-red *Rósza* (Rose). There is one fiery-hot paprika, *Eros*, which is made from small cherry peppers. Although a few grades of paprika are hot, Tibor explains that modern peppers have had most of the heat bred out of them. Previously, the heat was lessened by cutting open the peppers and scooping out the hot seeds and membranes with a knife.

To complete my paprika tuition, Tibor takes me to Szeged's premier restaurant, Czarda, where chef Faragó Sandor is charged with keeping alive some 80 traditional Hungarian dishes. The most famous local dish is Szeged fish soup, which he makes with sturgeon, pike, perch, carp or the huge local catfish, the dry-tasting spice marries perfectly with the earthiness of the freshwater fish.

My lesson is rounded out with some cooking tips. According to Faragó, there's really only one thing to remember when cooking with paprika: don't burn it. He goes on to describe how nearly every dish begins in the same way, by stewing finely chopped onions in lard over a low heat (vegetable oil deprives the dish of essential flavour, he insists). You then stir in several large tablespoons of paprika, being careful not to overheat it, before adding liquid or stock. The timing is vital: rapid frying of paprika will make it bitter and destroy its delicate flavour.

Not to be outdone, Tibor offers me his own recipe. Once a year, he and his father make 100kg of salami. They mix 100kg of minced pork (with plenty of belly pork) with 2kg of the best paprika and 500g of hot paprika. The mixture is then stuffed into skins and tied at the ends, ready to be smoked and hung up in a cool shed to dry.

Tibor offers a final tip: given paprika's delicate nature, it's worth taking the trouble to look after it. The small quantity of oil that gives paprika its charm also makes it susceptible to oxidisation. It will go off in time, so it should be stored in a cool, dry place away from heat and sunlight. Tibor takes his own piece of advice very seriously: he keeps his precious powder in the fridge.

Rich Pickings

The air is thick with a dizzying, heady aroma. It evokes memories of a quayside restaurant in a French Mediterranean port and a steaming bowl of *bouillabaisse*. It also summons up an image of Italy: a plate of lemon-yellow, butter-rich *risotto alla Milanese*. And Spain, the scent of a primrose-hued paella served at a beachside shack near Valencia.

Saffron. Its heavy scent is unmistakable. But this time I'm in the sitting room of a private home in Spain, near Albacete in La Mancha. The smell spreads from a charcoal brazier, where Granny is drying the precious filaments in a sieve.

Saffron is the orange stigma of the autumn crocus, *Crocus sativus*. It is the world's most valuable spice, and sells for around £100 per ounce. November is harvest time, and the whole Mas Ripoli family has assembled to gather and pick it over. Ramon, the eldest son, a police chief in Madrid, has taken his annual holiday to be here. The oldest family members and the youngest children sit side by side at a table overflowing with lilac-blue blooms.

They take each flower in turn, squeeze it to open the bud, and skilfully pluck the three stigmas, depositing them on a white enamel plate which grows more golden by the minute, like a fiery red setting sun. We are close to the eastern plains, a high, barren land, where temperatures drop to minus 21C in winter and rise to 40C at the height of summer. But these conditions suit the crocus crop.

Earlier in the day, I had joined the family on the high plateau to pick the crocuses. A biting wind blew as we moved, crouching, with grass baskets slung from our waists. Crab-like, we walked astride the rows, 100 metres long by three metres wide. These cultivated strips, or *celaminas* each yield between 500g and 1kg of filaments. We began picking at first light, aiming to finish before 11am. By this time, the blooms begin to open and the delicate stigmas risk being damaged by the wind.

There can be few lines of work as labour-intensive as the growing, collecting and sorting of this spice. Gathering is back-breaking work. The rows are picked for three days in succession, each plant averaging about five blooms. But this is the least of the labour involved.

The colourful red stigmas must now be extracted from each bloom. These contain the saffron, which will be dried and sold as threads or, more expensively, a fine powder. Some 250,000 blooms are required to yield 1kg of dried saffron. In some fields, paid pickers do the work, but the Mas Ripoli family is more typical – they band together to pick the crop themselves. The harvest represents a joint investment which will pay for luxuries and holidays.

We return to the family home in the picturesque village of Alcala de Jucar, which is built into a honeycomb of rocks above a winding river. Here, Granny, who is considered the most skilful member of the family, dries the threads judiciously in a sieve held at a safe distance over the dull embers of a charcoal fire. The threads need to lose as much as four-fifths of their weight, as any dampness will lead to decay when the harvest is stored.

Saffron is prized by cooks. Musky, pungent and mildly bitter, it gives taste, colour and fragrance to food. For thousands of years, it has been valued as a cure-all – an aphrodisiac, intoxicant and hangover remedy all in one. First described in Egyptian scrolls around 7000BC, it has been referred to by all the great writers, from Homer and Pliny through to Virgil and Shakespeare, who mentions it in *The Winter's Tale*: 'I must have saffron for my warden pies.' Wardens were large, hard pears.

Saffron was first brought to Britain by Phoenicians trading for Cornish tin, and it has continued to feature in the region's cuisine. The bakers, Blewetts of Truro, use it by the pound. Customers won't let them get away with other colouring for their famous Cornish saffron cake. Trade in saffron in the Middle Ages was highly profitable, and passing off 'false saffron' was a crime so serious that in Germany rogue traders were burnt at the stake. Trading in the root bulbs was punishable by death, so it was a bold man who smuggled corms to England in the mid-14th century.

In Tudor times, it was valued as a medicine and also as a food colouring for butter, cream, cheese and golden pastry glazes. Henry VIII was a major patron of the spice and bestowed on Chipping Walden – the centre of England's main saffron growing area – its present name, Saffron Walden. However, he also acted to limit its usage, issuing instructions forbidding women in his court to dye their hair with it: the pigment, crocin, produces a strong shade of yellow, so it was used as a dye for cloth, particularly in the East Anglian wool trade.

Today, saffron from Iran and Kashmir can be superb, but most of it comes from Spain (70 per cent of world trade) where Safinter is one of the most reputable producers, buying direct from the La Mancha pickers.

How to use saffron? John Humphries, saffron importer and author of *The Essential Saffron Companion*, has compared every known method. He adopts the less-is-best school of thought, and advocates making an infusion. You may need as few as three threads per person – a dozen will season a rice dish for four (I have to say, though, that in Valencia I have seen a cook using 10 times this amount). John heats a frying pan for 30 seconds, removes it from the heat and tosses in the filaments, shaking for about two minutes while they dry (be careful: if they burn, they are useless). In a mortar, he crumbles the saffron with the back of a spoon before pouring on a little boiling water. The longer it infuses, the stronger the colour – so leave it for an hour rather than 10 minutes.

Although not widely used in British kitchens, chefs are keenly introducing saffron into their repertoires. Rowley Leigh of Kensington Place in London was the first to place massive orders for 250g parcels of the stuff, adopting it as a *de rigueur* seasoning in his fish and mussel soups; while Simon Hopkinson famously invented saffron mash, inspired by a holiday in the South of France. Its use has spread from soups and rice dishes to desserts, even ice creams (like vanilla, saffron has an affinity with cream and milk). I, meanwhile, like to use it in a cakey fruit and spice loaf, delicious eaten in slabs, generously spread with good butter.

Saffron facts:

The quality of saffron is measured according to the proportion of crimson threads. Coupé is the most powerful grade, followed by Mancha Selecto, then Rio, then Sierra.

Good saffron is less than one year old. Look for threads which are a brilliant orange colour. Beware of imitations: safflower, marigold and turmeric are all used as substitutes. They give the colour but not the taste of saffron.

The World of Spice

We all love spices in our food. Their heady aromas alert the senses and arouse the appetite; their perfumes may lodge in the nose – as do vanilla, cardamom or cloves – creating anticipation of pleasures to come; or they may mask some of the less appealing odours of cooked food, for example, saffron or bay leaf can transform a fish soup.

On the tongue, spices set a challenge for the palate with their picquancy: sweet, sour, bitter and salty. Or they may simply be hot, such as ginger and peppercorns and chilli, mustard and horseradish and wasabi paste.

Spices often evoke exotic notions of faraway countries and other food cultures. They excite and exalt. You only have to think of Indian food and the way it orchestrates dozens of spices in infinite combinations.

Sugar and spice and all things nice – how would our food today be without them? Palaeolithic man, with his stone implements, eating roots and fruits, small animals, fish and birds, was grateful merely for survival. It took many thousands of years for him to master the use of fire and learn to indulge his palate, refining the plainness of his fare, introducing aromatic leaves and seeds and barks.

Flavour was only part of the story. Salt and sugar, as well as herbs and spices, were soon found to play a vital role in human subsistence, both as medicines and preservatives. Many herbs, such as thyme and rosemary, contain oils which are bacteriocidal – they kill germs.

The understanding and use of spices has evolved gradually. Salt sharpens flavour but, when it was found to be a preservative, it became the most essential resource on the planet. Salt draws out moisture from food and inhibits spoilage from airborne bacteria, so you can brine down meat, fish and vegetables for long storage.

The Chinese were the first to appreciate the medical character-istics of plants, seeds, barks and roots, skills explored by Indian (ayurvedic) and Greek healers.

But it was the luxurious qualities of spices that appealed to gourmets and led to the steady increase in trade from East to West. Eventually, some highly perfumed spices, such as cinnamon, nut-meg, cloves, ginger and peppercorns, became symbols of conspicu-ous consumption among the wealthy. Peppercorns were worth a king's ransom – they were actually traded by one Roman emperor to spare Rome from being sacked by the Goths, when they were at the gates of the city.

Centres such as Baghdad, Cairo, Venice, Genoa and Lisbon grew rich in turn, through the centuries, as they became hubs of the spice trade, spices being as precious as exotic perfumes (ambergris, incense and myrrh) or gold and silver and rare stones. The search for them and the profits they generated have shaped history, from Marco Polo opening up the East to Columbus discovering the Americas, and the East India Company establishing India as the 'Jewel in the Crown' of the British Empire.

Before the world-wide search for precious spices, though, medieval monasteries, the seats of learning in their day, all had herb gardens, or physic gardens as they called them. They studied herbal remedies as medicines long before cooks began to use spices and herbs to enhance and improve the flavour of dishes.

Nicholas Culpeper's *Complete Herbal*, published in the seven-teenth century, lists over 400 herbs and their uses, and cooking is not one of them. Not even saffron, today the world's most expensive spice, which was then grown in Cambridgeshire. is recommended for culinary use. 'It refreshes the spirits,' says Culpeper. 'It guards against fainting fits and palpitation of the heart, it strengthens the stomach, aids digestion, cleanses the lungs, is good for coughs. It is good in hysteric disorders. But some who have taken too large a dose,' he adds, 'have fallen into inveterate convulsive laughter which ended in death.' Nothing about food.

Paprika, the national spice of Hungary, was initially introduced by the church as a plant which they hoped might have medicinal properties. It didn't but it looked pretty in the garden, so it stayed.

People began to cook and eat it. It wasn't until the occupying Turks tried to place a ban on it that it started to have unrealistic value. Grown in secret, it developed into the ingredient so essential to Hungarian cooking that they use 5kg per head per year.

My own interest in spices, and in food in general, began when I lived in Hong Kong for 18 months. I wondered how it was possible that the Chinese, working with similar ingredients to our own, could produce such different-tasting and delicious food. The answer was by adding masses of fresh ginger, spring onions and garlic, and lots of Chinese five-spice powder with its powerful anise flavour, soy sauce, chilli and hoisin sauces.

Over the years, thanks mostly to my life as a food writer, I've been able to travel and enjoy most of the world's gastronomies – first in France, Italy, Spain, China, Morocco and Turkey, and then in the Americas, India and Sri Lanka, south-east Asia, Indonesia, Japan, Africa and Australasia.

Hunting down spices became an obsession, whether it was hot and fruity chillies in the Mercado de Abastos in Oaxaca, Mexico, or cardamoms in the 'spice trail' of Kerala, still a world centre for exotic spices.

My latest adventure was a trip, with my wife Heather, to Zanzibar, once a world hub of spice trading, where Arabians, Indians and Africans have bled into one identity under the banner of spices. As part of the Oman Empire it became the leading source of cloves in the world. The islanders brought seeds from the Dutch East Indies, captured slaves in the Congo to work the plantations, then sold produce to European traders.

We spent a day on a spice farm, under the shade of towering coconut palms and dense evergreen clove trees, whose scented pink flower buds had not quite opened (and were thus ready for harvesting). Our guide cut the rhizomes (thickened underground roots) from bamboo-like ginger and turmeric bushes. And we saw cardamom bushes with similar leaves, but with orchid-like flowers close to the ground.

We fingered the slim, young, upright branches of cinnamon trees, which would be peeled to make the quills. We picked nutmegs – and saw that each was wrapped in a red lace jacket, which would be dried in the sun to sell as mace.

We marvelled at the climbing peppercorn vines with their lush deep-green, heart-shaped leaves and tiny bunches of berries like so many miniature grapes. In dense shade, we found a vanilla vine, thick-leafed, with its 'beans' like French beans, tough and green. They had no aroma at all – the beans have to be picked from the vines and processed for months before the colour, texture and haunting flavour of vanilla develops.

By now our hands were perfumed and stained. We bought bags of spices from the spice shop and returned to the hotel for dinner. From the kitchen came the unmistakable aroma of the spices of Zanzibar sizzling on fresh grilled fish.

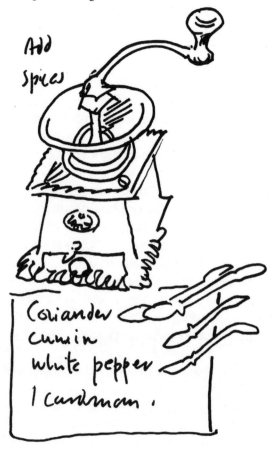

Spicy Lamb Stew – Ethiopia

The thick, spicy stews of this ancient land are known as *wots* – this one is called *yebeg wot*. The essential seasoning is the fiery chilli mixture known as *berberi* (pronounced 'bari-bari'). Sometimes hard-boiled eggs are added at the end of the cooking to make the stew go further.

Serves 4-6
2 tablespoons groundnut or sunflower oil
2 onions, finely chopped
50ml *berberi* red pepper paste (see below)
50ml clarified spiced butter (see below)
2.5cm ginger, grated
1 clove garlic, chopped
6 large tomatoes, peeled and chopped
Salt and freshly ground black pepper
1kg leg of lamb, off the bone, cut into 3cm pieces

In a heavy cooking pot, heat the groundnut or sunflower oil and fry the onions until soft. Add the red pepper paste and continue cooking for a few minutes. Then add the clarified spiced butter and cook for a further 10 minutes.

Stir in the ginger and garlic and cook gently for another 5 minutes. Add the tomatoes, season to taste with salt and freshly ground black pepper, and cook for 15 minutes.

Put the lamb into the mixture and simmer gently for 1 hour, stirring occasionally, until the meat is tender, adding a little water, if necessary. Serve with plain boiled rice.

Berberi Red Pepper Paste

This spicy mixture, which is added to most Ethiopian stews, is also served at the table as a condiment. Sometimes more chilli is added, making it very fiery indeed. It can be stored in the fridge for months.

Makes 1 jar
1 tablespoon chilli powder
1 tablespoon paprika
1 teaspoon coriander seeds, dry-roasted and ground
1 teaspoon freshly ground black pepper
Pinch of grated nutmeg
4 cloves
Pinch of ground cinnamon
Pinch of ground allspice
1 teaspoon ground cardamom seeds
4 shallots, chopped
2 cloves garlic, chopped
1 teaspoon salt
250ml boiling water
Olive oil, to cover

Mix all the ingredients, except the olive oil, in a blender, adding the boiling water to make a paste.

Put in an airtight jar with a topping of olive oil to seal. Store in the fridge.

Clarified Spiced Butter

Makes 1 jar
100g unsalted butter
50ml water
1 small onion, chopped
1 clove garlic, chopped
2.5cm ginger, grated

Heat the butter and water in a saucepan until the butter melts.

Add the onion, garlic and ginger, and bring to the boil until it starts to foam. Leave to settle and cool and then strain.

Store in a covered, sterilised jar in the fridge. It will keep for several months.

Sources of articles where known: Pan's People, *Penthouse*; All Vanity Fare recipe strips appeared in *Vanity Fair* in 1960s; Elizabeth David from *Cooking People*, Leslie Frewin Publishers, 1966; Good English Grub, *Vanity Fair*; Len Deighton from *Cooking People, ibid*; Collier's Cuppa, 9th July 1967, *Sunday Times*; Atticus, January 1969, *Sunday Times*; Badger Gammon is Off – may we recommend the hedgehog?, 12th August 1970, *Sunday Times*; What Makes One Run, Stops the Other, 22nd July 1973, *Sunday Times*; The Bland Leaders: 7th October 1973, 11th November 1973, 26th May 1974, 19th May 1974, 12th May 1974, 20th January 1974, *Sunday Times*; Stuffed Sweet Aubergine recipe from *Round the World in Recipes*, Hodder & Stoughton, 1993; Goodbye Fish Fingers…, 6th January 1974, *Sunday Times*; Self-Sufficiency, 6th January 1974, *Sunday Times*; Self-Sufficiency - Living off the Land, 1974, *Sunday Times*; The Skinny Side of Sausages, 1974, *Sunday Times*; A Hot Little Number, *Sunday Times*; Fat Chance These Ads Give You, 4th May 1975, *Sunday Times*; The Strange New Taste of Tomorrow, 19th January 1975, *Sunday Times*; Secret Super-Crop Down on the Marsh, 26th January 1975, *Sunday Times*; The Cost of Vitamin C, 3rd August 1975, *Sunday Times*; Good Beef about Bad Beef, 15th June 1975, *Sunday Times*; Whisker-Licking Good?, 5th October 1975, *Sunday Times*; Whatever Happened to Carnivores?, 12th October 1975, *Sunday Times*; Ginseng and Tonic, 2nd March 1975, *Sunday Times*; The Pie that Stares, *Sunday Times*; Black Pud gets Fishy Face-Lift, *Sunday Times*; Test your Nerves on Guga, 28th September 1975, *Sunday Times*; Even if it's only Eggs, Scramble Them with Style…, March 1975, *Cosmopolitan*; Baby Big and the Magic Milkmen, 16th March 1975, *Sunday Times*; A Taste of the Times, 22 January 1977, *Sunday Times*; The Good Prison Food Guide, 23rd July 1978, *Sunday Times*; Big Bang Beans, Aloo Baji and Æbleskiver, 19th March 1978, *Sunday Times*; Gourmet with a Conscience, September 8 1974, *Sunday Times*; Campaign for Real Bread, 13th January 1980, *Sunday Times*, 27th January 1980, *Sunday Times*; An ABC of French Wine, March/April 1983, *Hopper*; The Hidden Side of Majorca, 29th January 1984, *Sunday Express Magazine*; Gastronomic Grand Tour, 1984, *Sphere Magazine*; The World's Top Chef, 29th January 1984, *Sunday Express Magazine*; The Emergent Cookery of Australia, 1986, *Cuisine*; True Confessions on a Plate, 11th November 1989, *The Independent*; Smokescreen, Autumn 1993, *Egon Ronay Food*; Real Chickens Don't Eat

Sheep, 28th January 1990, *Independent on Sunday*; Snob Appeal on a Plate, January 1990, *Independent on Sunday*; Paella recipe *Round the World in Recipes, ibid*; Beyond Paella: Spanish Food gets Serious, 11th February 1990, *Independent on Sunday*; A Famine in the Classroom, 24th March 1991, *Independent on Sunday*; Safe and Sound, but Still not Stylish, 11th March 1990, *Independent on Sunday*; Heartening Times for a Fish called Wonder, 1st April 1990, *Independent on Sunday*; When Yellow is a Sauce of Courage, 10th June 1990, *Independent on Sunday*; Sixty Ways to Woo your Shopper, 1st July 1990; Red and Yellow and Tartrazine, 8th July 1990, *Independent on Sunday*; No Need to Beef About Meat, 26th August 1990, *Independent on Sunday*; A Steamboat Full of Eastern Promise, 23rd September 1990, *Independent on Sunday*; The Book of the Dish of the Day, 30th September 1990, *Independent on Sunday*; You Don't Have to Mortify the Flesh to be a Vegan, 14th October 1990, *Independent on Sunday*; Everything but the Quack, 4th November 1990, *Independent on Sunday*; A Little Bite of What You Fancy, 18th November 1990, *Independent on Sunday*; Designed by Italians...Eaten by Everybody, 9th December 1990, *Independent on Sunday*; Little Ears of Pasta recipe *ibid*; Treat Yourself to a Belly Full of Roots Recipes, 6th January 1991, *Independent on Sunday*; Reach for the Stars, Inspector Brown, 27th January 1991, *Independent on Sunday*; Eat Your Way to Perfect Health, 24th February 1991, *Independent on Sunday*; Hasty, Hasty, Very Very Tasty, 17th February 1991, *Independent on Sunday*; Homage to a Taste of Catalonia, 14th April 1991, *Independent on Sunday*; A Crustacean Worth Shelling Out For, 5th May 1991, *Independent on Sunday*; Grey Mullet for Grey Matter, 16th June 1991, *Independent on Sunday*; A Great Tradition goes up in Smoke, 25th August 1991, *Independent on Sunday*; Sophie's Choice, 21st April 1991 *Independent on Sunday*; How to Make the World of your Oyster, 1 Sep 91, *Independent on Sunday*; The Big Apple, 12th October 1991, *Independent on Sunday*; Cappuccino Crazy, 27th October 1991, *Independent on Sunday*; More than One Way to Souse a Herring, 3rd November 1991, *Independent on Sunday*; Rio is Cooking, 1999, *Conde Nast Traveller*; Feijoada recipe *Round the World in Recipes, ibid*; Some Like it Hotter, March 1999, *Waitrose Food Illustrated*; Rich Pickings, July 1999, *Waitrose Food Illustrated; The World of Spice* and recipes for Spicy Lamb Stew, Berberi Red Pepper Paste and Clarified Spiced Butter, Kyle Cathie 2003.